Meteor in Action

Meteor in Action

STEPHAN HOCHHAUS
MANUEL CHRISTOPH SCHOEBEL

MANNING

SHELTER ISLAND

Manning Publications Co.
20 Baldwin Road
PO Box 761
Shelter Island, NY 11964

Development editor: Dan Maharry
Technical development editor Kostas Passadis
Copyeditor: Liz Welch
Proofreader: Barbara Mirecki
Technical proofreader: Al Krinker
Typesetter: Dennis Dalinnik
Cover designer: Marija Tudor

ISBN: 978161729247
Printed in the United States of America
1 2 3 4 5 6 7 8 9 10 – EBM – 20 19 18 17 16 15

brief contents

contents

foreword

In 2011, Geoff Schmidt, Nick Martin, and I started writing Meteor, a new JavaScript application platform. Our plan was to make it possible for any JavaScript developer to built great web and mobile apps with a mimimum of fuss and confusion.

JavaScript is a remarkable technology. From its humble beginnings as a scripting tool for browsers, it has become the programming language that runs everywhere: inside a browser, on a mobile device, and in the cloud. It is favored by both experts and beginners, an unusual combination for the software industry. But the JavaScript ecosystem is highly fragmented, and the teams who choose JavaScript have to assemble and maintain complete application stacks from scratch and spend far too much of their time working on low-level technical tasks—like designing application-specific WebSocket messages—that have little to do with their actual application.

Meteor offers a simple and straightforward solution for JavaScript developers looking to build a modern application, and *Meteor in Action* includes everything you need to get started. It covers all the key parts of the Meteor stack: the data synchronization system that publishes new information from the cloud to each active user, reactive templates that redraw the screen as data changes, events and forms, Meteor's isomorphic user account system, routing, packages, and security.

More than that, though, *Meteor in Action* teaches the fundamentals of Meteor's application architecture. Meteor is a full-stack reactive platform, which means all its parts, from the database driver to the client-side template engine to hot code push, work together to respond to changes in real time. And Meteor is an isomorphic platform, meaning that wherever possible the JavaScript APIs you use are identical across the browser, mobile device, and in the cloud. With clear examples, the authors explain these principles and show how they add up to form the Meteor development experience.

Stephan and Manuel have been active in the Meteor community since our earliest releases. They've contributed on countless email and forum threads, and now they've shared their knowledge in an enjoyable and approachable book on Meteor.

Happy hacking!

MATT DeBERGALIS
FOUNDER, METEOR DEVELOPMENT GROUP

preface

I met Manuel in 2013 when a friend took me to the first Meteor Ruhr meetup. After too many years in the enterprise world I was about to start my own business based on a web platform built on PHP. What Manuel showed us in these early stages solved so many issues I had faced, and it made web programming seem like child's play. Highly motivated, I got back home and immediately collected more material on this new platform. I put the collection on my blog, and since I had just read an article on SEO that recommended using superlatives to attract people's attention, I boldly claimed to present the "Best Learning Resources for Meteor.js." And this is where it all started.

In March 2014, Manning contacted me and asked if I was interested in writing a book on the promising Meteor platform. They had found my blog post and were convinced I was knowledgeable enough to explain the platform to other developers. Of course I agreed, but even though I had collected the—what I thought to be—best learning resources, I had little idea of how to actually apply them. I was still stuck in PHP-land. Writing a book was an excellent opportunity to learn everything about Meteor, so I happily agreed, but not without first consulting Manuel and asking him to join me in this endeavor. Luckily for me, he agreed to write the book, so together we set out to explain this new platform.

Having written this book, I feel that the combination of Manuel's vast knowledge and my own ignorance helped us to avoid the pitfalls of assuming too much on the reader's part and strike a good balance on usefulness vs. theoretical depth. Do let us know if this strategy pays off.

We feel the contents of this book are sufficient to get you into good shape to write amazing applications. While we can't address each and every detail of working with Meteor, we hope that the fundamentals we teach you will help you understand the available documentation, packages, and source code much better. At the end of the day Meteor, and the *Meteor in Action* book, are about enabling you to turn your ideas into applications. Tell us what you built! You can find us on Twitter, use the book's GitHub repo, or post in the Author Online forum for this book. We'd love to hear back from you!

STEPHAN HOCHHAUS

acknowledgments

Looking at the cover, you will see only two names, Manuel's and mine, but there were so many wonderful people who contributed to our book, that it would be a shame to let them go unmentioned. First and foremost, thanks are due to the fine folks at Manning, most importantly Robin De Jongh, who believed that a book on Meteor was a good idea, and Ozren Harlovic, who made the first contact with me. Thanks also to our editors Sean Dennis and Dan Maharry, who helped turn our technical gibberish into intelligible words and graphics. Thanks to our copyeditor Liz Welch, who had to put up with dozens of *faux amis du traducteur*, and to our proofreader Barbara Mirecki, as well as to the many other folks at Manning who worked with us behind the scenes.

The Meteor community has been invaluable in the creation of this book. We'd like to thank all of the early (and latter-day) pioneers using Meteor and publishing articles on the web, writing packages, and pushing the boundaries of the platform. You know who you are!

Manning's editorial, production, and technical staff were amazing to work with, even though they kept pushing us hard in order to make this book the best we could. We appreciate the pestering; it was worth it!

Many reviewers read the manuscript at various stages of its development, and we'd like to thank them for providing invaluable feedback: Carl Wolsey, Charlie Gaines, Cristian Antonioli, Daniel Anderson, Daniel Bertoi, David DiMaria, Dennis Hettema, John Griffiths, Jorge Bo, Keith Webster, Patrick Regan, Subhasis Ghosh, Tim Couger, and Touko Vainio-Kaila.

Thanks also to our technical development editor Kostas Passidis, who made sure that our technical explanations were both accurate and understandable, as well as to Al Krinker for his thorough technical review of the final manuscript shortly before it went to press. And special gratitude to Matt DeBergalis for contributing the foreword to our book.

A huge thank you goes out to you, our readers, especially those who believed in the book early on and joined the MEAP early access program when only a few chapters were available. Your input, interest, and encouragement kept us going!

STEPHAN HOCHHAUS

I'd like to thank Said Seihoub for making me go to that Meteor meetup. Without him this book would have never been written. Huge thanks also to Manuel, who always knew an answer when I ran into problems. Writing is a lonesome business, so thanks also to the entire #meteor IRC channel who kept me company when I needed to procrastinate. Without you this book would probably have come out already in 2014!

Thanks also to Anton Bruckner, Johann Sebastian Bach, Joss Whedon, and Terry Pratchett for creating the right working atmosphere. Finally my thanks go out to my family, who showed a lot of patience when I told them once a month that I finished a chapter, only to return to the very same chapter the next week to rewrite and 'finish' it again.

MANUEL SCHOEBEL

Writing a book takes a lot more effort than I imagined, but it was a great journey that helped me to dig deeper into the details of Meteor. Thank you Stephan for getting me on board. As always, it was a pleasure working with you.

During the writing of this book I went on another journey as well, with my startup that took up just as much of my time. Christina, without your indulgence and patience and support I could not have worked on either project, so thank you for being as great as you are!

Having a family that is always behind you is a luxury that not everyone experinces. I know that and appreciate it very much—you give me peace of mind when things get difficult.

Last but not least, I thank everyone who is part of the group of people working on making the web more awesome every day. This includes not only the guys from Meteor itself, but also everyone who creates new packages, joins meetups, or is just starting to learn how to bring their ideas to the web. The web has given us freedom to learn and to explore, to work and to play—more freedom than we have ever known in the past. It is a playground in which you can even make a living. We invite you to play with us!

about this book

A common phrase you hear from experienced developers is that "building applications ain't rocket science." While it may not be as complicated as sending people into space, it can be quite daunting to the uninitiated. A huge number of tools and server components is typically required to put your applications on the web, not to mention mobile devices. Meteor aims to become a game-changer. As Nick Martin, one of Meteor's creators, puts it:

> At Meteor, we hope to democratize web app development by empowering anyone, anywhere to create apps.[1]

We have seen people with only the most basic understanding of HTML and CSS turn their ideas into code after less than a day with Meteor. As such we believe that it will make development easier. It will even open up development for people who never considered themselves developers.

Unless you have a good teacher you will probably need more than half a day to know your way around the Meteor platform. This is where *Meteor in Action* comes in. It is your personal teacher that walks you through all major aspects of creating applications, regardless whether you want to write a web or mobile app. Eventually you will be able to turn your own ideas into code. If you did this before Meteor, you will be amazed at how quickly Meteor solves some of the most common issues.

---

[1] http://blog.heavybit.com/blog/2014/04/01/meteor

When writing *Meteor in Action* we aimed to address both front-end developers that want to extend their skills to the server side as well as developers with a server background, making the transition from Java, Ruby, or PHP to full stack JavaScript. It is not a book for complete beginners; we expect that you have built (or at least tried) something for the web before.

As all tools that are still in use, Meteor is always changing and evolving. We took great care to lay a good foundation with this book to teach you the fundamentals of this platform. We have confirmed that all functionality described in the following chapters works well with version 1.1.

Roadmap

Meteor in Action is organized into three parts.

Part 1 gives a high-level overview of the platform. It introduces the various components and concepts that make up the Meteor stack. After a first look at Node.js, MongoDB, isomorphism, and reactivity in chapter 1, you will build your first Meteor application in chapter 2.

Part 2 teaches you about the fundamental building blocks for reactive applications. Each chapter focuses on a different aspect of writing applications. Chapter 3 starts with templates, chapter 4 explains how to work with data and perform CRUD operations. Chapter 5 brings together these two and highlights some important considerations when building reactive interfaces. Chapter 6 introduces a way to secure applications by bringing in user-related functionality. The following chapter 7 explains how to replace the automated data publication mechanism Meteor uses by default. It covers Meteor's pub/sub concept and how to use methods to implement another layer of security. Routing operations on both client and server using the popular Iron.Router library is discussed in chapter 8. Chapter 9 teaches you how to use packages to extend Meteor's core functionality, either by using existing Isopacks, npm packages, or writing your own. Chapter 10 concludes the second part of the book by looking at server-side methods for asynchronous operations, accessing external APIs, or uploading files.

Part 3 takes it one step further and covers building and deploying your applications properly. Chapter 11 explains Meteor's build system, debugging your code, and how to turn your code into both web and mobile applications. The final chapter 12 addresses various aspects of putting your Meteor application into production.

The book ends with three appendixes. Appendix A covers the installation of Meteor on all supported platforms. Appendix B sheds some light on the architecture of MongoDB and which components are used to achieve high availability. It also includes instructions on how to set up *oplog tailing*, an important technique behind Meteor's approach to scalability. Appendix C teaches you how to set up the reverse proxy nginx for load balancing between multiple Meteor servers, serving static content, and enabling SSL.

Prerequisites

To get the most out of this book, you'll need to have Meteor installed on your system. Instructions for installing Meteor can be found in appendix A and also on the official Meteor website (http://meteor.com).

Throughout the book we assume that you have at least basic knowledge of HTML, CSS, and JavaScript. You should know how to work with objects and have used a callback before. It is also helpful, yet not required, to have a basic understanding of how databases work. However, you do not need to have any experience with server-side JavaScript or even Node.js to be able to follow along.

Code

All code presented in this book is available as a download from the Manning website www.manning.com/books/meteor-in-action. You can also find it on GitHub at www.github.com/meteorinaction.

To make it easy to follow, each chapter is available as a separate git repository. Since not all code is printed in the book, we have added *tags* to each repository making it easy for you to get back on track if you ever get lost. For example, when you begin chapter 2, you can refer to the code tagged as begin to see what the starting code looks like. If you want to skip ahead to when we added fixtures upon server start, check out the code tagged listing-2.9.

Author Online

The purchase of *Meteor in Action* includes free access to a private forum run by Manning Publications where you can make comments about the book, ask technical questions, and receive help from the authors and other users. To access and subscribe to the forum, point your browser to www.manning.com/books/meteor-in-action. This page provides information on how to get on the forum once you are registered, what kind of help is available, and the rules of conduct in the forum.

Manning's commitment to our readers is to provide a venue where a meaningful dialogue between individual readers and between readers and the authors can take place. It's not a commitment to any specific amount of participation on the part of the authors, whose contributions to the book's forum remain voluntary (and unpaid). We suggest you try asking them some challenging questions, lest their interests stray!

The Author Online forum and the archives of previous discussions will be accessible from the publisher's website as long as the book is in print.

About the authors

Stephan Hochhaus started his development career when he accidentally found himself in a Perl class for linguists. After many years of working for large enterprises creating scalable web solutions and several flings with PHP, C#, and even Java, in 2013 he started his own business developing web apps for small and medium companies. Since he met Meteor he feels ready to settle down with JavaScript. Stephan also does consultancy work for teams introducing Scrum or Continuous Delivery. He holds a masters degree in linguistics and socio-psychology from the University of Bochum and is fluent in regular expressions.

Manuel Schoebel holds a diploma in business informatics from the University of Essen with a special focus on web entrepreneurship. Manuel spent much of his time coaching founders and developing MVPs and even founded several startups. He started with Meteor in 2012 when the platform was still in its infancy and quickly became a renowned expert in the Meteor community for his valuable blog posts. Since 2013, Manuel uses Meteor exclusively for his projects.

Together, Manuel and Stephan have established Meteor meetups in Cologne and the Ruhr area in Germany, bringing together Meteor developers to exchange ideas and present new developments.

About the title

By combining introductions, overviews, and how-to examples, the *In Action* books are designed to help learning and remembering. According to research in cognitive science, the things people remember are things they discover during self-motivated exploration.

Although no one at Manning is a cognitive scientist, we are convinced that for learning to become permanent it must pass through stages of exploration, play, and, interestingly, retelling of what is being learned. People understand and remember new things, which is to say they master them, only after actively exploring them. Humans learn *in action*. An essential part of an *In Action* book is that it is example-driven. It encourages the reader to try things out, to play with new code, and explore new ideas.

There is another, more mundane, reason for the title of this book: our readers are busy. They use books to do a job or solve a problem. They need books that allow them to jump in and jump out easily and learn just what they want just when they want it. They need books that aid them in action. The books in this series are designed for such readers.

about the cover illustration

The figure on the cover of *Meteor in Action* is a "Roustabout"—an unskilled laborer, deckhand, or dock worker, of seemingly pugnacious disposition. The illustration is taken from a nineteenth-century edition of Sylvain Maréchal's four-volume compendium of regional dress customs published in France. Each illustration is finely drawn and colored by hand. The rich variety of Maréchal's collection reminds us vividly of how culturally apart the world's towns and regions were just 200 years ago. Isolated from each other, people spoke different dialects and languages. In the streets or in the countryside, it was easy to identify where they lived and what their trade or station in life was just by their dress.

Dress codes have changed since then and the diversity by region, so rich at the time, has faded away. It is now hard to discern the inhabitants of different continents, let alone different towns or regions. Perhaps we have traded cultural diversity for a more varied personal life—certainly for a more varied and fast-paced technological life.

At a time when it is hard to tell one computer book from another, Manning celebrates the inventiveness and initiative of the computer business with book covers based on the rich diversity of regional life of two centuries ago, brought back to life by Maréchal's pictures.

Part 1

Look—a shooting star!

Part 1 serves as a high-level overview. It takes a look at the various pieces that make up the Meteor platform and how they work together. We'll introduce you to Node.js, MongoDB, and the concept of reactive programming. After a thorough look at the entire stack in chapter 1, you'll build your first Meteor application in the second chapter.

A better way to build apps

Meteors have a reputation of changing life as we know it. They're capable of making dinosaurs extinct or forcing Bruce Willis to sacrifice his life for humankind. This book is about a Meteor that impacts web development, but it doesn't threaten to destroy anything. On the contrary, it promises to offer a better way to build applications. Meteor takes several existing tools and libraries; combines them with new thoughts and new libraries, standards, and services; and bundles them to provide an entire ecosystem for developing web and mobile applications that are a delight to use.

Meteor is an open source, MEAN[1] stack–based app development platform designed to have a consistent JavaScript API across client and server with a focus on real-time, reactive applications, rapid prototyping, and code reuse.

As a developer, you know that once you open the source view of your browser all web applications are just a combination of HTML, CSS, and JavaScript. Giants like Google, Twitter, or Facebook achieve impressive results that look and feel like desktop applications rather than websites. The smoothness of Google Maps and the directness of Facebook's Messenger led to users having much higher expectations toward all sites on the internet. Meteor allows you to meet these high expectations because it provides all the infrastructure functionality like data subscriptions and user handling, allowing you to focus on implementing business functionality.

This chapter will tell you how Meteor makes your life as a developer easier. After a short look at why it was created, we'll focus on what it consists of and how you can use it to build your own applications that may take only a fraction of the time.

1.1 Introducing Meteor

If you look at the state of web development in recent years, you'll see two clear trends. First, applications become more powerful, often indistinguishable from desktop applications. Frankly, users don't care what the technology is that works behind the scenes; they simply expect a great user experience. This includes instant feedback on clicks, real-time interaction with other users, and integration with other services. The second trend is that the number of languages, libraries, tools, and workflows is increasing so quickly that it's becoming impossible for developers to keep up with all trends. As a result, we can summarize the current state of web development:

1. Users expect more convenience from applications.
2. Developers expect to worry less about making different libraries work well together or writing plumbing code.

1.1.1 The story behind Meteor

When Geoff Schmidt, Matt DeBergalis, and Nick Martin got accepted into the Y Combinator startup seed accelerator, they planned to build a travel recommendation site. But when they talked to fellow start-up companies, they realized how much they struggled with the same challenges they'd already solved when they worked on Asana, an online platform for cooperative project and task management. So they changed their plans and decided to come up with an open source platform to provide a sound foundation for web applications that are just as smooth to use as desktop applications.

---

[1] The MEAN stack refers to all applications built on top of MongoDB, Node.js, Angular, and Express.js. There are several variations of the MEAN stack, such as MEEN—MongoDB, Ember.js, Express, and Node.js. Sometimes the term is used loosely to indicate any infrastructure running on Node.js in combination with a NoSQL database.

On December 1, 2011 the Meteor Development Group (MDG) announced the first preview release of Skybreak,[1] which soon after got renamed to Meteor. Only eight months later, the project had arranged for $11.2 million in funding from big names in the industry such as Andreessen Horowitz, Matrix Partners, Peter Levine (former CEO of XenSource), Dustin Moskovitz (co-founder of Facebook), and Rod Johnson (founder of SpringSource). The Meteor GitHub repository has stayed in the top 20 most popular repositories since then and rose to become the 11th most popular repository on GitHub just days after its 1.0 release, having more stars than the Linux kernel, the Mac OS X package manager homebrew, and backbone.js.

Why did Meteor create such interest with developers? Because it takes away the need to create low-level infrastructure like data synchronization or to build pipelines to minimize and compile code and lets developers focus on business functionality. With over $11 million in funding, investors find Meteor very appealing. Similar to Xen, the free hypervisor for server virtualization, or JBoss, the Java application server, the MDG will eventually offer additional tools targeted at larger enterprises.

The MDG divides its projects into four areas:

- *Tools* such as a command-line interface (CLI), a hybrid between a build-tool like make and a package manager such as the node package manager npm, that takes care of entire build flows that prepare an application to deploy for the web or mobile devices
- A collection of *software libraries*, a suite of core packages that provide functionality that can also be extended with custom packages or Node.js modules installed via npm
- *Standards* like the Distributed Data Protocol (DDP), a WebSocket-based data protocol
- *Services* such as an official package server or a build farm

All of Meteor's projects are accessible using a unified API so that developers don't need to know which components make up the entire Meteor stack.

1.1.2 The Meteor stack

Simply put, Meteor is an open source platform for creating rich web applications entirely in JavaScript. It bundles and provides all required pieces under one umbrella. It consists of Node.js, MongoDB, the actual application code, and a powerful CLI tool that combines the power of npm and make. As such, it's more than a combination of server processes and libraries. Some like to refer to it as an entire ecosystem rather than a framework. But even if it goes beyond what other web frameworks offer, at its core it still relies on a stack to run applications.

The Meteor stack (see figure 1.1) is a member of the MEAN family, which means it's powered by Node.js on the server side. Node.js is an event-driven, highly scalable

---

[1] https://www.meteor.com/blog/2011/12/01/first-preview

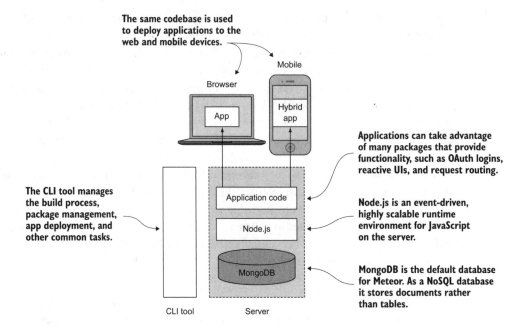

The same codebase is used
to deploy applications to the
web and mobile devices.

Mobile

Browser

App

Hybrid
app

The CLI tool manages
the build process,
package management,
app deployment, and
other common tasks.

Application code

Node.js

MongoDB

Applications can take advantage
of many packages that provide
functionality, such as OAuth logins,
reactive UIs, and request routing.

Node.js is an event-driven,
highly scalable runtime
environment for JavaScript
on the server.

MongoDB is the default database
for Meteor. As a NoSQL database
it stores documents rather
than tables.

CLI tool   Server

Figure 1.1   The Meteor stack runs applications powered by smart packages on top of Node.js and MongoDB.

runtime for JavaScript on the server. It serves the same purpose as an Apache web server in the LAMP (Linux, Apache, MySQL, PHP) stack.

All data is typically stored inside a MongoDB, a document-oriented NoSQL database. There are plans for Meteor to support other (SQL-based) database systems, but currently the only suggested database is Mongo. It provides a JavaScript API that gives access to all stored content in the form of documents or objects. The same language used inside the browser can be used to access data, which Meteor takes advantage of to implement true full-stack development.

All software and libraries required to create web applications from scratch are bundled in the shape of smart packages, so developers can get started right away. These packages include a reactive UI library (Blaze), user account management (accounts), and a library for transparent reactive programming (Tracker).

The Meteor CLI tool allows developers to quickly set up an entire development environment. There's no need to know how to install or configure any server software; Meteor takes care of the infrastructure aspect entirely. It's also both a build tool, comparable to make or grunt, and a package manager, such as apt or npm. For example, it can compile preprocessor languages such as LESS or CoffeeScript on the fly, without first setting up workflow, or add authentication via Facebook OAuth with a single command. Finally, the CLI tool bundles an application to run on different client platforms, inside a web browser or as native mobile apps.

All parts of the stack integrate seamlessly; all core packages are designed and tested to work well together. On the other hand, it's entirely possible to switch out parts of the stack for others, should the need arise. Instead of using Meteor in full, you could decide to use only the server components and use, for example, Angular.js on the client side, or use a Java back end that uses Meteor on the front end to provide real-time updates to all clients.

1.1.3 *Isomorphic frameworks: full-stack JavaScript*

Meteor runs on top of Node.js and moves the application logic to the browser, which is often referred to as *single-page applications*. The same language is used across the entire stack, which makes Meteor an isomorphic platform. As a result, the same JavaScript code can be used on the server, the client, and even in the database.

Although many frameworks use the same language on both client and server, most of the time they can't share code between the two instances because the frameworks aren't tightly integrated—for example, they use Angular on the front end and Express.js on the back end. Meteor is truly full-stack because it uses a simple and unified API that exposes all core functionality and can be used on the server, in the browser, and even to access the database. To get started you don't have to learn multiple frameworks, and it results in much better reusability of the code than only using the same language.

To allow you to access the database from the browser, Meteor includes mini-databases. They simulate the exact same API of a database. Inside the browser, *Minimongo* allows developers to use the same commands as they would in a MongoDB console.

All Meteor applications run on top of Node.js, a server that interprets application code written in JavaScript. In contrast to many other application servers, it uses only a single thread. In multithreaded environments, a single thread that writes to disk may block all other threads and put all further client requests on hold until a write operation finishes. Node.js, on the other hand, is able to queue all write requests and continue taking and processing requests, effectively avoiding race conditions (that is, two operations trying to update the same data simultaneously). The application code runs in sequence from top to bottom, or synchronously.

Long-running operations such as I/O to disk or database may be split off from the synchronous sequence. They'll be processed in an asynchronous way. Node.js doesn't wait until these finish, but it attaches a callback and revisits the results of an operation once it finishes, meanwhile working on the next requests in line. To better understand synchronous and asynchronous events, let's consider a familiar programming scenario: heating up a frozen pizza.

Figure 1.2 details all the steps required to prepare food from the freezer. Each step is an event, albeit a pretty small one in our lives. Every event that requires our attention takes place in a synchronous stream of events: we take the pizza from the freezer, unwrap it, preheat the oven, put the pizza in, and set an alarm. That's the point when we actually branch off a subprocess. At its core, cooking the pizza in the oven is a long-running I/O process. We set the alarm to be notified when it's done so we can

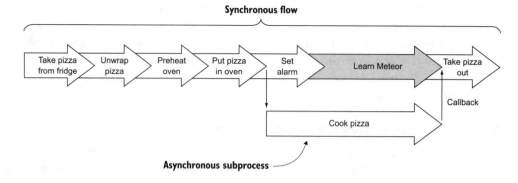

Figure 1.2   **Synchronous and asynchronous events when heating up a pizza**

attend to more important matters, like learning Meteor. When the alarm goes off, it calls our attention and puts the result of the subprocess back in our synchronous flow. We can take the pizza out and move on.

As you can see from this example, cooking the pizza doesn't block your flow. But if your colleague also wants a pizza and you have room for only one inside the oven, he'll need to queue his request—this effectively blocks all others in the office from heating up their pizza.

In Node.js the synchronous flow takes place as long as the server runs. It's called the *event loop*. Figure 1.3 shows how the event loop deals with processing user requests. It takes one event at a time from a queue. The associated code is executed, and when it finishes, the next event is pulled into the loop. But some events may be offloaded to a thread pool—for example, operations writing to disk or database. Once the write operation is finished, a callback function will be executed that returns the result of the operation back into the event loop.

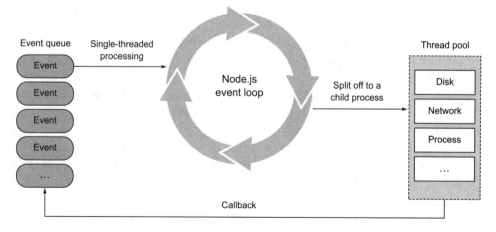

Figure 1.3   **The Node.js event loop**

Typically, developers need to know how to write code that takes full advantage of the event loop and which functions run synchronously and which asynchronously. The more asynchronous functionality is used, the more callbacks are involved and things can become quite messy.

Fortunately, Meteor leverages the full power of the event loop, but it makes it easy because you don't have to worry so much about writing asynchronous code. It uses a concept called *fibers* behind the scenes. Fibers provide an abstraction layer for the event loop that executes asynchronous functions (tasks) in sequence. It removes the need for explicit callbacks so that a familiar synchronous style can be used.

1.1.4 *Processing in the browser: running on distributed platforms*

When using a back end running a Java, PHP, or Rails application, processing takes place far away from the user. Clients request data by calling a URI. In response, the application fetches data from a database, performs some processing to create HTML, and sends the results to a client. The more clients request the same information, the more caching can be done by the server. News sites work particularly well with this paradigm.

In a scenario where each user has the means to create highly individualized views, a single processing instance can quickly become a bottleneck. Consider Facebook as an example: no two people will ever see the exact same wall—it needs to be computed for each user individually. That puts a lot of stress on the servers while clients idle most of the time, waiting for a response.

When the processing power of clients was relatively limited this made perfect sense, but these days a single iPhone already has more computing power than most supercomputers in the early days of the web. Meteor takes advantage of that power and delegates most of the processing to the clients. Smart front ends request data from the server and assemble the Document Object Model (DOM) only in the browser or mobile device (see figure 1.4).

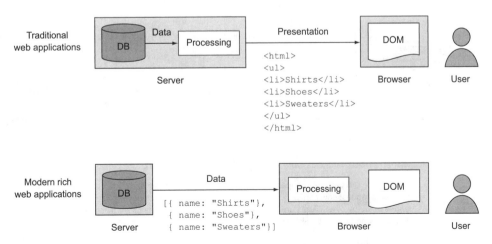

Figure 1.4 The difference between traditional and modern rich web applications

This client-centric approach brings two significant advantages:

- Less data needs to be transferred between server and client, which essentially translates into quicker response times.
- Processing is less likely to be blocked by other users due to long-running requests, because most of the work is done on each individual client.

Traditional client-server architectures are based on stateless connections. Clients request data once, the server responds, and the connection is closed again. Updates from other clients may happen, but unless users explicitly make a server request again, they won't see the updates but an historic snapshot of the site. There's no feedback channel from the server to the client to push out updated content.

Imagine you open your local movie theater's site and see only two seats are left to the new Joss Whedon movie premiere. While you debate whether you should go, someone else buys these tickets. Your browser keeps telling you two seats are available until you decide to click again, only to find out that the tickets are gone. Bummer.

Moving the processing from a single server to multiple clients involves moving into the direction of distributed computing platforms. In such distributed environments, data needs to be sent in both directions. In Meteor, the browser is a smart client. Connections aren't stateless anymore; the server may send data to the client whenever there are updates to subscribed content. Figure 1.5 shows the various architectures. To allow bidirectional communication between server and client, Meteor uses Web-Sockets. A standardized protocol named *Distributed Data Protocol* (DDP) is used to exchange messages. DDP is simple to use and can be used with many other programming languages like PHP or Java as well.

As a consequence of moving applications to the browser, all clients essentially become nodes of an application cluster. This introduces new challenges already

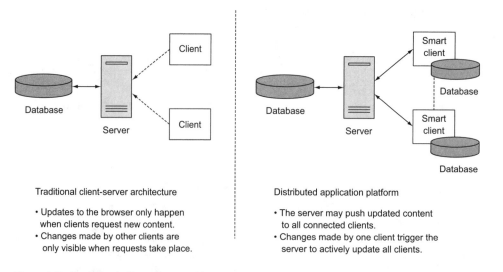

Traditional client-server architecture

- Updates to the browser only happen when clients request new content.
- Changes made by other clients are only visible when requests take place.

Distributed application platform

- The server may push updated content to all connected clients.
- Changes made by one client trigger the server to actively update all clients.

Figure 1.5 Traditional client-server architectures compared to distributed application platforms

familiar from distributed server farms, most importantly synchronizing data between all nodes. Meteor takes care of this by means of its reactive nature.

1.1.5 Reactive programming

Applications created by traditional programming paradigms are much like a golem[1] you sent off with a plan. No matter what happens, the golem will keep walking and following directions. As its creator, you must be diligent about each and every step you command. For example, in an application you must define that you want to listen to changes to a drop-down element and what actions to take when a new value is selected. Also, you need to define what the application should do if another user has meanwhile deleted the associated entry while the first wants to display its contents. In other words, traditional programming hardly reacts to the world but follows orders given to it in code.

The real world happens to be slightly different. Especially on the web, a lot of events happen and the more complex usage scenarios get, the harder it is to foresee in which sequence events will occur.

In a desktop environment reactivity is the norm. When you use a Microsoft Excel spreadsheet and change the value in one cell, all other values depending on it will automatically recalculate. Even charts will be adjusted without the need to click *refresh*. An event, such as changing a cell, triggers reactions in related parts of the sheet. All cells are reactive.

To illustrate how reactivity differs from procedural programming, let's look at a simple example. We have two variables: a and b. We'll store the result of adding a and b in a variable called c using the procedural way of doing things. With actual values, it looks like this:

```
a = 2;
b = 5;
c = a + b;
```

The value of c is now 7. What happens if we change the value of a to 5? c won't change unless we explicitly call the addition code again. A developer therefore needs to include a checking method to observe whether a or b has changed. In a reactive approach, the value of c will automatically be set to 10 because the underlying engine is taking care of observing change. There's no need to periodically check that neither a nor b has changed or even explicitly initiating recalculations. The focus is on what the system should do and not how to do it.

In a web environment, achieving the Excel effect can be achieved in various ways. Using poll and diff, you could check for changes every two seconds. In scenarios where a lot of users are involved and little change happens, this puts a lot of stress on

---

[1] A golem is a mythical creature. Usually made from clay, it's magically brought to life and carries out its master's wishes to the letter. Terry Pratchett's *Feet of Clay* is a good first introduction if you're a fan of the fantastic.

all components involved and is extremely ineffective. Increasing the polling interval makes the UI appear slow and sluggish. Alternatively, you can monitor all possible events and define actions writing a lot of code to mimic the desktop behavior. This option becomes a maintenance nightmare when you need to update various elements in the DOM, even if each event fires only a handful of update operations. A reactive environment offers a third option that enables low-latency UIs with concise, maintainable code.

Reactive systems need to react to events, load, failure, and users.[1] To do so, they must be nonblocking and asynchronous. Remember when we talked about full-stack JavaScript? Then you'll notice that reactivity and JavaScript are a natural fit. Also we discussed that Meteor applications run distributed and that the server isn't the only instance responsible for creating a user's view. Load can still be scaled across multiple servers, but it also scales across each client. Should one of these clients ever fail, it doesn't bring down the entire application.

Although you can still build a less-than-optimal system by not taking into account the principles of reactive systems, reactivity is built into the core of Meteor. You don't have to worry about learning a new programming style; you can continue to use the same synchronous style you're used to. In many cases Meteor automatically hooks up reactivity without you even noticing it.

All components, from the database to the client UI, are reactive. This means all changes to data are synchronized between clients in real time. There's no need to write any Ajax routines or code to push updates to users because this functionality is directly built into Meteor. Also, it effectively removes the need to write most of the glue code when integrating different components, thereby shortening development times significantly.

Reactive programming certainly isn't the best approach for every scenario, but it fits perfectly into the way web applications work because in most cases we need to capture events and perform actions on it. Beyond the user experience, it can help improve quality and transparency, reduce programming time, and decrease maintenance.

1.2 How Meteor works

Once deployed on a server, Meteor applications can hardly be told apart from other Node.js-based projects. The platform's real strength comes to light when you look closely at how Meteor supplements the development process. A CLI tool and a collection of packages enable developers to quickly achieve results and focus on adding functionality to an application. Infrastructure concerns such as data exchange between database and browser or integrating user authentication via external OAuth providers are taken care of by adding packages.

---

[1] The reactive manifesto defines how reactive systems should be designed and behave in production environments; see www.reactivemanifesto.org.

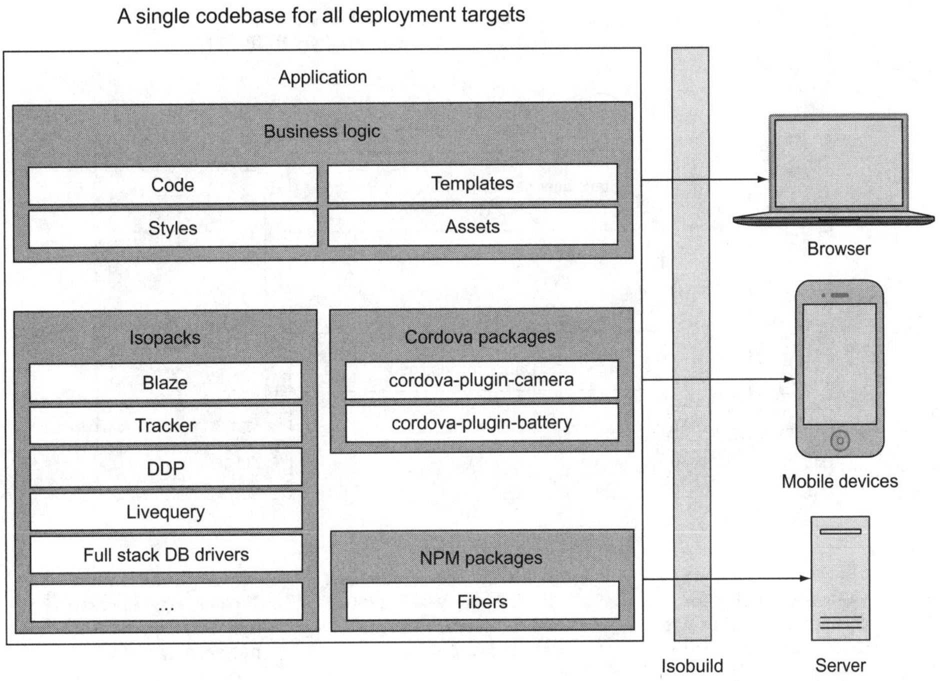

A single codebase for all deployment targets

Figure 1.6   Applications consist of business logic and various packages, which are compiled for the target platform using Isobuild.

Figure 1.6 shows the anatomy of Meteor applications. Developers define business logic that consists of code, templates and styles, and assets such as image files. Meteor can leverage the power of external packages from the Node.js ecosystem via npm and Cordova for mobile devices. Additionally, it defines its own package format called *Isopacks.*

Isopacks are designed to work in both server and client environments and may also contain templates and images. They may even extend Isobuild, the build process that outputs deployable code for all targeted platforms. Isobuild and Isopacks are Meteor's core ingredients.

Meteor applications communicate over both HTTP and WebSockets (see figure 1.7). The initial page request and all static files such as images, fonts, styles, and JavaScript files are transferred over HTTP. The applications running on client and server rely on the DDP protocol to exchange data. SockJS provides the necessary infrastructure. The client calls methods on the server using remote procedure calls. The client is calling a function over the network. The server sends back its responses as JavaScript Object Notation (JSON) objects. Furthermore, each client may subscribe to certain data publications. The Livequery component takes care of pushing out any changes to a subscribed dataset over DDP as well. The reactive Tracker library watches for those changes and triggers DOM updates in the UI layer via Blaze.

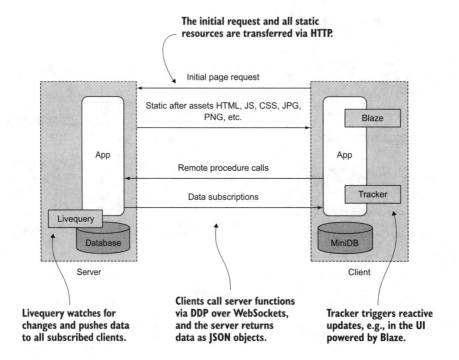

Figure 1.7   Communication between the server and client

1.2.1   Core projects

Meteor ships with a number of packages that provide commonly used functionality for web-based applications. A CLI tool allows you to create a new project and add or remove packages with a single command. New projects contain all core packages already.

BLAZE

Blaze is a reactive UI library, and one of its parts is the templating language Spacebars. Because developers usually (only) interact with the front-end lib via the templating language and Spacebars is relatively easy to use (in comparison to other templating languages), Blaze is simpler to use than React, Angular, or Ember.

The official documentation describes Blaze as a "reactive jQuery," a powerful library to update the DOM. But it doesn't follow the same imperative style jQuery uses ("find element #user-list and add a new li node!"), but a declarative approach ("render all usernames from the DB in this list using templates users!"). When content changes, Blaze re-renders only small fragments inside a template and not the entire page. It also plays nicely with other UI libraries such as jQuery-UI or even Angular.

TRACKER

The Tracker package provides the fundamentals of functional reactive programming (FRP). At its core Tracker is a simple convention that allows reactive data sources, such as data from the database, to be connected to data consumers. Remember this code from section 1.1.5:

```
c = a + b
```

a and b are reactive data sources, and c is the consumer. A change to either a or b triggers a recomputation of c. Tracker achieves reactivity by setting up a reactive context with dependencies between data and functions, invalidating the given context whenever data changes and reexecuting functions.

DDP

Accessing web applications is usually done over HTTP, which by definition is a protocol for exchanging documents. Although it does have advantages for transferring documents, HTTP has several shortcomings when passing data only, so Meteor uses a dedicated protocol based on JSON called DDP. DDP is a standard way to pass data over WebSockets bidirectionally, without the overhead of encapsulating documents. This protocol is the foundation for all reactive functionality and is one of the core elements of Meteor.

DDP is a standard approach to solving the biggest problem facing client-side JavaScript developers: querying a server-side database, sending the results down to the client, and then pushing changes to the client whenever anything changes in the database. DDP implementations are available in most major languages like Java, Python, or Objective-C. This means you can use Meteor just as a front-end component for an application and use a Java back end to communicate with it via DDP.

LIVEQUERY

Distributed environments like Meteor need a way to push changes initiated by one client to all others without needing a refresh button. Livequery detects changes in the database and pushes all changes out to the clients currently viewing affected data. At 1.0 Meteor is tightly integrated with MongoDB, but additional databases support is already on the roadmap.

FULL-STACK DATABASE DRIVERS

Many of the tasks performed on a client rely on database functionality, like filtering and sorting. Meteor leverages a seamless *database everywhere* principle. This means as a developer you can reuse most of your code anywhere in the stack.

Meteor comes with mini-databases that simulate an actual database inside the browser. The miniature database for MongoDB is called Minimongo, an in-memory, nonpersistent implementation of MongoDB in pure JavaScript. It doesn't rely on HTML5 Local Storage because it exists only in the browser's memory.

The in-browser database mirrors a subset of the actual server data and is used to simulate actions like inserts. It's also used as a cache for queries, so a client can directly access available data without any network activity. Because the connection between Minimongo and MongoDB is also reactive, the data is automatically kept in sync.

Latency is a key differentiating factor between desktop applications and the web. Nobody likes to wait, so Meteor uses prefetching and model simulation on the client to make it look like your app has a zero-latency connection to the database. The local Minimongo instance will be used to simulate any database operations before sending requests to the server.

The client doesn't have to wait for the remote database to finish writing, but the application assumes it'll eventually be successful, which roughly makes the vast majority of all use cases seem much quicker. In those cases where problems occurred when passing the write action to the server, the client needs to roll back gracefully and display an error message.

A typical flow of events is shown in figure 1.8. Once a user publishes a comment, it'll be validated first and then immediately stored in the Minimongo database in the browser. Unless validation fails, this operation will be successful and the user's view will be updated immediately. Because up to this point no network traffic is involved and all actions take place in memory, the user will experience no latency. In the background, though, the action is still ongoing.

The comment gets sent to the server, where again validations take place, and afterward the comment is stored in the database. A notification is sent to the browser indicating whether the storing operation was successful. At this point, at least one full server round-trip together with some disk I/O took place, but those have no impact on the user experience. From a user's perspective there's no delay in updating the view because latency compensation already took care of any updates in the fourth step. Eventually the comment gets published to all other clients as well.

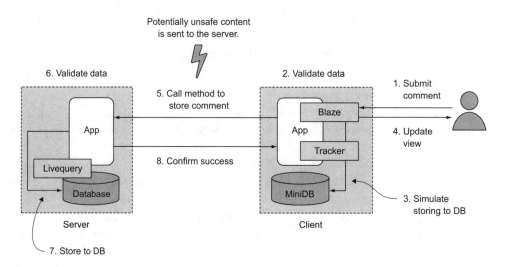

Figure 1.8   Data flow using latency compensation

ADDITIONAL PACKAGES

Besides the core packages many more packages are available as part of Meteor and are provided by the development community. They include functionality to easily integrate users and OAuth authentication via Twitter, GitHub, and others.

1.2.2 *Isobuild and the CLI tool*

On a computer with a Meteor installation, entering `meteor` on the command line will bring up the CLI tool. This tool is both a build tool comparable to `make` or `grunt` and a package manager such as `apt` or `npm`. It enables you to manage all tasks concerning your application:

- Create new applications
- Add and remove functionality in form of packages
- Compile and minify scripts and styles
- Run, reset, and monitor applications
- Access MongoDB shell
- Prepare an application for deployment
- Deploy applications to the meteor.com infrastructure

Creating a new project is a single command upon which the CLI tool creates all essential files and folder structures for a simple application. A second command starts a complete development stack, including a Node.js server and a MongoDB instance to enable a fully working development. Any file changes are monitored and directly sent to the clients in the form of hot code pushes so that you can fully focus on writing code instead of starting and restarting servers.

When starting a development instance or getting ready for production, Meteor gathers all source files, compiles and minifies code and styles, creates source maps, and takes care of any package dependencies. As such, it combines the power of `grunt` with `npm`.

There's no need to define processing chains if you use LESS instead of plain CSS; all it takes is to add the corresponding Isopack. All *.less files will automatically be processed by Meteor:

```
$ meteor add less
```

Add the `coffeescript` package to enable compiling from CoffeeScript to JavaScript.

1.2.3 *Client code vs. server code*

When you begin working with Meteor, you'll find that knowing which code should be executed in which environment is essential to writing applications. Theoretically all code can run anywhere in the stack, but some limitations exist. API keys should never be sent to the client—event maps that handle mouse clicks aren't useful on the server. To let Meteor know where to execute specific code, you can organize files in dedicated folders or use a check to verify in which context they're running.

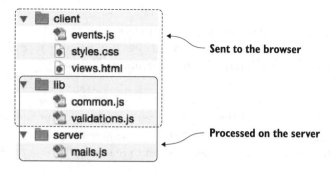

Figure 1.9   The file structure for a simple application

As an example, all code that handles mouse events might be placed inside a folder named client. Also, all HTML and CSS files won't be needed on the server side, which is why they'll also be found inside the client folder. Access credentials to a mail server or API secret keys must never be sent to the client—they'll be kept exclusively on the server (see figure 1.9).

All content from the server folder will never be sent to the client. To avoid redundancies, shared code can be saved to a file inside the shared folders such as lib, and it becomes available in both contexts. You can easily use front-end libraries like jQuery on the server as well.

Sharing code between both instances is especially helpful when it comes to input validation. The same method to validate that a user entered a correct credit card number can be used to display an error message in the browser and again on the server side to prevent inserting faulty data to the database on the server. Without Meteor you'd have to define one method in JavaScript for validation in the browser and another method in your server context because everything coming from the browser must be validated before working with it to establish a certain level of security. If your back end is written in a language like Ruby, PHP, or Java, not only is there redundant code, but also the same task needs to be done twice. Even if using JavaScript on the server side in other frameworks you'd need to copy and paste the validation section to a file on the server and a second file on the client. Meteor removes this need by processing the same file on both ends.

During the initial page load all JavaScript, styles, and static assets like images or fonts are transferred to the client.[1] As figure 1.10 shows, all files are available on the server but aren't executed as part of the application. Similarly, not all files are sent to the client, so developers can have better control over which code runs in which environment. Transferring files is done via HTTP, which is also used as a fallback for browsers that don't support WebSockets. After the initial page load, only data is exchanged via DDP.

---

[1] Technically, all JavaScript files are combined into a single app.js file, but for better traceability individual files illustrate the information flow.

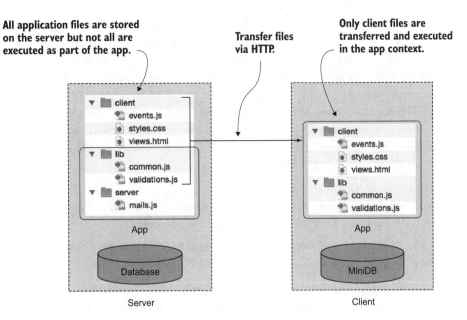

All application files are stored on the server but not all are executed as part of the app.

Transfer files via HTTP.

Only client files are transferred and executed in the app context.

Figure 1.10   Data exchange between server and client via HTTP and DDP

1.3   Strengths and weaknesses

As with any tool there are situations when Meteor will be a perfect fit, but there will always be scenarios in which using it might be a poor choice. Generally speaking, any application based on the principles of distributed application platforms will greatly benefit from using it, whereas the more static a site is, the less you'll gain from using Meteor.

1.3.1   Where Meteor shines

The Meteor platform offers all the tools required to build applications for different platforms—the web or mobile. It's a one-stop shop for developers and makes it much simpler to get started with than most other frameworks. The main advantages of Meteor are a single language across the entire stack, built-in reactivity, and a thriving ecosystem of packages to extend existing functionality. In summary, this translates to development speed.

Having one language across the entire application stack, a protocol that's designed for data exchange, and simple unified APIs removes the need for additional JavaScript frameworks such as AngularJS or Backbone that talk to sophisticated REST back ends. That makes Meteor extremely well suited for projects that require fast results while still meeting high user expectations.

EASY TO LEARN

Quickly achieving visible results is one of the best motivators for learners. Meteor leverages the power of the MEAN stack, which may be very powerful but also rather complex to learn. To increase developer productivity, Meteor exposes this power behind one common JavaScript API. New developers don't have to take a deep dive into the specifics of loosely coupled front-end libraries and back-end frameworks before they can achieve results. Knowing the fundamentals of JavaScript is sufficient to get started.

Meteor's common API also makes it easier to work with the Node.js event loop by allowing developers to write synchronous code instead of worrying about nested callback structures. Existing knowledge can be reused, because familiar libraries like jQuery or Underscore are part of the stack.

CLIENT-SIDE APPLICATIONS

With increasingly powerful clients, much of the application can be executed on the client instead of the server. This gives us two main benefits that are also valid for Meteor:

- Less load on the server as clients perform some of the processing
- Better responsiveness of actions in the user interface

To efficiently promote browsers to smart clients, it's important to provide a two-way communication infrastructure so that the server may push changes out to the client. With DDP, Meteor provides not only a transport layer but a full solution for communicating in both directions. These stateless connections are a core feature of the platform, and developers can take advantage of them without worrying about message formats.

INSTANT UPDATES USING REACTIVE PROGRAMMING

Much of an application's code is about handling events. Users clicking certain elements may trigger a function that updates documents inside the database and updates the current view. When using reactive programming, the code you need to write for handling events is reduced. Massive collaboration that consists of hundreds of events becomes much more manageable. For that reason, Meteor is especially suited for real-time chats and online games or even to power the Internet of Things.

HIGH CODE REUSE

Meteor delivers on the old Java promise: write once, run anywhere. Because of the isomorphic nature of Meteor, the same code may run inside the browser, on the server, or even on a mobile device.

For example, in REST architectures the back end must talk to the database in SQL while the clients expect JSON. Taking advantage of in-browser mini-databases, the server can publish a handful of records to a client, which in turn accesses this data as if it were in a real database. That enables powerful latency compensation with minimal coding requirements.

POWERFUL BUILD TOOLS

Out of the box, Meteor offers a CLI tool that acts as a package and build manager. It covers the entire build process, from gathering and compiling of source files to minification, source mapping, and resolving of dependencies. This Isobuild tool optimizes an application for the web or packages it as a mobile Android or iOS app.

1.3.2 Challenges when using Meteor

Although you can use Meteor to build any type of site, in some situations it's best to use alternatives. Given its relatively young age and positioning, you may encounter certain challenges when working with Meteor.

PROCESSING INTENSE APPLICATIONS

Especially when your application relies on heavy processing such as data-crunching extract, transform, and load (ETL) jobs, Meteor won't be able to handle the load well. By nature, any Node.js process is single-threaded, so it's much harder to take advantage of fast multiprocessor capabilities. In a multitier architecture, Meteor could be used to serve the UI, but it doesn't offer a lot of computing power.

The way to integrate more processing power into a Meteor application is similar to any other Node.js application: you delegate CPU-intense tasks to child processes. But this is also a best-practice architecture for any language, where multiple tiers are used to separate the number crunching from the user interface.

MATURITY

Meteor is relatively young and still has to prove itself in production environments in regard to scaling or search engine rankings. Scaling applications in particular requires a lot of knowledge about the components involved and possible bottlenecks.

Although Node.js has proven that it's capable of scaling to large loads, Meteor still has to show it can handle large deployments and a high number of requests. Conservative users might argue that it's safer to rely on an established foundation. Just keep in mind that any server stack and framework is likely to be slow if the application isn't written with scalability and performance in mind.

Even if the Meteor community is friendly and helpful, it is in no way comparable with the huge resources available for PHP or Java. The same goes for hosting options; there aren't yet as many dedicated Node.js or Meteor solutions available as for PHP or even Python. If you plan on hosting your application on your own infrastructure, several solutions are available.

As with all young projects, the number of tools available around the framework itself is rather limited with Meteor as of now. Velocity is a community-driven effort to create a testing framework, which has active developers but isn't part of the core Meteor projects. Also, debugging tools aren't as convenient as the ones available for Java or PHP.

FEW CONVENTIONS ON STRUCTURE

There are only few suggestions for structuring applications and code in Meteor. This freedom is great for single developers who can quickly hack on code, but it requires good coordination between team members when applications grow in size. It's up to developers' preference whether they use a single file or hundreds of folders and files. Some may embrace this freedom; others will find it necessary to define clear structures before being able to start coding.

USING SQL AND ALTERNATIVE DATABASES

The roadmap shows that someday Meteor will support SQL databases, but for now the only officially supported database is MongoDB. To use additional systems like MySQL or PostgreSQL, community packages must be used. Although several community members have successfully launched applications backed by SQL databases, no full-stack support exists for latency compensation and transparent client-to-server updates. If you need a rock-solid and fully supported stack with relational data high on your priority list, then Meteor is not yet for you.

SERVING STATIC CONTENT

Some sites like newspapers and magazines rely heavily on static content. Those are the sites that profit most from server-rendered HTML and can use advanced caching mechanisms that speed up the site for all users. Also, the initial loading times are much faster.

If initial loading times are important to your app, or it serves mostly the same content for a large number of users, you won't be able to leverage all the advantages of Meteor. In fact, you'll need to find ways to work around its standard behavior to optimize for your use case and you therefore might want to use a more traditional framework to build your site.

Who is using Meteor? (From the horse's mouth)

Despite its young history, Meteor is already powering many successful projects and even entire companies.

Adrian Lanning's Share911.com was one of the early adopters to the Meteor platform. In case of an emergency, the application enables you to simultaneously alert the people you work with as well as public safety personnel. The main criterion for picking a technology was speed—both in real-time behavior as well as development time. Adrian researched the event-driven technologies Netty (Java), Tornado (Python), and Node.js. After further evaluation of Tower and Derby.js, he decided to develop a prototype using Meteor, which took less than 10 days.

> *Happily, Meteor has been solid and we haven't needed to make a change. We have included other technologies but I am confident Meteor will be the core web tier for us for a long time.*
>
> —Adrian Lanning

Workpop.com provides a job platform for hiring hourly-wage workers. With a team of only two developers and just five months' time, CTO Ben Berman managed to create a modern take on what job boards on the internet should look like. Over $7 million in funding prove that their decision to go with Meteor has paid off. Workpop's philosophy is to keep technology out of the way and focus on their goal of getting people hired. Although very performant, both Spring (Java) and ASP.net were found to be too intensive, and even Rails was dismissed because it encourages building RESTful applications.

By sticking to familiar JavaScript and shipping with the best reactive UI kit on the web, Meteor delivers on its promise of rapid iteration for small teams.

—Ben Berman

With lookback.io, it's possible to record mobile user experiences and get insight into how people use your application at the push of a button. The initial version was built using Django, but lead developer Carl Littke switched to Meteor soon after. Achieving the same results using Django, Angular, and the associated REST APIs turned out to be a much more complex task than relying on Meteor's built-in reactivity, data APIs, and login. Speed of development was the most important aspect when choosing Meteor. This also made up for the areas where Meteor's young age is still showing.

The Meteor Development Group has done an exceptional job of developing a framework that solves some of the major pain points of developing web apps today. I wouldn't think twice about using Meteor for my next project.

—Carl Littke

Sara Hicks and Aaron Judd created the open source shopping platform ReactionCommerce.com. They consider Meteor's event-driven nature a perfect fit for enhancing sales using dynamic merchandising and real-time promotions and pricing. Having a single codebase for the web and mobile devices was a big plus. Meteor isn't the only technology used for the Reaction platform, but it forms the foundation. Additional libraries are added into the project, thanks to the support for all Node.js packages via npm.

Slow speed can cost retailers as much as 13 percent of sales. Thanks to Meteor's latency compensation the screen will redraw right away. This translates into happier customers and better sales figures.

—Sara Hicks

Sacha Greif created the popular Hacker News clone Telescope. When looking for the right stack, he narrowed his choices down to Rails and Node.js. With Rails he was worried about managing a large number of moving parts with hundreds of files and gems, and as a designer, he was already familiar with JavaScript. He made the decision for Meteor in 2012 despite its still limited feature set at that time. Today Telescope is powering sites like crater.io (news about Meteor) and bootstrappers.io (a community for bootstrapped entrepreneurs).

What really appealed to me was the all-in-one aspect: all these things that required piecing together multiple solutions with other frameworks were provided out of the box with Meteor.

—Sacha Greif

1.4   *Creating new applications*

We've discussed a lot of theory; now it's time to look at the code. Before you proceed, make sure you've installed Meteor on your machine. Refer to appendix A to guide you through the process.

Because Meteor is also a CLI tool, we'll need to perform the initial setup of our application in a shell environment. This allows us to install the framework and create new applications. All the steps in this section will be performed inside a terminal.

1.4.1   *Setting up a new project*

When Meteor is installed, the CLI tool is used to create a new project. Navigate to the folder you want to contain your application and type the following into the terminal (see figure 1.11):

```
$ meteor create helloWorld
```

Meteor creates a new project folder and three files automatically:

- helloWorld.css contains all styling information.
- helloWorld.html contains all templates.
- helloWorld.js contains the actual logic.

NOTE   Every project contains an invisible folder, .meteor (see figure 1.11), where runtime files such as the development database, compiled files, meta-information regarding used packages, and other automatically generated content goes. For development purposes, we can ignore this folder.

Figure 1.11   A basic Meteor application created with the Meteor CLI tool

You can now start creating your own application by changing the content of the existing files. For this project the three files will suffice, but for any other project that's even a little more complex, it's better to create folders and split your code into separate files to maintain a better overview. We'll take a close look at how to structure your projects in the next chapter.

1.4.2 Starting the application

The CLI tool of Meteor also starts the application with the following command:

```
$ meteor run
```

You can also start a Meteor server by calling the `meteor` command without any arguments; `run` is the default behavior. Behind the scenes, it starts both a Node.js server instance on port 3000 as well as a MongoDB listening on port 3001.

You can access the application with your web browser at http://localhost:3000 (see figure 1.12).

Should you need to change the port Meteor is listening on, you can do so by passing the argument `--port` to the `meteor` command. The following command starts Meteor on port 8080:

```
$ meteor run --port 8080
```

As you can see, the application is up and running and it has one button. If you click the Click Me button, the text below will update automatically, showing you exactly how many times you've clicked it since you loaded the web page. This is because the application already has an event binding included. Let's take a closer look at the file contents and find out how that binding works.

1.5 Dissecting the default project

The helloWorld application at this state is very simple. Because all files are in the root folder of the project, they're all executed on the server and sent to the client. Let's see what each file does.

Figure 1.12 Every new Meteor project is a simple application with a single button.

1.5.1   *helloWorld.css*

By default, this file is empty. Because it's a CSS file, you can use it to store your custom style information. If you put something into this file, the styles will immediately be applied to the application. Meteor automatically parses through all files ending with .css and will send those to the client for you. Try, for example, adding `body { back-ground: red; }`. Save the file and you'll see the background of your application in a beautiful red color.

1.5.2   *helloWorld.html*

The file shown in listing 1.1 contains the templates used in our project. Templates control the overall look and layout of an application. Although the file extension is .html, the code inside isn't fully valid HTML as you'd expect.

> **Listing 1.1   `helloWorld` template**

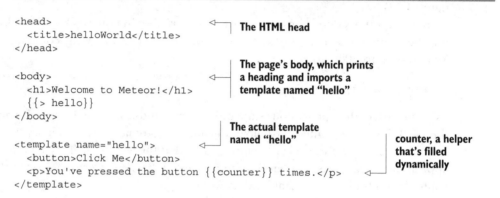

```
<head>
  <title>helloWorld</title>               The HTML head
</head>

<body>                                     The page's body, which prints
  <h1>Welcome to Meteor!</h1>             a heading and imports a
  {{> hello}}                             template named "hello"
</body>

                                          The actual template
                                          named "hello"                counter, a helper
<template name="hello">                                                that's filled
  <button>Click Me</button>                                            dynamically
  <p>You've pressed the button {{counter}} times.</p>
</template>
```

First, three different elements appear here: an HTML head, an HTML body, and a template named `hello`. As you can see, the opening `<html>` tag of a valid HTML document is missing. Meteor adds it automatically, so you don't need to worry about it.

The body consists of only an `h1` heading and a placeholder using Handlebars syntax. The curly brackets let you know that you're dealing with some sort of dynamic content. The greater-than symbol indicates that another template will be injected into the document at this position. It's followed by the name of the template. Therefore, the placeholder inserts a template named `hello` into the `body` element:

```
{{> hello}}
```

When starting the server, Meteor parses all files with an .html extension to collect all templates. It recognizes and manages any references and inclusions. For this to work properly, every template needs to have an opening `<template>` and closing `</template>` tag. The `name` attribute is needed to reference a template in order to include it. A template's name is case sensitive and must always be unique.

You also need to be able to reference the template somehow in your JavaScript to extend it with some functionality, as you'll see in the helloWorld.js file in the next section. Again, the name of the template is used to make that connection.

Finally, you need a way to inject data from the JavaScript code into the template. That's the purpose of {{ counter }}, a so-called *helper*. Helpers are JavaScript methods with a return value that's available to the template. If you look at your browser, you'll find that instead of {{ counter }} you can see the number of clicks. Let's look at the corresponding code.

1.5.3 helloWorld.js

The JavaScript file of a basic project contains several fundamental concepts of Meteor. The first snippet we want to show you is this:

```
if (Meteor.isClient) {
  //...
}

if (Meteor.isServer) {
  //...
}
```

There are two if statements, both relating to a Boolean variable of the global Meteor object itself. Remember that all code that you write is available to both the client and the server unless you apply any restrictions. Being available also means code gets executed in both environments. Sometimes, though, you need to specify whether code should run only on the server or only on the client. By checking for these two attributes of the global Meteor object, you can always find out where you are.

In any project, the code block in the first if statement will run only if the context is the client and the code block in the second if statement will run only if the context is the server.

You should be aware that the entire code from this file is available on the server and the client. That means you must *never* put security-related code (like private API keys) into an if (Meteor.isServer) block because doing so may send it directly to the client as well. Anyone opening the source view inside a browser could simply read the lines of code and with those any security-related information, and you definitely don't want this to happen.

> **NOTE** When creating a new project, Meteor puts developer productivity first. That means initially projects won't be secure enough to be deployed into production. Throughout the book we'll discuss how to develop production-ready and secure applications.

Of course, there are simple and standard ways to handle sensitive code, and we'll cover this topic in the upcoming chapters when we discuss how to structure a project.

For now, we'll only use this single JavaScript file. For simple applications, checking the current context is good enough.

The next snippet looks like this:

```
if (Meteor.isClient) {
  // counter starts at 0
  Session.setDefault("counter", 0);

  Template.hello.helpers({
    counter: function () {
      return Session.get("counter");
    }
  });
//...
}
//...
```

Here you see two global objects in use: `Session` and `Template`. `Session` allows you to store key-value pairs in memory. The `Template` object enables you to access all templates, which you defined in the HTML file, from your JavaScript files. Because both objects are only available on the client, they can't be called on the server. That would lead to reference errors, which is why this code is wrapped inside the `isClient` context.

As long as `Session` variables aren't declared, they remain `undefined`. The `Session.setDefault()` command initiates a key-value pair inside the `Session` object with the key `counter` and a value of 0.

In this snippet you access the `hello` template defined inside the helloWorld.html file and extend it with a so-called *template helper*. This template helper is named `counter` and is a function that returns the content of the `Session` value for the key `counter` as a string. Now you see why the `hello` template is different from what you actually see in the browser. The template helper in the `hello` template `{{ counter }}` is in fact a function that returns the string that you see in the browser.

On the one hand, you have templates to define the HTML that should be rendered, and on the other hand, you have template helpers that extend templates and make it possible to use functions and substitute placeholders with dynamic content.

Remember what happens when you click the button? This is where event binding comes in. If you click the button, a `click` event is fired. This in turn increases the counter on the page by 1. The following code increases the counter, which is stored inside the `Session` object:

```
if (Meteor.isClient) {                          ◁——  Handling mouse clicks is
  Template.hello.events({                             only useful on the client.
    'click button': function () {                                                    Define a function to
      // increment the counter when button is clicked                   ◁——         call when the input
      Session.set("counter", Session.get("counter") + 1);   ◁——                      button is clicked.
    }
  });}                                                                  Increases the Session
                                                                        variable by 1
```

Every template has the function events() and with that you can define event handling for a specific template. The object to pass to the events() function is called an event map, which is basically a normal key-value JavaScript object where the key always defines the event to listen to and the value is a function that's called if the event is fired.

To specify the event, always use a string in the form 'event target', where the target is defined by standard CSS selectors. You can easily change the previous example to use a CSS class or ID to further specify the button. Also note that these events are only fired in the context of this template. This means any input in a different template such as clicking on an input element wouldn't call the function specified here.

You can go ahead and click the button a couple of times, and you'll note how the browser renders your new string. Only the placeholder is updated and not the entire page.

Notice that there's no code involved that updates the template directly; you rely on the reactive nature of Session. The template helper counter is rerun whenever the value inside the Session object changes. The event simply changes the data source, and Meteor takes care that all places that use this value are recomputed instantly.

The last snippet we'll look at is this one:

```
if (Meteor.isServer) {
  Meteor.startup(function () {
    // code to run on server at startup
  });
}
```

As the comment indicates, you can define a function that should be run at the startup of your application. You could also call the Meteor.startup function multiple times and pass different functions in order to run several different functions at the startup of the application. Meteor.startup can also be used on the client side to run functions at the start of the client-side application. This sample application doesn't use any server-side code, so this block and the startup function remain empty.

Now that you've looked at the helloWorld example code and you have a solid understanding of the basic concepts, you'll extend these files to develop your own first Meteor application.

1.6 Summary

In this chapter, you've learned that

- Meteor is a full-stack or isomorphic JavaScript platform, similar to the MEAN stack.
- Developers can run the same code only on the server, the client, or in all contexts.
- Clients are active parts of the application logic, which means Meteor applications leverage the power of distributed computing environments.
- Using a standard protocol called DDP, servers and clients communicate via Web-Sockets instead of HTTP, enabling bidirectional message exchange.

- Meteor uses the principle of reactive programming to minimize the need for infrastructure code.
- Development productivity is enforced by reusable packages called Isopacks, which are used to provide common or specialized functionality.
- One codebase is used to provision HTML apps for the browser or hybrid applications for mobile devices on iOS, Android, or Firefox OS.

My fridge! A reactive game

This chapter covers

- Building a reactive app with Meteor
- Understanding the basic architecture for Meteor projects
- Including jQuery-UI to enable drag-and-drop interfaces
- Using the Meteor CLI to deploy to meteor.com

In this chapter, you're going to build your first Meteor application. You could create a new project from one of the included example applications, but creating a small reactive game from scratch gives you a much better understanding of how things work together. At the end of this chapter, you'll have written fewer than 60 lines of JavaScript and even less HTML to create a game that stores data to a database and updates all connected clients in real time.

You'll see how templates and code work together and include jQuery-UI in your project. To share your application with the world, you'll also deploy it to the meteor.com infrastructure with a single command.

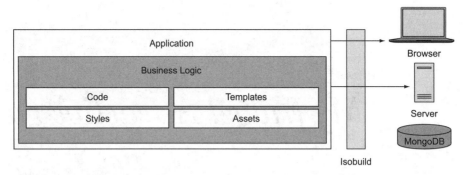

Figure 2.1   Only business logic is required for the My fridge! application.

2.1   Application overview

My fridge! is a small real-time application that shows the contents of a fridge and allows you to drag products in and out. Unlike a physical refrigerator, this one can be accessed from anywhere in the world and all changes will be visible to every client connected to the server.

Although our application is merely a simulator, you could use My fridge! as a notepad to remember what's in your actual fridge at home. Or if you're a hardware hacker, you could connect your actual fridge to the internet and use Meteor to display its contents in real time. That way, if your friends take out the last bottle of juice, you can check this from your office and grab some OJ on the way back home.

As you build this application, you'll keep things simple and rely on the functionality enabled in every new Meteor project. You're going to add code, styles, templates, and assets (see figure 2.1). You won't use any additional packages in this chapter.

First you'll create the views using Spacebars, Meteor's templating language. All products will be stored in a MongoDB database, so you need to define a database connection. You'll use static images to represent each product in the fridge. Finally, you'll learn how to include an external JavaScript library and use jQuery-UI to enable dragging items in and out.

Meteor's own reactivity will take care of keeping all clients synchronized and updating the views. All you need to take care of is the actual functionality—that is, the dragging and dropping to update the location attribute for a product inside the database. In this application you won't allow users to add additional products easily, and you won't be applying strict security measures. Those topics will be covered in later chapters. At the end of this chapter your fridge will look like the one shown in figure 2.2.

2.2   Initial setup

Before you continue, make sure you've installed Meteor on your machine. Refer to appendix A to guide you through the process. Remember that Meteor also comes with a CLI tool? You'll use it to perform the initial setup of the application in a shell

Figure 2.2 The final state of the My fridge! application

environment. This allows you to create new applications. You'll perform all the steps in this subsection inside a terminal.

2.2.1 Setting up a new project

With Meteor installed, its CLI tool becomes available. Creating a Meteor project involves typing just one line into a terminal:

```
$ meteor create myFridge
```

That line creates the project folder containing three files: one for HTML templates, one for JavaScript code, and one for CSS styling information.

Navigate to the project folder and use the CLI tool to start the application with the following commands:

```
$ cd myFridge
$ meteor run
```

Move the terminal console to the background; you'll now start coding in your editor of choice. It'll be useful to check whether it shows any error messages, but you won't need to restart the server for the rest of this chapter. Each change to a file and even adding new files will be handled by Meteor automatically. If you pay close attention, you'll notice that with every file change the console will either show that the server was restarted or that the client code was modified and has been refreshed. Figure 2.3 shows the output.

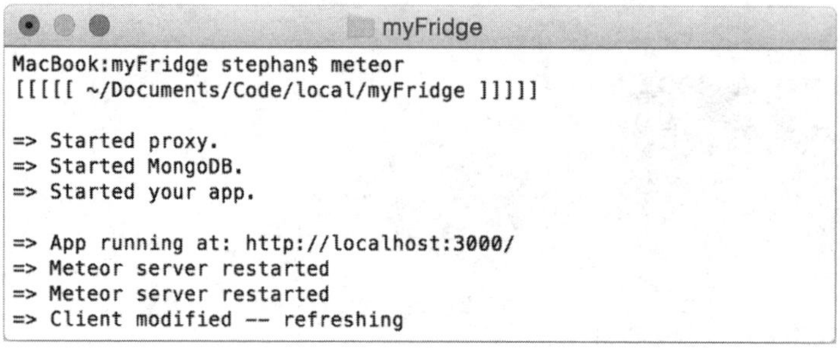

```
MacBook:myFridge stephan$ meteor
[[[[[ ~/Documents/Code/local/myFridge ]]]]]

=> Started proxy.
=> Started MongoDB.
=> Started your app.

=> App running at: http://localhost:3000/
=> Meteor server restarted
=> Meteor server restarted
=> Client modified -- refreshing
```

Figure 2.3   The `meteor` **command automatically restarts the server when application code changes.**

2.3   Creating a layout

The first step of building our game requires us to think about the layout. For My fridge! we need a simple layout with a fridge on the left side and a product shelf with a list of items on the right side. Items should then be draggable from one side to the other.

So to create the layout, you'll create some templates, add images, and add a way to iterate through a list of products.

> **NOTE**   Because this book is about Meteor and not CSS, we won't discuss the styling in depth. You can refer to the associated code example to browse through all styles.

2.3.1   Setting the styles

For a basic structure, we want to have a fridge and a product list side by side, as shown in figure 2.4.

Your first step is to set the styles for the general layout inside myFridge.css according to listing 2.1 so that you can then focus on the HTML templates. Define the container's `width` setting and make sure that the fridge is displayed on the left and that the product list (on the right) is a little smaller.

Listing 2.1   General layout styles

```
.container{
  width: 95%;
  position: relative;
}

.left{
  float: left;
  width: 60%;
  margin-right: 2%;
}

.right{
  float: right;
  width: 37%;
}
```

These are only the positioning elements; check the code samples for the full code.

Figure 2.4   The three main DIV containers for the My fridge! layout

Listing 2.1 defines three classes to position the DIV containers. Because you want our application to work on a mobile phone as well, you use percentages to make the layout responsive.

2.3.2   *Adding the templates*

For each of the DIVs you'll use an individual template, even for the container. When you're finished you'll have a head section, a body, and four templates:

- container—for the general layout
- fridge—to display the fridge on the left
- productList—to display the supermarket on the right
- productListItem—to show items on either side

Listing 2.2 Skeleton template structure

```
<head>
  <title>myFridge</title>
</head>

<body>
  {{> container}}
</body>

<template name="container">
  <div class="container">
    <div class="left">
      {{> fridge}}
    </div>
    <div class="right">
      {{> productList}}
    </div>
  </div>
</template>

<template name="fridge">
  <div id="fridge">
    ...
  </div>
</template>

<template name="productList">
  <div id="supermarket" class="box">
    ...
  </div>
</template>
```

Include contents from a subtemplate.

Subtemplates are referenced by name.

The container template takes care of the basic layout of the application. It puts the fridge on the left and the product list on the right. Technically we could use a single template for all HTML code, but splitting things up provides a better overview and control over what happens where.

Now that you've created the skeleton layout, let's make the left side look like an actual fridge. The fridge should be represented by an image of an open fridge. At this point we need to extend our project to be able to add image files. Because in the sample application no images were used, create a new folder called public in the application root. This is where you'll put all images.

NOTE The public folder is treated in a special way by convention. Every file you put into the folder is accessible at the root path of your URL. If you put a file named image.jpg into the public folder, you can access it via http://localhost:3000/image.jpg.

To include an image of the empty fridge in the browser, you'll use a file called myFridge/public/empty-fridge.jpg from this chapter's source code. To reference it from a template, you don't need to include /public in the path—just use the following:

```
<img class="image-responsive" src="/empty-fridge.jpg" />
```

Our fridge should contain an unsorted list of items on the right, also represented by images. We can't tell how many items will be in the fridge at any given time, so we need a flexible solution we can iterate through. Therefore, we're going to use a dedicated template for the item list.

Iterating through an array of objects inside a template can be done with a helper named {{#each}}. The # in front indicates that it doesn't substitute the placeholder for a string but provides some sort of logic. You'll create an unordered list and iterate over an array called products. The following listing shows how it looks in action.

Listing 2.3   Looping through products in the productsList template with the each helper

```
<template name="productList">
  <div id="supermarket" class="box">
    <ul id="products">
    {{#each products}}
        <li>{{> productListItem}}</li>
    {{/each}}
    </ul>
  </div>
</template>
```

For each object in the array you pass to this helper, the contents between the each tags is rendered once. In this case you want to render a list element for every product you pass to the helper. The list element you render contains a template that you want to insert here {{> productListItem}}. The advantage of using a template inside the loop is that you can reuse the same template, productListItem, again for your product list on the right side of our application, which means you can write less code.

Add a new template to the bottom of your HTML file as shown in the following listing.

Listing 2.4   Template for each productListItem

```
<template name="productListItem">
  <img src="{{img}}"
       data-id="{{_id}}"
       class="image-responsive product-image draggable" />
</template>
```

Next let's adjust the fridge template in the myFridge.html file so that it looks like the code in listing 2.5.

Listing 2.5   Looping through each product inside the `fridge` template

```
<template name="fridge">
  <div id="fridge">
    <img class="image-responsive" src="/empty-fridge.jpg" />
    <ul>
      {{#each products}}
        <li>{{> productListItem}}</li>
      {{/each}}
    </ul>
  </div>
</template>
```

As you can see, you're reusing the `{{> productListItem}}` template for both the fridge and the supermarket. Next we want to be able to render some products—the product list as well as the fridge is currently empty.

2.4   Adding content to the database in real time

Now that the layout is in place, we can focus on the back end. All items, regardless whether they're in the fridge or not, should be available from our database. Once they're in the database, they should be sent to the client, so we need to add a connection between the database and the templates.

2.4.1   Storing items in the database

Meteor comes with a bundled MongoDB database that's used by default. Due to the tight integration, we don't need to specify a connection string or credentials to use MongoDB. To communicate with the database, we need to declare a new *collection*. MongoDB uses collections instead of database tables because it's a NoSQL or documents-oriented database. Collections contain data in the form of one or multiple documents. Chapter 4 covers the details of working with databases; for now we'll focus on getting the fridge into a fully functional state.

You'll use `Mongo.Collection` to define a new database collection to insert, remove, update, and find documents. Because the collection is going to store products, you'll name it accordingly and place it inside the JavaScript file, as shown in the following listing.

Listing 2.6   Declaring a `products` collection on the client and server

```
Products = new Mongo.Collection('products');

if (Meteor.isClient) {
    //...
}

if (Meteor.isServer) {
    //...
}
```

You should put this line on top of the file, outside of any `Meteor.isServer` or `Meteor.isClient` block, because it should be available on both the client and the server.

All of our products will have three attributes:

- A name—for example, *Bread*
- An associated image file in the /public folder, such as *bread.png*
- A current location—that is, either *fridge* or *supermarket*

Using the JavaScript console inside the browser

Because Meteor applications run at least partly inside the browser, you need to switch to the JavaScript console sometimes to see debugging output or to be able to issue commands. All major browsers have developer tools that allow you to access the console by using a simple keyboard shortcut.

Chrome:

- On the Mac, press the keys Option-Command-J.
- On Windows, press the keys Ctrl-Shift-J.

Firefox:

- On the Mac, press the keys Option-Command-K.
- On Windows, press the keys Ctrl-Shift-K.

Internet Explorer:

- On Windows, press F12 and click the Scripts tab.

Opera:

- On the Mac, press the keys Option-Command-I.
- On Windows, press the keys Ctrl-Shift-I.

Safari:

- On the Mac, press the keys Option-Command-C.

To add some data you can open up the JavaScript command-line tools in a browser and add a product using the following:

```
Products.insert({img: '/bread.png', name: 'Bread', place: 'fridge'});
```

In response to this function call, you get the document ID of the newly inserted product. With this ID you can also get the document out of the database like this:

```
Products.findOne({_id: 'X6Qw8v3ChcsZKaKan'});
```

Because you know only a single object can have this ID, you'll use the findOne() function. The response is a single product object from the database (see figure 2.5).

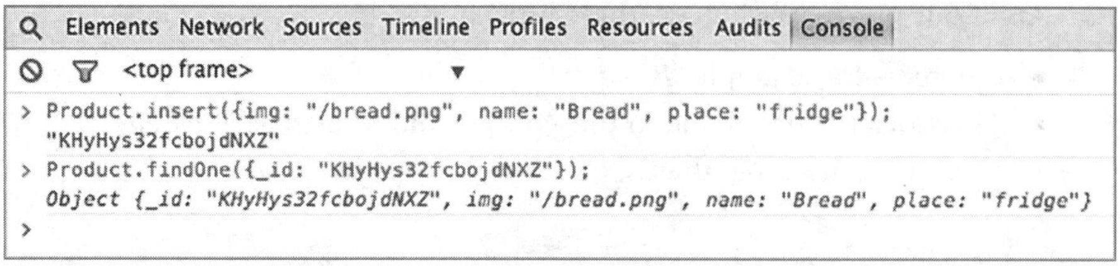

```
  Q   Elements  Network  Sources  Timeline  Profiles  Resources  Audits | Console |
  ⊘   ▽  <top frame>                  ▼
> Product.insert({img: "/bread.png", name: "Bread", place: "fridge"});
  "KHyHys32fcbojdNXZ"
> Product.findOne({_id: "KHyHys32fcbojdNXZ"});
  Object {_id: "KHyHys32fcbojdNXZ", img: "/bread.png", name: "Bread", place: "fridge"}
>
```

Figure 2.5   Using the browser's JavaScript console to insert and look up data in the database

Developer productivity vs. security

Although it's convenient to use the Developer Console to add and remove items from the database, it's also a security risk. If you can do it, then anyone else using your application will also be able to do it.

New projects always contain a package called `insecure`, which disables authentication checks and allows anyone to read and write to any collection. Together with its sibling `autopublish`—which automatically makes all collections from the server side and their content available to the client—it makes developers' lives much easier because it lets them focus on building functionality first, without having to struggle with authentication issues during the early stages of development.

During development you'll most likely introduce a permissions scheme and limit publishing data to what the authenticated user has access to. When that time comes, you can get rid of both packages using the following command line:

```
$ meteor remove insecure
$ meteor remove autopublish
```

Querying data by its location is also quite simple. Instead of using the `_id` field, you can look at individual attributes as well. You expect more than a single result, so you'll use `find()` and look for all database entries that have `fridge` as their `place` attribute:

```
Products.find({place: 'fridge'});
```

Now that you've added some data to the database, you can access and view the data in the browser.

2.4.2   *Connecting data to templates*

In the `fridge` template, you'll want to iterate over all products where the attribute `place` is `fridge`. To do so, you'll extend the template with a helper called `products` that returns all products you want to show in the fridge. Let's look at the template again:

```
<template name="fridge">
  ...
</template>
```

You can access each template by its name with the global `Template` object that comes from Meteor. Every `Template` object has a function called `helpers` that takes an associative array where the values are accessible in the template through its keys:

```
Template.fridge.helpers({
  products: function(){
    return [];
  }
});
```

⟵─ **The each tag inside the template expects an array.**

For the fridge, you'll want to iterate through an array of products that you get from the database. The helper's job is to look up the data from the database and pass it to the template. Remember that to display the data you created a loop inside the templates using `{{#each products}}`...`{{/each}}`:

```
<template name="fridge">
  <div id="fridge">
    <img class="image-responsive" src="/empty-fridge.jpg" />
    <ul>
      {{#each products}}
        ...
      {{/each}}
    </ul>
  </div>
</template>
```

⟵─ **Loop through all items returned from the products helper.**

To extend the template `fridge` with the `products` helper, you pass it to the `helpers` function of the `Template` object. To do so, replace all code inside the `Meteor.isClient` block in the myFridge.js file with the code from the following listing.

Listing 2.7 Setting up a `products` helper for the `fridge` template

```
Template.fridge.helpers({
  products: function () {
    return Products.find({
      place: 'fridge'
    });
  }
});
```

The `products` helper is a function that returns every product where the attribute `place` is `fridge`, just as you want it. Because you've added a product to the fridge already, it should directly be added to your view. Make sure you also placed the associated image into the public folder. If you've added the bread document to your collection and the corresponding image to the public folder, the application will look like figure 2.6 now.

For the `productList` template on the right side, you can now do the same thing but with a query that looks for a different value of the `place` attribute. You don't want

Figure 2.6   The fridge shows an image of a loaf of bread.

to show all products from the database, but only those that are currently in the super-market. To do so you need to query the database, as in the following listing.

Listing 2.8   Setting up a `products` helper for the `productList` template

```
Template.productList.helpers({
  products: function () {
    return Products.find({
      place: 'supermarket'
    });
  }
});
```

If you insert some more products to the fridge or the supermarket using the Java-Script console, you'll see how they get added automatically to the screen. Also, the insertion of products is done in real time already. Open another browser and you'll see products being added immediately (see figure 2.7).

So far you've created the UI and set up the required data structures for the fridge application. The last thing you have to add is the user interaction that allows visitors to put products into the fridge and remove them from it, too.

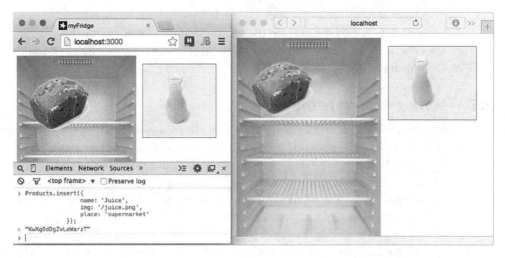

Figure 2.7   Changes to the database are reflected in other browsers in real time.

2.4.3   Adding a defined set of products

Although it's sometimes helpful to be able to add products manually, you can use the server to add a defined set of products upon startup. That way, you'll have a known state to work with, regardless of how much testing has been done in a previous run.

Inside the JavaScript file the code from listing 2.9 will remove all products from the database every time the server starts. Afterward, it'll put milk in the fridge and bread in the supermarket.

Listing 2.9   Adding a defined dataset to the database upon server start

```
if (Meteor.isServer) {                        This gets executed whenever
  Meteor.startup(function () {                the server restarts.

    Products.remove({});                      Removes all products
                                              from the database
    // fill the database with some products
    Products.insert({
      name: 'Milk',
      img: '/milk.png',                       Inserts some
      place: 'fridge'                         products into
    });                                       the database

    Products.insert({
      name: 'Bread',
      img: '/bread.png',
      place: 'supermarket'
    });
  });
}
```

Stop your Meteor server by pressing Ctrl-C and start it again. If you copied over the images for milk and bread from the sample code into your public folder, you can now see a bottle in the fridge and bread on the right. As a final touch, let's add interactivity via drag and drop.

2.5   *Moving items into the fridge*

Our goal is to make the products draggable from the product list into the fridge, and vice versa. This isn't specific to Meteor but a standard front-end task. We'll use the jQuery-UI library for the dragging and dropping and make the necessary connections to your templates. Because we also want to update the database as a result of dragging and dropping, we'll need to supplement the front-end actions with a back end that's capable of storing content in the database.

We'll start by adding the jQuery-UI library to the existing project. It'll provide drag-and-drop functionality that works across all major browsers. Once the library is available, we'll define both the fridge and the product list as possible drop targets where items may be placed. Finally, each product list item will be marked as draggable so that it can be moved to either of the drop containers.

2.5.1   *Adding jQuery-UI to the project*

You don't have to add the jQuery-UI library to your project files, but you can include the online version instead. This works the same way in Meteor as in any other HTML file: by adding it to the <head> area of your myFridge.html file (see following listing).

> **Listing 2.10   Loading jQuery-UI from a CDN**

```
<head>
  <title>myFridge</title>
  <script src="//code.jquery.com/ui/1.11.4/jquery-ui.js"></script>
</head>
```

The library is now loaded from jquery.com. Obviously you need to have a connection to the internet in order to use the content delivery network (CDN) to provide the JavaScript file. Alternatively you can download the library from http://jqueryui.com and put the file jquery-ui.min.js into a folder called client. Meteor will automatically serve and load this file on the client. If you add the file locally, make sure to not include the `script` tag in the `head` section of the template file.

2.5.2   *Defining drop targets for items*

You'll use the jQuery API for drag and drop to define both `fridge` and `productList` as possible drop targets. Because the `fridge` and the `productList` have to be rendered into the DOM before you can use jQuery-UI to perform any modifications on them, you have to wait until each template is rendered. A callback function available to every template makes this very easy[1]:

```
Template.fridge.onRendered(function() {
  var templateInstance = this;

  templateInstance.$('#fridge').droppable({
    drop: function(evt, ui) {
      // do something
    }
  });
});
```

> Instead of parsing the entire DOM, we limit jQuery's scope to this template instance.

Scoped DOM parsing with jQuery

Every time you see `$()` in your code, you can be certain that jQuery is involved. Usually it also means that the entire DOM tree is parsed, which is rather slow and often not what you want. When you try to set the background color for `body` it's perfectly acceptable to use `$('body')`. But most of the time you want to avoid one template having side effects that change other templates. Besides the full DOM parsing, which affects performance, debugging will become a nightmare.

Meteor offers a simple solution to limit jQuery's activity to the current template scope: `Template.instance()` contains an object that represents the current template. Inside the `created`, `rendered`, and `destroyed` callbacks the same object is available as `this`. You can limit jQuery's scope to this object and safely use, for example, the `.dateinput` class in multiple templates without having the `formTemplate` suddenly creating datepickers all over the place.

Because using `this` directly can be confusing, you should use a more meaningful identifier such as `templateInstance` in the code example earlier.

When the `fridge` template is rendered, you define `<div id="fridge">` as a droppable target. This means DOM elements may be added to it dynamically by simply dragging them into the `div` area. Basically you're listening for an event (that is, a user moving an item to the container), so you have to define an event handler to determine whether something was dropped in the container. The event handler will also need to perform an update to the associated item in the database and update its location.

The event handler will be called `drop`, and it'll change the `place` attribute once a product has been dropped. To identify the database entry that corresponds to the product that was dropped, you need to pass a data ID to it. In the JavaScript event handler, you use a function with two arguments: the `event` and a `ui` object. You'll use the `ui` object of the `drop` callback to identify the ID of the dropped product. You can tell which HTML item was dragged by looking at the `ui.draggable` argument. The `ui.draggable` object will always be one of the `productListItem` items. It's easy to

---

[1] Using jQuery within the current template's scope is covered in more detail in chapter 3.

identify which HTML element was dragged, but you also need a link back to the database, which is where the `data-id` attribute comes in:

```
<template name="productListItem">
  <img src="{{img}}" data-id="{{_id}}" class="image-responsive product-image
    draggable" />
</template>
```

You added a data attribute to the `<img>` named `data-id`. The value of the `data-id` attribute is set to `_id`, which represents the database ID of a product. When you drag an image, you have an easy way to identify which product in your database is affected, and you can change its `place` attribute accordingly. Using a similar syntax like you did for inserting new products, you can update existing ones by calling the `update()` function for our `products` collection. All you need is to pass the database ID and set the `place` attribute to the location it was dropped in, as shown in listing 2.11.

Remember that `data-id`, and with that the `_id` of the related product of the dragged image, is available via the `ui.draggable` object.

Using jQuery to access element attributes

To minimize the amount of code you have to write, you'll use a shorthand notation to get the ID of any product. You'll use jQuery to access an element from the HTML5 dataset API.

Unlike jQuery UI, the basic jQuery functionality is bundled with Meteor, so you don't need to include it for any project. The HTML5 dataset API specifies that every element in the DOM may hold additional attributes with a `data-` prefix. It's useful to attach meta-information to any element on a page. In combination with newer jQuery versions (starting with 1.4.3) you don't have to access the attribute via `attr('data-id')` but with `data('id')`.

Accessing the `data-id` attribute for a product is therefore done like this:

```
$(ui.draggable).data('id')
```

You can even further shorten the code by dropping the surrounding `$()` so that only the `ui` object remains:

```
ui.draggable.data('id')
```

You can use either of those two variants.

Listing 2.11   Declaring `fridge` as a droppable target and updating the product location

```
Template.fridge.onRendered(function () {
  var templateInstance = this;

  templateInstance.$('#fridge').droppable({
    drop: function(evt, ui) {
      var query = { _id: ui.draggable.data('id') };      ◁──  Get the database ID from the HTML attribute data-id.
      var changes = { $set: { place: 'fridge' } };        ◁──  Set the update statement to set place to fridge.
```

```
        Products.update(query, changes);      ◁─┐  Perform the
    }                                            │  database update.
  });
});
```

You create a query that addresses the correct product document in our `Products` collection. The first argument passed to `Products.update()` works just like before: it returns a document based on its ID. The second argument uses the `$set` functionality to specify that you want to update a field in this document. The data you want to set is the `place` attribute, and because it's the drop event that's called if an item is dropped over the fridge, you want to change the `place` attribute to `fridge`.

The product list is also a drop target and therefore needs almost the same code but with two small, yet important, differences. Again the `rendered` function of the `productList` template has to be used to wait for the DOM. Also, if an item is dropped over the `productList` template, the `place` attribute of the product document has to be changed. This time you need to set it to `supermarket` instead of `fridge`. The following listing shows the required code.

Listing 2.12 Declaring `productList` as a droppable target

```
Template.productList.onRendered(function() {     ◁─┐  productList is the template
  var templateInstance = this;                      │  name used by Meteor.

  templateInstance.$('#supermarket').droppable({   ◁─┐  supermarket is
    drop: function(evt, ui) {                          │  the div ID.
      var query = { _id: ui.draggable.data('id') };
      var changes = { $set: { place: 'supermarket' } };  ◁─┐  Set the place attribute
      Products.update(query, changes);                      │  to supermarket when
    }                                                        │  products are dropped.
  });
});
```

2.5.3 Allowing items to be draggable

You've set up the droppable targets, but you also have to define elements that may be dropped: the draggable items. In this application, each `productListItem` element should be draggable. Again, you'll rely on jQuery-UI to mark the list items as draggable, so you use the `rendered` function of the `productListItem`. For every `productListItem` that's rendered, this `rendered` callback will be executed once, effectively making each food movable (see the following listing).

Listing 2.13 Declaring `productListItem` as a draggable item

```
Template.productListItem.onRendered(function() {
  var templateInstance = this;

  templateInstance.$('.draggable').draggable({
    cursor: 'move',
    helper: 'clone'
  });
});
```

Note that listing 2.13 uses `templateInstance.$('.draggable')` in order to access the HTML element that's dragged. In our case this is the `<img>`. Using jQuery in this template's context allows Meteor to search for an element only inside the `productList-Item` template rather than the entire DOM tree, which makes it more efficient.

2.6 Deploying to meteor.com and using the fridge

You now have an application in which you can drag an image from a product list on the right to the fridge on the left, and vice versa. When the image is dropped, the underlying product document will be updated accordingly. The changes reactively change the UI and the product is rendered in the correct place automatically.

To share your fridge with the world, you can deploy it on one of the Meteor test servers with the `deploy` command. Just pick a name that's not yet taken that should be used as the subdomain under which your app will be available. If the subdomain is taken already, you'll see an error message.

Let's deploy our project to mia-ch02-myfridge by using the following:

```
$ meteor deploy mia-ch02-myfridge
```

To make sure only you can access, update, or delete the application from the test server, it'll be associated with your personal Meteor developer account that's based on your email address. Therefore, you must provide your email when deploying for the first time. Meteor will memorize your address on your working machine. Also, you'll get an email response that explains how to secure your account with a password. When the deployment is finished, you can access your application on a meteor.com subdomain with the name you picked—in our case, http://ch02-mia-myfridge.meteor.com.

Now you can share this URL with a friend (or simply open up two browsers on the same computer) and start dragging and dropping products back and forth. You'll see that all changes will be available on all clients almost instantly. Meteor takes care of keeping all connected clients in sync, even though you never defined any specific code for that. You also never had to write any code to poll the server for any database updates. This is full-stack reactivity in action.

In the following chapters, we'll look at how all the parts that seem to work magically fit together, and you'll see that there's no magic behind all of this at all but just good-old JavaScript.

2.7 Summary

In this chapter, you've learned that

- For development purposes, the `meteor` CLI tool runs the entire Meteor stack in the background.
- Spacebars is the templating language used by Meteor.
- Collections are used to interact with the database.
- Static files like images are served from the public folder.
- Changed data is reactively pushed to all clients.

Part 2

3, 2, 1—impact!

Now that you're familiar with the basic concepts of the Meteor platform, you'll learn about the building blocks for reactive applications in detail. Beginning with the UI and templates (chapter 3), we'll slowly work our way through the stack. We'll explain how to work with data and use reactive editing (chapters 4 and 5), add users (chapter 6), manage data publications (chapter 7), use routing (chapter 8), structure code in packages (chapter 9), and write synchronous and asynchronous code on the server (chapter 10).

Working with templates

This chapter covers

- Creating templates
- Using Meteor's default templating syntax
- Organizing JavaScript and HTML
- Using event maps to make templates interactive
- Understanding the template life cycle

Everything your web browser renders is HTML eventually. If you open any website in source view you'll find that each page has hundreds of lines of HTML. Not only is writing everything by hand tedious, error-prone, and highly inefficient, it's also impossible when you're working with web applications because much of the content is dynamic and you can't know in advance what exact code needs to be rendered.

Templates allow you to define blocks of HTML that can be reused as often as you like. As a result, you have to write less code, and your code is easier to read and much simpler to maintain.

In this chapter, you'll learn how to write templates and what you can do with them. We'll first take a look at Blaze, Meteor's reactive UI library, and Spacebars, its default templating language.

3.1   Introduction to templates

Templates are the building blocks for our UI. Templates are snippets of HTML that contain placeholders, which can be filled by content returned by the application logic. They can be reused to ensure the same look and feel on all sites and all elements.

Another important aspect of templates is *separation of concerns*. This means a template is intended only for the representation of data and is ultimately rendered as HTML to the DOM. A template should have as little programming logic inside it as possible. Everything that needs computation and creates a specific output shouldn't be inside a template but separated into a JavaScript file. This approach helps to increase the readability, and it's basically the same concept of separating the styling of HTML into its own Cascading Style Sheets (CSS) files instead of cluttering the HTML with styling definitions.

Think about a simple list of users, as shown in figure 3.1. For each person you're going to display the name along with a phone number. Because you don't know how many people need to be shown in this list, you'll use a dynamic template to generate the necessary HTML code.

In this example, you use an `<h5>` element that wraps around the name and you put the phone number inside a `<p>` element. To tell the template processor where you want the content to go, you use placeholders that include double curly brackets. Using pseudocode, the required template would look like this:

```
<h5>{{NAME}}</h5>
<p>Phone: {{PHONE}}</p>
```

Figure 3.1   A list of people and their phone numbers

Because the placeholders may contain multiple elements, you need the template to be able to create any number of list items. Just like in JavaScript code, you can use a loop that takes an array as input and iterates over each of the array contents, taking care of filling the placeholders for *name* and *phone* with information about the person. In this example, you'll create a list of people that reuses the `profile` template. For each person, it should contain the following:

```
<ul>
    <!-- for every user render this: -->
    <li>{{ LOOP_THROUGH_PERSON_LIST_USING_TEMPLATE }} </li>
</ul>
```

Hooking up the templates with the back-end logic will return the HTML code shown in the following listing.

Listing 3.1 Rendered HTML from template

```
<ul>
    <li>
        <h5>Christina</h5>
        <p>Phone: 1234-567</p>
    </li>
    <li>
        <h5>Stephan</h5>
        <p>Phone: 666-999-321</p>
    </li>
    <li>
        <h5>Manuel</h5>
        <p>Phone: 987-654-321</p>
    </li>
</ul>
```

The advantage of using templates is you write them only once and use them for an infinite amount of data (in our case, people) you want to render. Having a single place to manage the appearance of an element is also convenient. Think about what you need to do if you don't want the <h5> element but only a normal <p> element for a person's name. You only have to change it in a single template, and it instantly updates for any person that you render with the help of the profile template.

3.2 Working with templates

Unless you're writing a server-only application, every web application written in Meteor should have at least one template. Displaying content in a browser without using a template isn't possible. This section discusses the foundations of working with templates.

3.2.1 The Blaze engine

Behind the scenes, Meteor uses a reactive UI library called *Blaze*. It's responsible for processing templates and is an important part of what's often referred to as the magic of Meteor. As you can see in figure 3.2, Blaze consists of two major components:

- A runtime API
- A build-time compiler

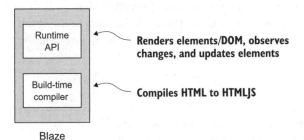

Figure 3.2 The Blaze components

The *runtime API* renders elements, keeps track of their dependencies, and updates them through their complete life cycle as those dependencies change. That means if the phone number of a person is changed in the database and a user currently views a page listing this person's information, the number gets automatically updated on the screen. This is because the placeholder depends on the actual value stored in the database, which is a reactive data source.

The runtime API works with JavaScript in order to apply reactivity; it can't deal with HTML directly, which is why the second component of Blaze is a *build-time compiler*. Meteor ships with a compiler that translates HTML into JavaScript (HTMLJS to be precise). By default, it processes templates using Spacebars. Optionally, it's possible to use packages to switch the compiler to a different templating language such as Jade.

Both components work separately, so it's entirely possible to bypass the build-time compiler and not use any templates but instead write code that directly targets the runtime API. Because this isn't very practical for most users, we won't worry about the runtime API itself but concentrate on using Spacebars.

> **NOTE** Meteor's templating language is called Spacebars. It's a direct descendant of Handlebars, with which it shares most of its syntax and functionality.

Blaze uses live page updating, so whenever a template-related file is changed on the server (HTML, CSS, or JavaScript), it gets updated instantly in the browser. How does Blaze find templates inside a project?

3.2.2   *Organizing template files*

When working with templates, you usually have four types of files to deal with, though only one is technically required for a template:

- The actual template stored in an HTML file
- Optional JavaScript code in a JS file that runs inside the client context and provides functionality to templates
- Optional styles in one or more CSS files[1]
- Optional static resources such as images or fonts inside the public folder

Without a JavaScript counterpart, templates may only be static and can't be filled with dynamic content, which is why in most cases you'll need at least two files for working with templates. To keep everything organized, it's best to keep each template in a dedicated HTML file. Meteor will find them anywhere in your project folders.[2] All the front-end code can be stored in a single JS file, or you can use HTML/JS pairs so that each template consists of two files, which we recommend if your projects grow more complex:

```
<template name>.js
<template name>.html
```

---

[1] Also, Less, Sass, and other styling languages can be used; CSS is just an example.
[2] There are exceptions to this rule, which we'll explore in depth in chapter 10.

In this chapter we won't worry about styling elements because this works just like in any other web application. We covered the public folder in the previous chapter, so let's focus solely on the first two elements: HTML and JavaScript files.

3.3 Creating dynamic HTML templates

Meteor comes with its own templating language called Spacebars. If you're familiar with Handlebars or Mustache, you already know enough to start using it immediately. Even if you haven't used any of these languages, you'll find that the general syntax is fairly simple to work with.

Templates written using Spacebars look almost like regular HTML. Template tags are easily spotted because they're always enclosed in multiple curly braces. The four major types of template tags are

- Double-braced tags {{ ... }}
- Triple-braced tags {{{ ... }}}
- Inclusion tags {{> ... }}
- Block tags {{#directive}} ... {{/directive}}

3.3.1 Double and triple-braced tags (expressions)

Template tags that can enhance static HTML code by being replaced with dynamically generated content are also called *expressions*. They depend on a data source or some kind of application logic that returns a value.

Template tags can only be used inside a template context. A basic template tag is shown in the following listing.

Listing 3.2 Double-braced template tags

```
<template name="expressions">
    {{ name }}
</template>
```

As you can see, every template has an opening and closing `<template>` tag and a mandatory `name` attribute. The `name` attribute has to be a unique identifier for a template inside the application. Using the name of a template, you're able to access it from a JavaScript file, which we'll do later on.

DOUBLE-BRACED TAGS

Double-braced template tags are used to insert strings into the HTML. No matter what return value they're dealing with—an array, an object, or a string—it's always rendered as a string. Let's assume you have a template named `expressions` from listing 3.2 and you want to replace the template tag {{ name }} with `<strong>Michael</strong>`.

The accompanying JavaScript code must return the substitute string as shown in listing 3.3. Remember that the code must be wrapped in a `Meteor.isClient` environment—it can't be run on the server side because templates aren't available inside the server scope.

Listing 3.3   JavaScript code for a helper called name

```
if (Meteor.isClient) {
  Template.expressions.helpers({
    name: function () {
      return "<strong>Michael</strong>";
    }
  });
}
```

◁——— The template can only be used on the client; it's undefined on the server.

Together the HTML and JavaScript code will render as shown in figure 3.3.

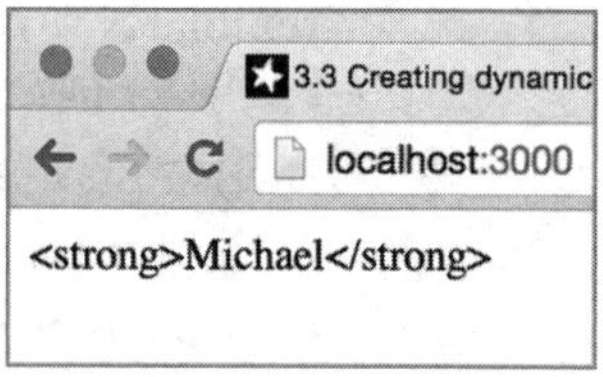

As you can see, double braces process the string and escape all possibly unsafe characters. This is useful if you want to avoid return values being accidentally interpreted as HTML or even JavaScript. Sometimes, though, you may want to avoid any processing of the string. In that case, you need to use triple brackets.

Figure 3.3   Tags in double curly braces always render strings and escape HTML and script tags.

TRIPLE-BRACED TAGS

If your template tag starts and ends with three curly braces {{{ ... }}}, its contents will be rendered exactly as you passed them to the template tag. Extending the example from listing 3.3, let's now use {{{ name }}} instead of {{ name }}. Meteor won't escape any characters or tags and will pass the output to the browser unaltered (see figure 3.4).

As you can see, the HTML tags are rendered as HTML into the DOM and not as simple strings.

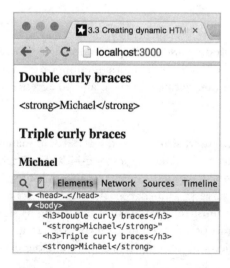

Figure 3.4   Strings in triple curly braced tags are rendered as HTML.

WARNING If you use triple curly braces to display data entered by a user, you must ensure that it's been sanitized first (that is, check for potential malicious scripting content). If you don't, your website is vulnerable to cross-site scripting attacks. The simplest way to deal with user-generated data is to let Meteor sanitize it for you before it gets displayed and stick with double curly brackets whenever possible.

Peeking inside Blaze's build-time compiler: turning HTML into HTMLJS

Blaze uses its runtime API to transform HTML code from a Spacebars template into JavaScript. Each compiled template file can be found in the directory .meteor/local/build/programs/web.browser/app.

The template in listing 3.2 produces the following code:

```
Template["expressions"] = new Template("Template.expressions",
                        (function() {                          ◁──────  The template
    var view = this;                                                    named
    return [ HTML.Raw(                  Blaze.View                      expressions is
            Blaze.View("lookup:name",  ◁── constructs a reactive        converted into
            function() {                    region in the DOM.          a function.
                return Spacebars.mustache(view.lookup("name")); ◁──┐
            }
        )                               Spacebars returns the
    ];                                  actual value for name.
    }));
}));
```

This HTMLJS code enables Meteor to reactively update templates and even just parts of them. Every template is accessible through the global `Template` object by its `name` attribute.

Although it's possible to call `Blaze.View` directly from inside a template helper, there's rarely a need to do so. Only when you decide to build your own runtime API for Blaze, replacing Spacebars with something else such as Jade or Markdown, will you need to familiarize yourself with the internal processing structures.

Until an API documentation for this becomes available, you can find out more by looking at the contents of the `blaze` and `spacebars` packages, which are part of Meteor's core.

3.3.2 Inclusion tags (partials)

In addition to inserting strings or HTML, you can insert a template into another template. Because they represent only a part of the whole template, these subtemplates are also known as *partials*. Inserting a template into another is achieved using the > sign enclosed within two curly braces like this:

```
{{> anotherTemplate }}
```

Inclusion tags are an important tool to keep templates small and let them represent only one thing. If you want to render a complex UI, we advise you to split everything the user can see into smaller, logically encapsulated templates and subtemplates.

MONOLITHIC TEMPLATES

For example, say you need a profile page that displays not only an avatar image and the name of a person but also a news stream. You could put everything into one template, as shown in the following listing.

Listing 3.4   Full profile page template

```
<template name="partials">                              ◁─────  The template representing
  <div class="left">                      ◁─┐                  the partials page
    <img src="{{image}}">                    │  Place this div
    <p>{{name}}</p>                           │  on the left side.
  </div>
  <div class="right">                     ◁─┐  Place this div on
    <ul class="news-stream">                 │  the right side.
      <li class="news-item">Yesterday I went fishing, boy this was a blast</li>
      <li class="news-item">Look, cookies! <img src="cookies.jpg"></li>
    </ul>
  </div>
</template>
```

If your UI gets more complex, you can imagine that your profile template could become big. This is bad for readability and code maintainability. It's better to separate everything with its own logical function into a dedicated template and combine them in a main template. That way, your templates stay small and are easier to read and maintain. Two developers could split up the profile and news stream work and make independent changes much more easily.

MODULAR TEMPLATES

Listing 3.5 shows our first template, partialsSplit. This is the main template that represents the site and contains two smaller templates. Two small templates represent the actual user profile (partialsUserProfile) and the news stream (partialsNews-Stream). Also note that the layout is contained in the main partialsSplit template—in this case, the simple <div class="left"></div> and <div class= "right"></div>.

Listing 3.5   Splitting the profile page template

```
<template name="partialsSplit">            ◁─┐  The template that represents
  <div class="left">                           │  the profile page
    {{> partialsUserProfile}}              ◁─┐  The user profile is included in the
  </div>                                       │  parent template as a subtemplate.
  <div class="right">
    {{> partialsNewsStream}}               ◁─┐  The news stream is also
  </div>                                       │  included in the parent
</template>                                    │  template as a subtemplate.
```

```
<template name="partialsUserProfile">
  <img src="{{image}}">
  <p>{{name}}</p>
</template>

<template name="partialsNewsStream">
  <ul class="news-stream">
    <li class="news-item">Yesterday I went fishing, boy this was a blast</li>
    <li class="news-item">Look, cookies! <img src="cookies.jpg"></li>
  </ul>
</template>
```

TIP Avoid putting layout information into subtemplates. Let the parent template define the look and feel as well as the size of the elements they include.

Not having layout definitions buried inside subtemplates greatly improves reusability. Because there are no layout definitions in the `partialsUserProfile` template, you can easily reuse it on another page template and put it onto the right side into a `<div class="right">{{> partialsUserProfile }}</div>`.

DYNAMICALLY INCLUDED TEMPLATES
In addition to using static texts to include subtemplates, you can dynamically include a template based on the return value from a helper (see listing 3.6). That way, you can reactively switch templates without having to maintain complex if/else structures inside templates. In combination with reactive data sources like a session variable, they can be quite powerful.

Listing 3.6 Inserting subtemplates dynamically with helpers

```
// meteorTemplates.html
<template name="dynamicPartials">
  <div class="left">
    {{> Template.dynamic template=templateNameLeft }}        ◁───┐   The name of the
  </div>                                                           subtemplate comes
  <div class="right">                                              from a helper.
    {{> Template.dynamic template=templateNameRight }}       ◁───┘
  </div>
</template>

// meteorTemplates.js
Template.dynamicPartials.helpers({
  templateNameLeft: function () {
    return "partialsUserProfile";                            ◁───┐   Helpers return a string
  },                                                               that can either be
  templateNameRight: function () {                                 dynamic or static.
    return "partialsNewsStream";                             ◁───┘
  }
});
```

3.3.3 *Block tags*

In contrast to *expressions* or *partials*, which are essentially placeholders, *block tags* change the behavior of the enclosed block of HTML. They start with double curly braces and a #. A sample block template tag may look like this:

```
<template name="myTemplate">
  {{#name arguments}}
      <p>Some content</p>
  {{/name}}
</template>
```

The opening of a block template tag has a name and optional arguments.

The content of the block template tag

The closing of a block template tag must always have the same name as in the opening tag.

Block tags are used not only to display content but also to have control over the processing of a template. You can either define your own block tags or use Spacebars:

- #if—Executes a content block if a condition is true or the else block if not
- #unless—Executes a block if a condition is false or the else block if not
- #with—Sets the data context of a block
- #each—Loops through multiple elements

THE IF/UNLESS TAG

One of the built-in tags is the #if block tag. It works like a normal if block in JavaScript. It checks a condition, and if it evaluates to true, the contents of the block are processed—that is, they're rendered. Any value that's considered to be true in a regular JavaScript context is also considered to be true by the #if tag. If a common falsey[3] JavaScript value like null, undefined, 0, "" (empty string), or false is passed to #if, the following block won't be rendered (see table 3.1). Listing 3.7 shows an image tag only if there's an image helper and it evaluates to true.

Listing 3.7 Using an if block

```
<div class="cookies">
  <p>Look, more cookies!</p>
  {{#if image}}
    <img src="{{image}}" />
  {{/if}}
</div>
```

The `<img>` tag is rendered if the value for image evaluates to true.

Table 3.1 Input values and their interpretation by #if

Input value	Evaluates to
false, 0 (zero), "" (empty string), null, undefined, NaN, [] (empty array)	false
Strings (including "0"), arrays, objects (including empty objects)	true

---

[3] Anything that evaluates to false is considered falsey, even if the actual value is not false. Values that evaluate to true are considered truthy.

The counterpart to an #if block tag is the #unless block tag. It processes the block contents only if the condition evaluates to false (see the following listing).

Listing 3.8   Using an `unless` block

```
<template name="unlessBlock">
  {{#unless image}}
    <p>Sorry, no image available.</p>
  {{/unless}}
</template>
```

> ◁⋯ **The `<p>` tag is rendered if image evaluates to false.**

Both #if and #unless can be combined with an else tag in order to render one thing if the condition is true and another if it's false. Listing 3.9 uses #if but it works just the same with #unless.

Listing 3.9   Using `else` in an `if` block

```
{{#if image}}
  <img src="{{image}}" />
{{else}}
  <p>Sorry, no image available.</p>
{{/if}}
```

> ◁ **Whether if or unless is used defines whether the case for true or false is handled first.**
>
> ◁ **The `<p>` tag is rendered if `{{image}}` returns a falsey value.**

NOTE   There's no tag {{elseif}}. To deal with more cases than true and false, you'll either need to use nested if-else structures inside your template or, preferably, adjust your JavaScript code so that it can do the processing instead of the template.

Block tags and template tags always have to include valid HTML; otherwise Meteor will run into an error. That means you have to take care that tags that are opened are closed as well. Also, every element that opens inside a block must also be closed inside that block. You can't, for example, include an opening <div> tag in an #if block tag and close after the {{else}} because this would result in invalid HTML for your page upon rendering. If you have errors in your templates, the application will crash and produce an error message. Figure 3.5 shows the resulting error message for the following code block:

```
{{#if highlightBox}}
  <div class="box box-highlighted">
{{else}}
  <div class="box ">
{{/if}}
  <p>Welcome!</p>
</div>
```

> ◁ **This isn't allowed because it's not a valid HTML tag pair.**
>
> **A closing `<div>` tag without an opening one isn't allowed inside a template.**

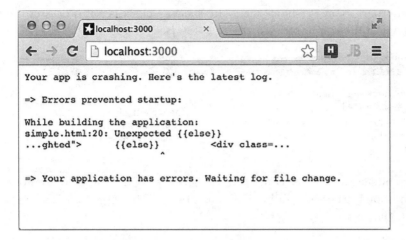

Figure 3.5   Output for invalid HTML in templates

It's perfectly all right, though, to use a block tag inside of an HTML attribute value:

```
<div class="box {{#if highlightBox}}box-highlighted{{/if}}">
    <p>Welcome!</p>
</div>
```

If showBox is a truthy value, the box string is included in the class attribute.

THE EACH/WITH TAG

If you wish to pass multiple values to a template, the most common way is to use an array. When an array is passed to a template, you can iterate over its contents using an #each tag. #each takes an array as its argument and renders its block content for every item inside the array. In listing 3.10 `skills` is passed as an argument. This defines the so-called *data context* of the block. Without a data context, #each doesn't render anything.

Listing 3.10   Using the #each tag

```
// HTML file
<template name="eachBlock">
  <ul>
    {{#each skills}}
      <li>{{this}}</li>
    {{/each}}
  </ul>
</template>

// JavaScript file
Template.eachBlock.helpers({
  skills: function(){
    return ['Meteor', 'Sailing', 'Cooking'];
  }
});
```

The #each block tag takes an array as a parameter.

You can access the current object of the array with *this*.

Whereas #each requires the template to have a data context, #with allows you to define a data context. The data context is the actual association between a template and any data.

Setting the data context using the #with tag requires a single attribute that will become the data context for the following block. Listing 3.11 shows an example where the data context for the template withBlock is explicitly set to profileJim.

Listing 3.11 Using the #with tag

```
// meteorTemplates.html
<template name="withBlock">
  <ul>
    {{#with profileJim}}          ◁─┐  The profileJim
      <p>{{name}}</p>                │  object is defined as
      {{#each skills}}              │  the data context.
        <li>{{this}}</li>
      {{/each}}
    {{/with}}
  </ul>
</template>

// meteorTemplates.js
Template.withBlock.helpers({
  profileJim: function () {
    var jim = {
      name: 'Jim "Sailor Ripley" Johnson',
      skills: ['Meteor', 'Sailing', 'Cooking'],
    };
    return jim;
  }
});
```

There's no need to explicitly specify a data context; using a helper automatically provides a context. Some more advanced use cases require you to do so. We'll look at them when we talk about reactive data sources in the next chapter.

Technically, all built-in block tags are helpers. Let's have a look at how you can create your own template helpers.

3.3.4 Helpers

When dealing with templates, you may often find it necessary to apply the same functionality again, such as formatting seconds into the HH:mm:ss format or applying control structures. This is when helpers are needed.

Helpers are JavaScript functions that can perform any kind of processing. They can either be limited to a single template or be made available globally. Global template helpers may be reused in all available templates, and it's good practice to define them in a dedicated JavaScript file instead of the individual template JS files.

LOCAL TEMPLATE HELPERS

A local template helper is used to extend one specific template only. It can't be shared between other templates and exists only within the namespace of a template. In their simplest form, local template helpers look similar to *expressions*.

Every Template object has a helpers function, which takes an object that can contain multiple key-value objects. Typically the key represents the placeholder name that can be used inside a template, whereas the value is a function that returns something. The function's return value doesn't have to be a string, but it can be any static value like a number, an array, an object, or even a function that returns another value.

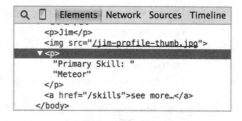

Figure 3.6   Resulting code from local helpers

To simplify things, we've shown both the contents from the HTML file as well as the JavaScript file in listing 3.12. Some of the helpers return only a static value (name); others return an array (skills), an object (image), and even a function (has-MoreSkills). The rendered HTML code can be seen in figure 3.6.

Listing 3.12   A profile template using different local helpers

```
// meteorTemplates.html
<template name="localHelpers">
  <p>{{name}}</p>
  {{#if image}}
    <img src="{{image.thumb}}">
  {{/if}}
  {{#if skills}}
    <p>Primary Skill: {{skills.[0]}}</p>
    {{#if hasMoreSkills skills}}
      <a href="/skills">see more...</a>
    {{/if}}
  {{/if}}
</template>


// meteorTemplates.js
Template.localHelpers.helpers({
  name: 'Jim',
  image: {
    large: '/jim-profile-large.jpg',
    thumb: '/jim-profile-thumb.jpg'
  },
  skills: ['Meteor', 'Sailing', 'Cooking'],
  hasMoreSkills: function (skills) {
    return skills && skills.length > 1;
  }
});
```

Accesses the local helper name that is the simple string 'Jim'

You can access object values as you would in normal JavaScript using dot notation.

If the array is empty, it wouldn't render the block content.

Skills is an array and you can access a special index with via array.[index].

The #if block content is rendered if the returned value of the helper function hasMoreSkills returns true. In this case hasMoreSkills has the skills helper as a parameter.

Returns true if the skills parameter is passed and has more than just one skill

Image is an object and thus a truthy value; the content block is rendered.

To pass parameters to a helper function, simply write the parameters you want to pass after the helper function (separated by a whitespace). The order in which you pass the parameters will be the same as defined in the function itself.

Have a look at listing 3.12 again. The built-in helper #if evaluates the following expression to determine whether it is true or false:

```
{{#if hasMoreSkills skills}}
```

In this case it checks hasMoreSkills, which is a function that itself requires an input value. Therefore, instead of the standard behavior of using if followed by a single expression, a second placeholder is passed: skills. The content of the skills object is passed to the function represented by hasMoreSkills. If a person has multiple skills it'll return true, so the if condition passes.

GLOBAL HELPERS

Oftentimes you have some helper that you need in more than just one template but you want to write it only once. Let's say you want to create a helper that returns true if an array has more than n items. Let's call this helper gt (as in greater than). This helper should be used in multiple templates, so create a globalHelpers.js file and put the helper code in there. Remember to wrap it in an if(Meteor.isClient){...} block because helpers—just like templates—are only available in the client scope.

You want the new helper to be available in all templates, so you can't use Template .<templateName> to define it. Instead, use Template.registerHelper; the following listing shows how local and global helpers are combined.

Listing 3.13 Using global helpers to determine array length

```
// meteorTemplates.html
<template name="globalHelpers">
  {{#if gt skills 1}}
    <a href="/skills">see more...</a>
  {{/if}}
  {{#if gt images 4}}
    <a href="/images">see more...</a>
  {{/if}}
</template>

// meteorTemplates.js
Template.globalHelpers.helpers({
  skills: function () {
    return ['Meteor', 'Sailing', 'Cooking'];
  },
  images: function () {
    return ['/jim-profile-large.jpg', '/jim-profile-thumb.jpg'];
  }
});

// globalHelpers.js
if (Meteor.isClient){
  Template.registerHelper('gt', function(array, n){
    return array && array.length > n;
  });
}
```

skills contains three items so the global gt helper returns true.

images contains only two items; the global gt helper returns false.

Local helpers for the globalHelpers template

Using the registerHelper function you can create helpers that are available to all templates.

CUSTOM BLOCK HELPERS

Also globally available and very useful are *custom block helpers*. They allow you to build reusable UI components or widgets. Note that the actual helpers may be used even without any JavaScript.

Suppose you define a new block helper named `#sidebarWidget`; you also need to define a template of the same name. The template will be injected where the block helper is called. Inside the template you use the partials syntax to include the output of `Template.contentBlock`. You can also access any other elements from the data context that may be passed to the block helper. This example will produce a sidebar widget with a title and some content.

When `#sidebarWidget` is called from within a template, it places its own contents between the `{{#sidebarWidget }}` and `{{/sidebarWidget }}` tags by including `Template.contentBlock`. Listing 3.14 shows how `sidebarWidget` can be used to wrap block contents in any template. The fact that it's reusable makes it ideal for building UI components or widgets.

Adding `{{> coderOfTheMonth }}` to the body of an application creates the output shown in figure 3.7.

> **Listing 3.14   Custom block helpers with `Template.contentBlock`**

```
<template name="coderOfTheMonth">
  {{# sidebarWidget title="Coder of the month"}}        ◁─┐
    Manuel                                                  Data context
  {{/sidebarWidget}}                                        can be set for
</template>                                                  custom block
                                                            helpers as well.
<template name="sidebarWidget">
  <div class="sidebar-widget box">
    <div class="title">{{ this.title }}</div>          ◁
    <div class="content">
      {{> Template.contentBlock}}
    </div>
  </div>
</template>
```

This is the content that gets displayed.

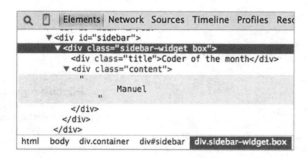

Figure 3.7   Reusable UI components or widgets can wrap any content using custom block helpers.

Besides the `Template.contentBlock` there's a `Template.elseBlock` (see listing 3.15) that relates to the content block after an `{{else}}` template tag. This way, you can enhance block helpers with simple control structures.

Listing 3.15   Using `Template.elseBlock`

```
// meteorTemplates.html
<template name="templateElseBlock">
  {{#isFemale gender}}
    Mrs.
  {{else}}
    Mr.
  {{/isFemale}}
</template>

<template name="isFemale">
  {{#if eq this 'w'}}
    {{> Template.contentBlock}}
  {{else}}
    {{> Template.elseBlock}}
  {{/if}}
</template>

// meteorTemplates.js
Template.templateElseBlock.helpers({
  gender: function () {
    return 'm';
  }
});

Template.isFemale.helpers({
  eq: function (a, b) {
    return a === b;
  }
});
```

Custom block helper called isFemale, to which we pass the gender variable that comes from the template helper

The isFemale block helper also has a helper function, eq, that takes two arguments and checks if they're both equal. *this* relates to the gender parameter in this case.

If the gender is 'w' then the #if statement is truthy and the contentBlock should be rendered.

If not, the elseBlock should be rendered. Because the gender is 'm' the elseBlock would be rendered.

The isFemale block helper also has a helper function, eq, that takes two arguments and checks if they're both equal. *this* relates to the gender parameter in this case.

MOVING LOGIC INTO HELPERS

Using helpers to return a value that should be rendered is generally the better way to dynamically display content. The less logic exists within a template, the easier it is to troubleshoot and extend an application.

If you don't require different HTML code for different cases, it's best to define a helper that calculates the correct content to be displayed. This way, you can avoid using `#if` and `#unless` in your templates. Listing 3.16 uses a template, `logicBy-Helper`, that displays the correct salutation based on a single-character gender value that may be stored in a database. All processing is done by the helper function, not the template itself.

Listing 3.16   Moving template logic into a JavaScript helper

```
// meteorTemplates.html
<template name="logicByHelper">
  {{genderLabel gender}}
</template>
```

In the double-braced tag, we call the helper function genderLabel and pass the parameter gender.

```
// meteorTemplates.js
Template.logicByHelper.helpers({
  gender: 'm',
  genderLabel: function (gender) {
    if (gender === 'm') {
      return 'Mr.';
    } else {
      return 'Mrs.';
    }
  }
});
```

The genderLabel helper function returns "Mr." in this case, because gender has the value 'm'.

As you can see, you can define lots of different helpers for a template that can be static values or even functions that return some computed value.

You've learned how to use Spacebars to create and extend templates so that it's easy to generate some HTML at the end. Now that you know how to create the HTML code of an application, let's enable the user to interact with the rendered HTML using events.

3.4 Handling events

One of the main differences between a static site and an application is that applications allow for user interaction. They need to handle events such as button clicks and react to them. The response most of the time is basically the modification of the DOM in order to show users something that's useful to them. To achieve this, there must be a way to do two things:

- Define the events the application listens to
- Define the actions that are triggered by an event

Meteor uses event maps to define events and their actions. DOM events are used in conjunction with CSS selectors to specify which elements and which events should be watched. Although you may use any DOM event for an event map, their behavior might differ between various browsers, but the events in table 3.2 should behave the same across all major browsers.

Table 3.2 Event types that work alike across all major browsers

Event type	Use
click	Mouse click on any element, including links, buttons, or `div`s.
dblclick	Double-clicks using the mouse.
focus, blur	Text input or other form control fields that gain or lose focus. Any element with a `tabindex` property is considered focusable.
change	Check boxes or radio buttons that change state.
mouseenter, mouseleave	Entering or leaving an element with the mouse pointer.

Table 3.2   Event types that work alike across all major browsers *(continued)*

Event type	Use
mousedown, mouseup	Pressing and releasing the mouse button.
keydown, keypress, keyup	Pressing and releasing keys on a keyboard; keydown and keyup are mostly used for modifier keys such as Shift.

3.4.1   Template event maps

Every template has its own event map. It's defined inside a JavaScript file similar to the following listing.

Listing 3.17   Event map for `layout` template

The key of the object defines what event should be triggered on which element.

Each template has an events function that takes the event map object as its parameter.

The value of the object is a function that's called in case the button is clicked. This event handler takes the event object itself as the first parameter and the template instance as the second parameter.

```
if (Meteor.isClient) {
  Template.layout.events({
    'click button': function (event, template) {
      $('body').css('background-color', 'red');
    },
    'mouseenter #redButton': function (event, template) {
      // start fancy animation
    }
  });
}
```

Moving the mouse cursor over the element with ID redButton might start an animation.

Meteor uses jQuery to call the actual event handler functions. In this example, if the user clicks any button within the `layout` template, the corresponding event handler is called and the background color of the body is set to `red`. Clicking any button outside of the `layout` template wouldn't trigger an action because the associated event map is only relevant for anything inside the `layout` template. But what happens if we use a child template and send an event to it? Change the code according to listing 3.18 and click either button to see.

Listing 3.18   Listening for events in a subtemplate

```
// meteorEvents.html
<body>
  {{> layout}}
</body>
<template name="layout">
  <button>Turn red</button>
  {{> green }}
</template>

<template name="green">
  <button id="green">Turn green</button>
</template>
```

Clicking the button would make the body element's background color red because the event would also call the handler of the layout template after the green handler was executed.

```
// meteorEvents.js
Template.layout.events({
  'click button': function (event, template) {
    $('body').css('background-color', 'red');
  }
});
Template.green.events({
  'click button': function(event, template) {
    $('body').css('background-color', 'green');
  }
});
```

Even though we have two distinct event maps and two buttons, any click on a button in the updated code will turn the background to red, even clicking the Turn Green button. Why is that?

3.4.2   *Event propagation*

The phenomenon you can see at work here is called *event propagation*, or *event bubbling*. That means every event is first processed where it occurs and then passed upward in the DOM tree. There it may trigger another action.

In a best-case scenario, you'd cleverly use this as chaining; in the worst case—which this example shows—you'll end up overwriting the action you wanted to take place with another.

> **NOTE**   Event propagation may have unexpected side effects when working with event maps. Remember to stop it; otherwise, it'll bubble up the DOM tree.

As you can see in figure 3.8, there are three template instances: the body, a layout template, and a green template. If the user clicks <button>Turn green</button> the event listener of the green template is called, because it listens for clicks on buttons inside its template scope. The first action that takes place sets the background-color attribute of body to green. But the event propagation isn't done yet.

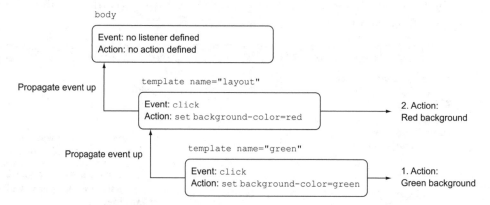

Figure 3.8   Action sequence for a click in the green template

The event is passed upward to the `layout` template, which also acts on click events. It calls its own event handler. Now a second action takes place, which sets the `background-color` attribute to red.

Technically the background color was green for a brief moment in time, but only as long as it took the event to propagate up. Therefore, the event handler of the `green` template has no visible effect.

Finally, the event is passed to the body element, and if it had an event map defined, it might even trigger a third action.

If you don't want an event to be handled by multiple templates you can—and should—always stop the event propagation. Add `stopImmediatePropagation()` to your template's event map to prevent events from bubbling up the DOM. Fix the event map for the `green` template by updating your code to the following listing.

> **Listing 3.19 Stopping event propagation within an event map**

```
Template.green.events({
  'click button': function(event, template) {
    event.stopImmediatePropagation();          ◁── This stops the event from
    $('body').css('background-color', 'green');     bubbling up the DOM.
  }
});
```

Now clicking the button turns the background color to green, regardless of whether the `layout` template also listens to button clicks. If you want to have even more control over event handling, you can also call `evt.stopPropagation()`. Doing so doesn't prevent other event handlers from being executed, but if you prefer you can call `evt.isPropagationStopped()` to check whether `stopPropagation()` was called somewhere in the event chain. Using this technique, you can add an event handler to the body and react to the click event in the `green` template as well as in the body but not trigger the `layout` event handler.

3.4.3 Preventing the browser's default behavior

Something you also want to prevent in many circumstances is the browser's default event handling. For example, if you click a normal link (`<a href="url">Go To</a>`), the browser would open the URL specified in the `<a>` element's `href` attribute and reload the page. Of course, in an application you build with Meteor you don't want the browser to reload the page at any time. To prevent this, you can call `event.preventDefault()` (see listing 3.20) and the browser's default behavior is prevented.

> **Listing 3.20 Preventing the browser's default behavior**

```
Template.layout.events({
  'click a': function(event, template){
    event.preventDefault();            ◁── Prevents the browser from
    console.log('Please do not leave yet');    executing the default action—
  }                                              that is, following the link
});
```

Before we move on to see how to integrate data into a template, the last topic we need to cover is the template life cycle.

3.5   *The template life cycle*

Putting a template inside the DOM and making it visible for the user is only part of its life cycle. Each template goes through three steps (figure 3.9) in order to get rendered in the browser. Each stage has an associated callback, which is useful to add custom behavior.

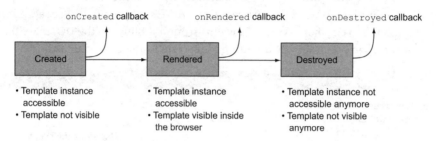

Figure 3.9   The template life cycle

The first step when inserting a template into the DOM is called `created`. Although the actual template isn't visible yet, the template instance is already accessible. The associated callback `onCreated` is especially useful if you want to initially create some properties for the template instance before it's rendered and visible to the user. All properties that you set in the `onCreated` callback are available in the other life-cycle callbacks as well. You can even use them in your helpers and event handlers. To access a template instance from within a helper or event handler, use `Template` `.instance()`.

> **NOTE**   As you saw in chapter 2, jQuery's scope can be limited to the current template instance and its subtemplates using `template.$()` or `template.find()`.

The second state for a template is called `rendered`. The associated `onRendered` callback is used to initiate objects that are inside the DOM already. Typical examples are jQuery plug-ins like datepickers, calendars, or datetables. They require a rendered DOM element, so they're initiated in the `onRendered` callback as shown in listing 3.21. Here we extend all elements inside the `formTemplate` that have a `.dateinput` class with a datepicker.[4]

---

[4]   To actually use a datepicker, you also need to add the required datepicker libraries to your project.

Listing 3.21   Initializing a jQuery plug-in to create a datepicker on an input element

```
Template.formTemplate.onRendered(function() {
  var templateInstance = this;

  templateInstance.$('.dateinput').datepicker({
    // additional options
  });
});
```

The third callback, `onDestroyed`, is used to clean up anything that you set up during the lifetime of a template. After it executes, the template instance is neither visible nor accessible anymore.

All three callbacks are just executed once and won't be repeated, even if data on the page changes.

Let's consider a simple scenario with a single placeholder expression:

```
<body>
  {{> profile}}
</body>
<template name="profile">
  {{!-- demonstrating the lifecycle --}}    ◁── You can use comments
  <p>{{placeholder}}</p>                          inside templates like this.
  <button>Button</button>
</template>
```

Listing 3.22 adds an explicit callback to each stage in a template's life cycle. When the profile template is created, you attach a property `lastCallback` to the template object, set it to `created`, and print the object in the JavaScript console. This is also the place where you could already read the data context of a template. Inside the `onRendered` callback, you change the value for `lastCallback` to `rendered`. Using `Template.instance()`, the helper can read the value for `lastCallback` and the button click is able to update its value. The `onDestroyed` callback can't be observed inside the browser console. All console messages are shown in figure 3.10.

Listing 3.22   The template life-cycle callbacks

```
Template.profile.onCreated(function () {
  this.lastCallback = 'created';
  console.log('profile.created', this);      ◁─┐   Prints out the instance of the
});                                              profile template. You can set
Template.profile.onRendered(function () {        variables to the template
  this.lastCallback = 'rendered';               instance like this.foo = 'bar'
  console.log('profile.rendered', this);   ◁─   that you could use later. You can
});                                             also read the data context, but
Template.profile.onDestroyed(function () {      you can't set it here.
  this.lastCallback = 'destroyed';
  console.log('profile.destroyed', this);  ◁─┘
});
```

```
Template.profile.helpers({
  placeholder: function () {
    console.log('profile.placeholder', this);
    console.log('profile.tplInstance',
                  Template.instance().lastCallback);
    return 'This is the {{placeholder}} helper';
  }
});
Template.profile.events({
  'click button': function (event, template) {
    Template.instance().lastCallback = 'rendered and clicked';
    console.log('profile.clicked', this);
    console.log('profile.clicked.tplInstance', template);
  }
});
```

You can still access the template instance in template helpers and events.

Prints out only the data context. You have no access to the template instance via *this*.

In the event handlers you don't need Template.instance() because the template instance is passed as the second parameter directly.

Figure 3.10   Console messages for template callbacks

3.6   Summary

In this chapter, you've learned that

- Meteor uses its own reactive UI library called Blaze.
- Spacebars is Meteor's default templating language and is an extended variation of Handlebars.
- Spacebars uses expressions, partials, blocks, and helpers to create small and modular templates.

- Helpers may be limited to a single template or available globally.
- Event maps are used to associate actions to events and elements.
- Each template goes through three steps—create, render, and destroy—in order to get rendered in the browser. Each stage has an associated callback, which is useful to add custom behavior.

Working with data

As you saw in chapter 1, Meteor doesn't rely on a traditional, server-focused architecture. It runs code and processes data on each client as well. To do so, it uses a mini-database to mimic the API of a real database inside the browser. That means you can access data in the same manner, regardless of whether you're making a database lookup or accessing the results of a query on the browser.

All data that's available only in a single client will obviously be lost once the client disconnects and hasn't sent its updates back to a central server. Meteor will take care of persisting data automatically by synchronizing client and server state.

Some information is relevant for only a single client, such as state information, which tabs have been clicked, or which value was selected from a drop-down list.

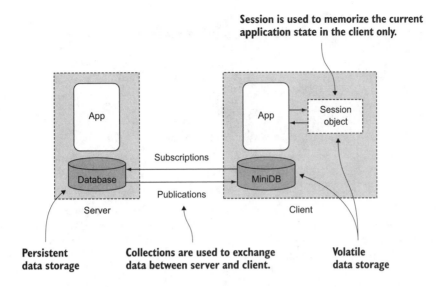

Figure 4.1 *Database everywhere* **means persistent data on the server but volatile data on the client.**

Information that's relevant only to an ongoing user session doesn't need to be stored on the central server and doesn't get synchronized. Figure 4.1 illustrates the general architecture. At the end of this chapter, you'll be able use `Collections` for data inside databases and `Sessions` for client-only information.

At its core, each web application captures, stores, and processes data. Creating, reading, updating, and deleting data, often referred to as *CRUD*, is the foundation on which advanced functionality can be built. CRUD in itself is only the most basic functionality, though. When two users read the same document from the database and one of them performs an update, we want this update to be published to the other client immediately. At least we should tell the second user that the document has changed since she first accessed it. In most languages and frameworks, you must manually set up a synchronization process that ensures all clients work with fresh data. Meteor takes care of managing the data flow properly by means of *reactivity*.

This chapter introduces you to the key components of reactivity and how to leverage it for CRUD operations in Meteor. To illustrate the principles, we'll turn a real-world problem into an application: imagine you go on a trip and ask a friend to take care of your plants and leave him with a note to water the red flowers once a week. We're building a house-sitter application.

When you've finished this chapter, you'll be familiar with the most important data sources in Meteor. You'll also be able to work with both volatile and persistent data, meaning you can store and retrieve data from a database and perform full CRUD

houseSitter: become a better friend using Meteor

When Manuel goes on vacation, he asks his friend Stephan to water the red flowers once a week. He's left his instructions on a sticky note requesting a simple action: watering the flowers. When should this action be carried out? When a week has passed. Although this seems like a simple task, we should build an application that helps us keep track of when and which plants we need to water.

To comply with Manuel's request, any good friend will have to factor in two data sources: the flowers and a calendar. The latter isn't explicitly mentioned, but it plays an important role in determining whether an action should be executed on the flowers. As with most situations in the real world, these instructions leave out some details. For starters, they don't define when the week starts or even how much water to use.

Naturally, a true friend will provide the missing context. To determine whether to water the flowers, Stephan relies on his calendar. A calendar is just a regular data source in itself, but adding a dependency to water the flowers each week turns it into a reactive data source. While Manuel is gone, Stephan is going to look at his calendar each day, and if it's a Monday, he'll go over and water the red flowers. To react to changed data, Stephan has created a mental dependency. The event "Monday" is linked to an action, "water the flowers."

Although there's room for error, it's much more convenient if Stephan is capable of making some sensible assumptions. This would allow Manuel to use a sticky note rather than having to write a 1,000-word essay on what to do while he's gone.

Meteor also links data sources and actions and provides an out-of-the-box behavior that allows developers to work with reactive data.

operations. We'll also discuss how to implement two-way data binding using Meteor's reactive approach by means of a so-called edit object.

We're going to implement functionality into an application by making use of two standard packages in Meteor: autopublish and insecure. As the names suggest, these packages make development easier by taking care of publishing data automatically across all clients and giving us more freedom during the development process by waiving strict security. That way, we can focus fully on adding functionality without constantly having to refactor security settings. Eventually, when we get to chapter 7, we'll discuss how to remove them to prepare an application for deployment.

4.1   *Meteor's default data sources*

In web applications, you typically deal with two types of data that are each associated with a specific type of data source:

- Volatile data, or short-term memory (for example, RAM)
- Persistent data, or long-term memory (for example, files and databases)

Volatile or short-lived data is used to deal with things like accessing the currently logged-in user. There's no reason to put this data into a database and share it across all clients, so it's generally only available in the client instance where the session takes place. Once a browser window is closed, all volatile data is typically gone, unless it's stored in the form of a cookie or the browser's local storage. But a user may have configured his browser to delete those on quit, so it isn't safe to assume the data stored inside is still available the next time a user visits a site.

Persistent data is anything that's actually stored by an application. This can include blog articles, comments, user profiles, or products in a web shop. Persistent data sources are available to some or all users of a web application. Meteor's default behavior is to share all persistent data sources across all connected clients. This is great during the early stages of development, but not if the amount of data grows into hundreds or even thousands of datasets. Transferring everything to clients regardless of whether they'll ever see the data can be avoided by using customized publications that clearly define what data gets transferred. They can also help by adding a security layer to avoid sending sensitive data that should be available only for some users to all connected clients. Again, this is a topic you'll learn about in chapter 6.

Meteor is designed to work well with NoSQL databases and so doesn't use tables (like MySQL or Oracle do) but instead stores data as documents. Collections are comparable to database tables and may hold one or multiple documents. Later in this chapter we'll talk more about databases.

> **NOTE**   By default, Meteor publishes all data from a database to all clients unless the `autopublish` package is removed. We'll do this in chapter 6 when we cover publications.

Regardless of whether they're used to store volatile or persistent data, all built-in data sources in Meteor are reactive by default. Table 4.1 gives an overview of the most common data sources and what they're used for. Let's take a closer look to understand what makes them different from nonreactive data sources.

Table 4.1   Most common data sources and their typical use

Data source	Typical use	Type
Session variables using the `Session` object	Selections or current step in multistep actions	Volatile
Collections (database queries)	Database content	Persistent

4.1.1   *What makes a data source reactive?*

If something happens in consequence to another thing that happened before, it's commonly known as a *reaction*. The same holds true for Meteor. To apply reactivity, we need data and actions, and we must create a trigger mechanism that links both together.

There's no need to constantly evaluate whether the flowers in a friend's house need water. Instead, by using a calendar we already have a data source that can be used to determine whether an action is required. We have an action, "check whether the flowers should be watered," which we defined to be executed each Monday. As such, we need to use a calendar as our data source in order to tell if today's day of the week has changed. If it has changed, we must perform the check once and can then wait for the next day until we check again.

It isn't effective to create a large list of all actions and every relationship that eventually may occur; it becomes tedious to keep such a list up to date. Also, what happens if we forget to check the calendar? In most frameworks we'd have to implement a frequent check to monitor possible changes to the calendar, which is similar to sitting at a desk and constantly looking at the clock in order not to miss the next day to possibly water the flowers.

Meteor makes things easier by using a declarative approach to define relationships between data and functions. A regular calendar becomes reactive due to the linked dependency on the check action, and it behaves just like an alarm clock for weekdays. That way, we can take advantage of reactivity, which means we execute the check based on the alarm initiated by our data source (see figure 4.2). There's no need to explicitly check whether the current day has changed—we'll be notified by the calendar when it happens.

By adding a relationship in form of a dependency, we turn any regular data source into a reactive data source. Not only can a reactive data source be passively accessed, but it's also capable of actively initiating a function to run by invalidating it. The `Tracker` package is responsible for creating and tracking dependencies as well as managing computations, which are the foundation of the platform's reactivity.

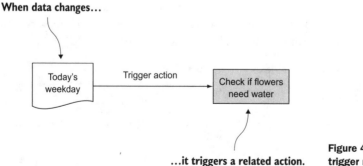

Figure 4.2   Data changes trigger related actions.

> **Tracker: dependency tracking behind the scenes**
>
> The fact that all built-in data sources are reactive by default means that Meteor automatically takes care of creating and tracking dependencies. It does so via a package named *Tracker*. This package is used to declare dependencies for a data source, invalidate computations, and trigger recomputations.
>
> As long as you only work with `Session` and `Collection` objects inside of templates, you might not need to use Tracker directly. For advanced techniques, it's helpful to understand the basic principles behind this small package that consists of less than 1 kilobyte of code. For the moment, we'll rely on Meteor to keep track of all dependencies for us without explicit declaration. We'll look at observing changes again in chapter 7.

4.1.2   *How reactive data is connected to functions*

Although we've told you that reactivity is built into Meteor and you get it for free, keep in mind that reactivity will only be used if you set up your code to do so. For that matter, Meteor provides *reactive contexts* in which reactivity takes place. These contexts can be created by using one of the following:

- Templates
- `Blaze.render` and `Blaze.renderWithData`
- `Tracker.autorun`

We looked at templates and Blaze in chapter 3. We'll be using `Tracker.autorun` in section 4.3 when we look at the `Session` object.

Once you've created a reactive context, a function inside this context will become a *computation*. A computation gets executed once and is executed again if it gets invalidated. Invalidating a function happens when a reactive data source is changed.

When computations are invalidated they're rerun, which makes them valid again. That prevents functions from running constantly and creating a chaotic and nondeterministic state of the application. The invalidation is a direct consequence of a data change and triggers an action. As long as the data doesn't change, the computation isn't invalidated and therefore isn't executed again. Because there can be various reactive contexts with varying dependencies, Meteor keeps track of all dependencies in a list (see figure 4.3).

When you first work with Meteor, you may not be aware that you're using reactive computations. When sending data to a template, Meteor takes care of re-rendering if any of the data changes. For example, if you have a template that displays a reminder to water the flowers, it'd be automatically updated if a reactive data source were used, as shown in listing 4.1.

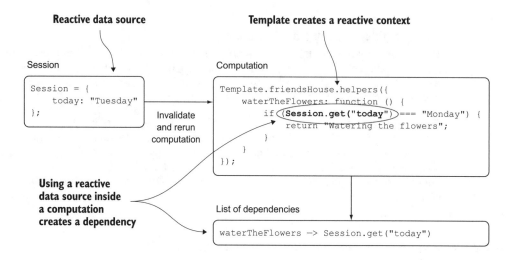

Figure 4.3   Changes to reactive data sources invalidate computations and trigger them to rerun.

Listing 4.1   Setting up a reactive context using template helpers

Creates a
reactive
context
```
Template.friendsHouse.helpers({
  waterTheFlowers: function () {
    var day = Session.get("today");
    if (day === "Monday") {
      return "Watering the flowers";
    }
  }
});
```

**Functions inside reactive
contexts are called
computations.**

**Session is a reactive data source
that will invalidate the computation
when its contents change.**

NOTE   Functions inside reactive contexts are called *computations*. Reactive data sources invalidate computations when data changes, which causes computations to reexecute. All reactive data sources used inside a computation are automatically associated with the computation.

Now that we've looked at the things Meteor will do automatically for us, let's focus on the things we have to do to work with and display data.

4.2   *Building a house-sitter app*

Let's revisit the example of our friend watering the flowers. Not only is he taking care of people's plants, but he's now a professional house sitter for many people and he tracks all of them in a database. This is also where he keeps all instructions for watering the plants. He's going to use a simple web application to look up each house and make a note when he's finished with a visit. Such an application would use the following data sources:

- A database to store all friends, instructions, and notes
- Session variables to store the currently selected house

Figure 4.4 shows the user interface along with some annotations. All data coming from a collection is shown in darker boxes, and all temporary data inside a `Session` object is depicted in a lighter box. If we view it from a high level, the app looks up all entries in a database and retrieves a single full document based on the value of a temporary session variable. Eventually it lets the user store changes made to the database.

Create a new project using Meteor's CLI tool:

```
$ meteor create houseSitter
```

Let's organize our code in different folders to make it easier to follow which code goes where. That removes the need to add `Meteor.isServer()` or `Meteor.isClient()` around any of the code.

We'll have code that should only be executed on the client. This goes into client/client.js. All templates will be put inside client/templates.html. Code that's executed only on the server goes into server/server.js, and collections will be stored in

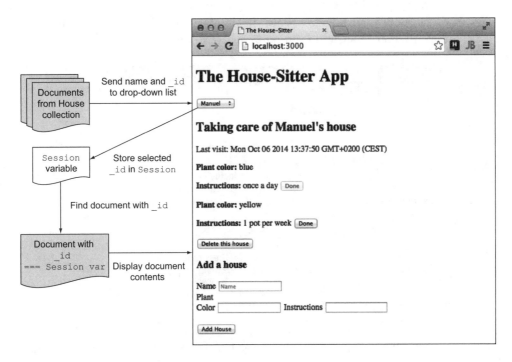

Figure 4.4   User interface and data sources for the house-sitter app

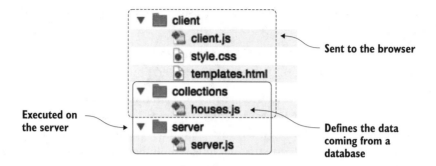

Figure 4.5   Organization of the house-sitter app

collections/houses.js because they should be available on both client and server. See figure 4.5 for reference.

4.2.1   *Setting up templates*

Before you start working with reactive data, you must set up a skeleton structure. List-ing 4.2 shows the body of our site. It includes three subtemplates: selectHouse, which allows users to select a house; showHouse, which displays all relevant details of a data-base entry; and houseForm, which allows users to add and edit database entries. These will be defined inside the same file in the upcoming sections—all templates will remain rather small, and splitting them up isn't necessary.

Listing 4.2   Basic template structure in client/templates.html

```
<head>
  <title>The HouseSitter</title>
</head>

<body>
  <h1>The House-Sitter App</h1>
  {{> selectHouse }}          Inclusion tags
  {{> showHouse }}            for additional
  {{> houseForm }}           templates
</body>

<template name="selectHouse">
</template>
                              These templates
<template name="showHouse">   remain empty
</template>                    for now.

<template name="houseForm">
</template>
```

NOTE   If you're including templates that aren't available, Meteor will display an error. You can avoid running into these errors by either creating an empty tem-plate or removing the inclusion tags from the body until they're actually needed.

The application doesn't need any styling definitions, so the client/style.css file remains empty. If you wish to add styles to make the house-sitter app prettier, this is where you can put them.

4.2.2 *Connecting to a database and declaring collections*

Although you'll learn about collections at section 4.4, you need to define one now because you require some data to be available. We'll discuss the details of working with collections later in this chapter.

MongoDB is a document-oriented, or NoSQL, database. It doesn't store its contents in tables but in documents. Multiple documents are grouped in collections. Therefore, you'll going to define a new `Collection` object called `HousesCollection` that will store its contents inside a MongoDB database in a collection named `houses`. Create a file inside a collections directory and add the code from listing 4.3.

> **Listing 4.3 Collection declaration in collections/houses.js**

```
HousesCollection = new Mongo.Collection('houses');
```

Also, you should make sure there's some data inside the database to work with, so you'll add some server-side code that checks upon start whether there's any data available inside the `HousesCollection`. If there are no entries, our code will insert a new document into the database (see listing 4.4). You can add more houses to the `houses` array if you require more data to be available.

> **NOTE** Wrapping code in a `Meteor.startup()` block works on both server and client. Whereas on the server the code gets executed once when the Node.js instance starts, it gets executed on each client once the DOM is ready.

Wrapping the code inside a `Meteor.startup()` block ensures that it runs only when the server starts. Theoretically you could also add this code to the client, but `Meteor.startup()` would be executed every time a client successfully connects. Because of the conditional `if`, nothing would happen, so you can just as well limit the fixtures to the server only.

> **Listing 4.4 Adding fixtures in server/server.js**

```
Meteor.startup(function () {                          ◁── Execute only once when
  if (HousesCollection.find().count() === 0) {   ◁──     the server starts.
    var houses = [{                              ◁──
      name: 'Stephan',
      plants: [{                                     Check whether there are any
        color: 'red',                                entries in the collection yet.
        instructions: '3 pots/week'
      }, {                                           Define all fixtures as
        color: 'white',                              array elements.
        instructions: 'keep humid'
      }]
    }];
```

```
      while (houses.length > 0) {
        HousesCollection.insert(houses.pop());    ◁
      }
      console.log('Added fixtures');    ◁
    }
});
```

▷ Insert all objects from the houses array into the database.

▷ Console logging also works on the server.

NOTE   The console.log() command works well in the browser console, but it can also be used inside the server context to print out messages. The output can be viewed inside the terminal running the meteor command.

4.3   *Working with the Session object*

Traditionally, accessing a website via HTTP is stateless. A user requests one document after another. Because there's often the need to maintain a certain state between requests—for example, to keep a user logged in—the most essential way to store volatile data in a web application is the session. Meteor's concept of a session is different from languages such as PHP, where a dedicated session object exists on the server or in a cookie. Meteor doesn't use HTTP cookies but uses the browser's *localStorage* instead—for example, for storing session tokens to keep a user logged in.

A dedicated Session object that's just available on the client and lives in memory is useful only for keeping track of current user contexts and actions.

4.3.1   *The Session object*

The Session object holds key-value pairs, which can only be used on the client. It's a reactive dictionary that provides a get() and a set() method. Until a session key is associated via set(), it remains undefined. You can avoid this by setting a default value using setDefault(), which works exactly the same as set(), but only if the value is currently undefined. Checking for a session value is a common operation, which can be done more efficiently by using the Session object's equals() function. It isn't necessary to declare a new Session variable using the var syntax, because the variable becomes available as soon as a set() or setDefault() method is used. The corresponding syntax is shown in the following listing.

Listing 4.5   Using the Session object

setDefault() sets a value for a key only if the key is undefined.

```
Session.setDefault("key", "default value");    ◁
Session.get("key");
Session.set("key","new value");    ◁
Session.equals("key","expression");    ◁
```

Returns default value ▷

Assigns a new value to a key

Translates to Session.get("key") === " expression" but is more efficient

TIP   Although a Session variable is typically used with strings, it can also hold arrays or objects.

Let's see how you can apply the `Session` object to the houseSitter app. Consider `Session` to be the app's short-term memory for keeping track of the currently selected house.

4.3.2 *Using Session to store selected drop-down values*

For the `selectHouse` template, all you need is a drop-down list so users can select a house from the database. The idea is to retrieve all documents from the database and show all available names. Once a name is selected, it'll define the context of all other templates and a single house will be displayed. You'll be using the code shown in listing 4.6.

An `{{#each}}` template helper is used to iterate through all houses returned from the database. The data context is set explicitly by passing `housesNameId`[1] as an argument. Both `{{_id}}` and `{{name}}` are attributes of the `house` object coming from the database, so there's no need to define helpers for them.

> **Listing 4.6 Drop-down list code in the `selectHouse` template**

```
<template name="selectHouse">
  <select id="selectHouse">
    <option value="" {{isSelected}}></option>          Begin the list with an
    {{#each housesNameId}}                              empty option to select.
      <option value="{{_id}}" {{isSelected}}>{{name}}</option>
    {{/each}}
  </select>
</template>
```

Begin the list with an empty option to select.

each iterates over all objects returned by a helper called housesNameId.

In the client.js file you define a helper that provides the `housesNameId` data context. Because we haven't looked at the details of working with collections yet, you'll just return all documents and fields for now. Because `housesNameId` is defined inside a `Template` object, it's reactive. This means if you add or remove documents from the database, the return value will automatically be adjusted and the select box will reflect your changes without the need to write dedicated code.

You'll use a `Session` variable called `selectedHouseId` to store the drop-down selection. The select box should reflect the actual selection, so you need to add a `selected` attribute to the currently selected option. To do so, you'll define a second helper named `isSelected` that returns an empty string or returns `selected` if the value of `_id` equals that of your `Session` variable.

The last step is to set the value for the `Session` variable based on the user's selection. Because it involves an action coming from the user, this requires an event map.

Whenever the value for the DOM element with the ID `selectHouse` changes, the event handler will set the `selectedHouseId` variable to the value from the selected

---

[1] For now `housesNameId` contains more than just a name and an ID, but don't worry. We'll make that more efficient in a bit.

option element. Note that you need to pass the event as an argument to the JavaScript function that sets the Session value in order to access its value (see following listing).

Listing 4.7   JavaScript code for selecting houses

Returns all documents from the collection

Returns selected if the _id for the currently processed house equals that stored inside the Session variable

```
Template.selectHouse.helpers({
  housesNameId: function () {
    return HousesCollection.find({}, {});
  },
  isSelected: function () {
    return Session.equals('selectedHouseId', this._id) ? 'selected' : '';
  }
});
Template.selectHouse.events = {
  'change #selectHouse': function (evt) {
    Session.set('selectedHouseId', evt.currentTarget.value);
  }
};
```

Remember to pass the event as an argument so the function can assign the selection value to the Session variable.

You can test that everything works correctly by opening the JavaScript console inside a browser and selecting a value from the drop-down list. You can get and set values for the variable directly inside your console as well. If you change the value to a valid _id, you can see that the drop-down list instantly updates itself as a result of the isSelected helper, as shown in figure 4.6.

Changing the selected value sets the value for selectedHouse.

Check the current value using Session.get in the console.

Setting a value for selectedHouse automatically changes the display value of the drop-down list.

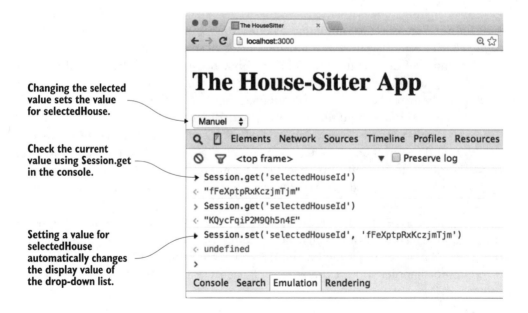

Figure 4.6   Getting and setting the Session variable via the JavaScript console

4.3.3 Creating a reactive context using Tracker.autorun

When working with JavaScript code, you'll often need to check for the value of a variable to better understand why an application behaves the way it does. You can use the `console.log()` method, one of the most important tools for debugging, to keep track of variable contents. Because you're dealing with reactive data sources, you can also take advantage of computations to monitor the actual values of those sources. In this section you'll learn how to print the contents of the reactive `Session` variable any time it changes by creating a reactive context for the execution of `console.log()`.

In section 4.1 you saw that besides templates and Blaze there's a third way to establish a context that enables reactive computations: `Tracker.autorun()`. Any function running inside such a block is automatically rerun whenever its dependencies (that is, the reactive data sources used within it) change. Meteor automatically detects which data sources are used and sets up the necessary dependencies.

You can keep track of the value for `Session.get("selectedHouseId")` by putting it inside an `autorun` function. Place this code at the very beginning of the client.js file, outside any template blocks (see listing 4.8). Whenever you use the drop-down list to select another value, the console immediately prints the currently selected ID. If no house is selected, it'll print `undefined`.

> **Listing 4.8   Using `Tracker.autorun()` to print a `Session` variable to the console**

```
Tracker.autorun(function () {
  console.log("The selectedHouse ID is: " +
    Session.get("selectedHouseId")
  );
});
```

As you can see, the `Session` object is simple to work with and can be extremely useful. It can be accessed from any part of the application and maintains its values even if you change source files and Meteor reloads your application (a process known as *hot code pushes*). If a user initiates a page refresh, all data is lost, though.

Keep in mind that the contents of a `Session` object never leave the browser, so other clients or even the server may never access its contents. This is what collections are used for. Let's take a closer look at working with collections.

4.4   Working with MongoDB collections

Meteor comes with its own instance of MongoDB, an open source, document-oriented NoSQL database. Each time you start your server with the `meteor run` command, a dedicated database server is also started and listens to connections on port 3001. By default, Meteor uses this instance as its database engine and stores all content inside a database called meteor. There's no need to define any database connection strings. But you can use environment variables like `MONGO_URL` to point your Meteor server to another database instance. Chapter 12 goes into detail on how to use external databases instead of the default local one.

What is a document-oriented database?

MongoDB is a document-oriented, NoSQL database. In contrast to relational (SQL) databases, every entry is self-contained and isn't spread across multiple tables to specify relationships. Each database entry is basically a JSON object.

To better understand document-oriented databases, consider all data you want to store to be written on a piece of paper (a "document"). If you want to keep track of all the houses you're house-sitting for, you'd create one form per house and then write down all the instructions. The advantage of document storage is that all relevant information is in a single place. Just grab a single piece of paper and you have all the info you need to take care of that house. The downside is that if multiple houses have the same plants and science has discovered that red flowers in fact need four instead of three pots of water each week, you'll have to change the instructions on every single piece of paper.

Every document is self-contained and may even have different information on it ("fields"), which reflects that at some houses you take care of the plants whereas in others you might also need to feed the rabbit. You don't write down any areas that you don't have to take action in, so even though two documents may be from the same collection, they don't necessarily contain the same fields:

```
Name: Stephan
Plants:
  - Color: Red
    Instructions: 3 pots/week
  - Color: White
    Instructions: water daily
Animals:
  - Name: Danbo
    Instructions: 1 carrot/day
```

```
Name: Manuel
Plants:
  - Color: Red
    Instructions: 3 pots/week
  - Color: Yellow
    Instructions: keep humid
```

If you've worked with SQL databases such as MySQL or Oracle before, the following table translates common SQL terms to their document-oriented equivalents.

SQL term	Document-oriented term
database	database
table	collection
row	document
column	field

If data is meant to be stored for an extended period of time, or if it should be shared across clients, collections are the way to do it. New database collections are declared using the `Mongo` object. The following statement makes the content from a MongoDB collection named `mycollection` available inside a Meteor application as `MyCollection`:

```
MyCollection = new Mongo.Collection("mycollection");
```

Because the collection should be accessed from both the server and the client, you need to make sure this line is executed in both contexts, so it shouldn't be wrapped inside any `isClient()` or `isServer()` blocks. Also note that it doesn't use a `var` declaration, which would limit its scope to a single file.

> **NOTE** Collection names in Meteor usually start with a capital letter and have plural names. If you want to be more explicit you can add `Collection` to their names to make your code more readable. Collections are best defined in one or more dedicated files accessible to both client and server.

The fundamentals of working with a collection are based on the way MongoDB works, so if you're already familiar with the syntax used to query Mongo databases you can reuse this knowledge with Meteor, even from inside the browser.

4.4.1 *Querying documents in MongoDB*

Querying documents in MongoDB is done using either `find()` or `findOne()`. The first returns all matching documents; the latter retrieves only the first document that matches specified search criteria. These criteria are passed to the query as an object called the *query document* or *selector*. If no selector is defined, then all documents match.

To find one document where the name is "Stephan", we need to make sure the selector contains the search field (name) and the desired value ("Stephan"). Field names or keys don't require quotes:

```
MyCollection.findOne({name: "Stephan"});
```

The `findOne()` operation is executed on the collection named `MyCollection`. It matches and returns the first document where the value of the field `name` equals `"Stephan"`.

Finding all documents that have instructions for watering a white plant requires a more advanced query. This time `find()` is executed, so all matching documents inside `MyCollection` are returned. The query document specifies that inside a `plants` key must be another key called `color`. The term `$exists: 1` translates into the field being present inside all matches.

```
Collection.find({"plants.color" : {$exists: 1 } });
```

To check whether the field contains a specific value, you can use `$in` instead of `$exists`. If you want to find all documents that contain a plant with a `color` attribute of `"White"`, you use the following query:

```
Collection.find({"plants.color" : {$in: ["White"] } });
```

In addition to search criteria, a second object may be passed to the query operations. It's called the *projection,* and you can use it to limit the fields that should be returned, change the sort order, or apply any kind of operation on the search results before returning them. Projections can be used with or without a query document. If no search criteria are needed, an empty selector is passed to the `find()` function.

The following query returns only the name field and value from each document. The term `name:1` can be read as "set the field name to visible" because 1 represents true. Using 0, you define the fields you want to exclude from retrieval:

```
Collection.find({},{name:1})
```

As you can see from these examples, using collection queries is quite different from using SQL. It's helpful to keep in mind that you aren't dealing with tables and rows but with documents that behave like objects.

> **NOTE**   More details on using MongoDB can be found in the official documentation at http://docs.mongodb.org/.

4.4.2 *Working with Meteor collections*

At the most basic level, you can store data to a collection as a document and search and retrieve one or more documents when you need to display data. Let's start by populating the houses collection.

The most important functions when working with collections are listed in table 4.2.

Table 4.2 **Overview of most important functions when working with collections**

Function	Use case	Return value
`Collection.find()`	Finds all documents that match the selector	Cursor
`Collection.findOne()`	Finds the first document that matches selector and projection criteria	Object
`Collection.insert()`	Inserts a document in a collection	String (document _id)
`Collection.update()`	Modifies one or more documents in a collection	Number of documents affected
`Collection.upsert()`	Modifies one or more documents in a collection or inserts a new document if no match is found	Object
`Collection.remove()`	Removes documents from a collection	Object

INTRODUCING CURSORS: THE DIFFERENCE BETWEEN FIND() AND FINDONE()

A single document can be retrieved from a collection by using `findOne()`. This function returns a JavaScript object that can be dealt with just like any other object. Using the find() function to retrieve multiple documents doesn't return any documents but instead returns a *cursor*. The cursor is a reactive data source, not the collection.

You can think of a cursor as being the query that eventually gets executed against the database. Cursors allow you to send data in batches. When dealing with large datasets, you'll find it's not efficient to always return all documents from a query but to iterate over results and send them in batches.

For now, we won't deal with cursors directly because Meteor is capable of knowing how to handle the results from a Collection.find() just fine. We'll revisit this topic once we discuss more advanced use cases in chapter 9.

4.4.3 Initializing a collection

For each house you need to take care of, you'll have one document inside the database. This document will include the name and plants you need to take care of. To have better traceability throughout the application code, you'll use a verbose name to help you keep track of the collection object. You've added the necessary code in section 4.2.2 already, so there's no need to add this line again. HousesCollection will provide an interface to all database entries:

```
HousesCollection = new Mongo.Collection("houses");
```

There's no need to create any data structures inside a collection. When the first entry is added to a collection, Meteor automatically creates a collection inside the database if it's not yet present.

The server code we defined during the setup of our application in section 4.2.2 takes care of both creating a database collection and filling it with data. As you saw in chapter 2 with the fridge example, you can also use the browser console to add new data. We'll add security mechanisms that prohibit this when we discuss publications and methods in chapter 6. For now let's focus on adding functionality instead of getting ready for production.

An important side effect of using fixtures is that you have an idea of what the data structure looks like. Because you're dealing with a NoSQL database, each document may have a completely different structure and it's good to have reference entries at hand. Although there may be other fields (such as animals or kids), the expected fields for each house document are shown in table 4.3. You're only taking care of plants in this example.

Table 4.3 Expected fields for the houses collection

Field name	Contains	Notes
_id	Unique ID for each house; string	Automatically assigned by MongoDB
name	Display name for each house; string	

Table 4.3 Expected fields for the `houses` **collection** *(continued)*

Field name	Contains	Notes
`lastvisit`	Timestamp for last action; `Date`	Generated by application logic
`plants`	Household plants to take care of; array of objects	
`plants.color`	Unique plant color per house; string	No database constraint, uniqueness must be ensured by application logic
`plants.instructions`	Watering instructions for a plant; string	

4.4.4 *Querying collections*

It's convenient to rely on everything being reactive in a development environment, but with larger datasets having every function react on any data change will have a visible impact on performance. For the drop-down list of houses, it doesn't matter whether someone adds or removes plants to/from a document, so you're going to limit reactivity to the `name` and `_id` fields only.

RETURNING SPECIFIC FIELDS ONLY

In the previous section, you defined the `housesNameId` helper to return everything from `HousesCollection`; now you'll limit the return value to only the fields `name` and `_id` as shown in listing 4.9. The selector object remains empty, but you pass a second object with a `fields` property to the cursor. Inside it you may set individual fields to 1, which means they'll be returned. Alternatively you could set fields to 0 to exclude them from being returned. You can't mix inclusion (1) and exclusion (0) styles. All keys mentioned must be set to either 1 or 0.

Listing 4.9 Limiting the fields returned to the drop-down list

```
Template.selectHouse.helpers({
  housesNameId: function () {
    return HousesCollection.find({}, {fields: {name: 1, _id: 1} });
  },
  // isSelected definition
});
```

RETURNING A FULL DOCUMENT

Once the user makes a selection from the drop-down list, you want to show the house document in full. In this case you obviously need to return all the fields inside the document. You'll create another helper that'll return exactly one document with all fields based on the value of the `Session` variable `selectedHouseId`. This helper will be used inside a template called `showHouse`, so you need to add this block to the client.js file, as shown in listing 4.10.

Listing 4.10 Returning a database document to a template based on ID

```
Template.showHouse.helpers({
  house: function () {
    return HousesCollection.findOne({
      _id: Session.get("selectedHouseId")
    });
  }
});
```

This time you're using a query document but pass no options to the `findOne()` function. As a result you'll get the full document stored inside MongoDB as an object. This object can be accessed like any other in JavaScript.

4.4.5 Display collection data in a template

Meteor templates make it easy to access data inside an object returned by a helper. All you need is a double-braced tag referencing the name of the object and the specific field you want displayed. To show the name stored inside the document returned by `house`, you can use `{{house.name}}`. To eliminate the need to prefix each object property with `house`, though, you'll find that a `#with` block that sets the data context is useful because it makes the template more readable.

To enhance the user experience, you'll add a conditional to check whether a valid selection has been made. If no selection has been made, the template should ask the user to make a selection.

Each plant should be displayed with information regarding its color, instructions for watering, and a button to mark a plant as watered.

For displaying the document's contents, you can either put everything inside the `showHouse` template or use a dedicated subtemplate. Using a subtemplate gives you greater flexibility and manageability in the future when you might want to support pets, kids, or cleaning.

When you include a template, it inherits the parent's data context. That way, you don't have to define a new helper and need to write less code. In the example in listing 4.11, you can see that the data context isn't taken from the parent directly but is further specified by `{{#each plants}}`. From the subtemplate, the current `plant` object from the loop is the defined context. You can still use the same expressions as you would in the parent, but remember that now you're at a deeper level inside `house`. To access parent attributes such as the house ID, you must use the `../` notation.

Listing 4.11 Template code for showing a house with all plants

```
<template name="showHouse">
  {{#with house}}
    <h2>Taking care of {{name}}'s house</h2>
```

Setting the data context for the template explicitly

Each database field is a property of the house object and can be accessed using dot notation.

```
    {{#each plants }}
       {{> plantDetails }}
    {{/each}}
  {{else}}
     You need to select a house.
  {{/with}}
</template>

<template name="plantDetails">
  <p>
    <strong>Plant color:</strong> {{color}}
  </p>
  <p>
     <strong>Instructions:</strong> {{instructions}}
       <button class="water" data-id="{{../_id}}-{{color}}" {{isWatered}}
         Done
       </button>
  </p>
</template>
```

each further narrows the data context for the subtemplate.

A subtemplate, plantsDetails, is included.

Adding both templates to the application, you can now select a house and view its contents, regardless of the number of plants.

ReactiveVar: **the power of** Session **with a local scope**

Session requires a globally unique name, or technically speaking, it lives inside the global scope. Sometimes you want a variable to be available everywhere in your app, but there are many cases where their usage is limited to a single part of the application—or even a single template.

As a rule of thumb you should avoid putting too much into the global scope, especially not variables that are used only locally, such as the watered state. To keep things simple we focus on working with the Session object, let's accept this limitation for the house-sitter app.

For bigger projects and if you wish to improve the code you can use locally scoped reactive variables—the aptly named ReactiveVar. The ReactiveVar package is part of Meteor core, but you have to add it manually via the command line:

```
$ meteor add reactive-var
```

Both ReactiveVar and Session use get() and set() functions, but ReactiveVar doesn't pollute the global namespace and can be limited to a local scope. You can reuse it with different values for the same template.

Just like Session, ReactiveVar stores key-value pairs. It may store whole objects as values. Updating objects inside the ReactiveVar container requires the use of set(). Because it's scoped to a template context, you must declare a new ReactiveVar inside the created callback for a template. There's no setDefault() function, but you can pass a default value to ReactiveVar when a new instance is declared:

```
Template.plantDetails.onCreated(function () {
  this.watered = new ReactiveVar();
  this.watered.set(false);
});
```

(continued)

Here, the keyword `this` refers to the currently available data context (which happens to be the content of a single `plants` object). Inside an event map you can set its value to `true` when the button is clicked. You must use the second argument to the function, `tpl`, which holds a reference to the template. Because `watered` is a property of the template, you can set it like this:

```
Template.plantDetails.events({
  'click button': function (evt, tpl) {
    tpl.watered.set(true);
  }
});
```

And finally, from within the helpers the current value can be accessed. Here you must access the current template instance using the corresponding `Template.instance()` syntax:

```
Template.plantDetails.helpers({
  watered: function () {
    return Template.instance().watered.get() ? 'disabled' : '';
  }
});
```

EVENT MAPS AND DATA ASSOCIATION

Besides simply presenting the data from a document, you also want to be able to mark a plant as watered. Clicking a button triggers an event that sets a plant to `watered`, but if you switch between houses you want to keep the state of a plant. To accomplish that, you'll use a `Session` variable again. This time you can't set the name in the application code because you don't know how many plants each house has. Therefore, you'll dynamically create an ID for each plant, consisting of the document `_id` in combination with the `color` attribute. You can do this because you defined `color` as a unique identifier for each plant inside a house.

It's common practice to use the HTML attribute `data-id` to pass unique element IDs to the application code. The event map watches for a click on any button with the class `water` and stores the value of `data-id` for the currently clicked button consisting of both the document ID and the `color` value. The event map shown in listing 4.12 can use `data-id` without having to create the compound ID itself.

Once the button is clicked, a `Session` variable with the new compound ID value is set to `true`. There's no need to set a default value for the `Session` variable. Remember, technically it's a key-value store inside the `Session` object, so you can add new keys at any time.

Listing 4.12   Event map for watering the plants

```
Template.plantDetails.events({
  'click button.water': function (evt) {
    var plantId = $(evt.currentTarget).attr('data-id');      ◁── data-id contains
    Session.set(plantId, true);                                   a unique ID for
  }                                                               each plant.
});
```

Whenever a plant is watered, you want to disable the button as an indicator that this plant doesn't require any more attention. You'll do this with a helper (listing 4.13) similar to the one you used to determine the currently selected house in the drop-down list. Because you're using globally available `Session` variables, you can water the red plant in Manuel's house, switch to Stephan's house, and then back to Manuel's and still find the button disabled.

Unless the user forces a page reload, all contents stored inside a `Session` object will remain available globally throughout an application.

Listing 4.13 Template helper for disabling the Done button

```
Template.plantDetails.helpers({
  isWatered: function () {
    var plantId = Session.get("selectedHouseId") + '-' + this.color;
    return Session.get(plantId) ? 'disabled' : '';
  }
});
```

4.4.6 *Updating data in a collection*

You update data inside a collection via the `Collection.update()` function. Although it can modify one or more documents at the same time when invoked on the server, the `update()` function is limited to manipulating a single document based on its `_id` when running on the client side. This is to avoid accidental bulk operations that may block the server for all users. If you need to update more than a single document at a time, you can do so using server-side methods (see chapter 6).

When using `update()`, you need to specify which documents to update, how to update them, and optionally define options as well as a callback (using an error as the first return value and the number of affected documents as a second value):

```
Collection.update(selector, modifier, options, callback);
```

Only two options are available, both of which are Booleans:

- `multi`—The default is `false`; if it's set to `true`, all matching documents are updated; otherwise, only the first match is updated.
- `upsert`—The default is `false`; if it's set to `true`, it inserts a new document if no matching documents are found.

To call `update()` from the client, you must provide a single `_id` as the first argument. This is part of the first argument, which is called the selector. It can be either an object with an `_id` attribute or a string that holds a valid document ID. The modifier uses standard Mongo syntax to define how to modify present data. Table 4.4 gives an overview of some of the most common operators. The following command updates a document with an `_id` of `12345` and sets the field `name` to `Updated Name`:

```
Collection.update({_id: "12345"}, {$set: {name: "Updated Name"}});
```

NOTE Not all functionality available in MongoDB is available in Minimongo, the client implementation. You can check the NOTES file inside the mini-mongo package for an overview of the current limitations.

Table 4.4 Overview of frequently used update modifiers for collections

Update operator	Description
$inc	Increments the value of a field by the specified amount
$set	Sets the value of a field in the document
$unset	Removes a field from the document
$rename	Renames a field from a document
$addtoSet	Adds elements to an array if they don't already exist
$push	Adds an item to an array
$pull	Removes all array elements that match a specified query

TRIGGERING UPDATES VIA EVENTS

So far we've only shown you how to use `Session` variables to store data, which means all data is gone once the browser window is closed or the user forces a reload. To keep track of when each house was last visited, you'll extend the event handler to store the current date to the database. A field, `lastvisited`, will be used inside each `house` document. Again, you don't have to define the database structure before you can add data—you just add a new field to an existing document.

Inside the client.js file you'll extend the existing event handler for the `plant-Details` template with two lines (listing 4.14). A new variable called `lastvisit` will be assigned a current timestamp. It'll be used in the `update()` function for the current document.[2] Be careful because you're now dealing with two IDs: one for the plant and another for the house. Let's leave `plantId` untouched and for the document ID use the `selectedHouseId` session variable to specify the ID in the `update` statement.

Listing 4.14 Extended event map for adding a last-visited date

```
Template.plantDetails.events({
  'click button.water': function (evt) {
    var plantId = $(evt.currentTarget).attr('data-id');
    Session.set(plantId, true);
    var lastvisit = new Date();                    ◁─┐ lastvisit contains a
    HousesCollection.update({                         │ current timestamp.
      _id: Session.get("selectedHouseId")
    }, {
```

---

[2] The browser implementation Minimongo doesn't support the full feature set provided by MongoDB. Therefore, using the `$currentDate` modifier isn't possible on the client.

```
      $set: {
        lastvisit: lastvisit
      }
    });
  }
});
```

The lastvisit field inside the currently selected document is set to the current timestamp.

Every time any of the plants inside a house is watered now (that is, the Done button is clicked) the `lastvisit` field gets updated. To verify that this update happens, you'll extend the `showHouse` template to display the value of `lastvisit`, as shown in the following listing.

Listing 4.15   Adding the `lastvisit` timestamp to the `showHouse` template

```
<template name="showHouse">
  {{#with house}}
    //...
    <p>Last visit: {{lastvisit}}</p>
    //...
  {{/with}}
</template>
```

Add this line to show the timestamp stored as lastvisit.

Clicking the button for either plant will automatically disable the button and update the timestamp in the database, as shown in figure 4.7.

Because of latency compensation, the value in the local Minimongo instance is updated first and the result is shown immediately. At the same time, the update is sent to the server, where the last visit date will be persisted. Should the connection to the

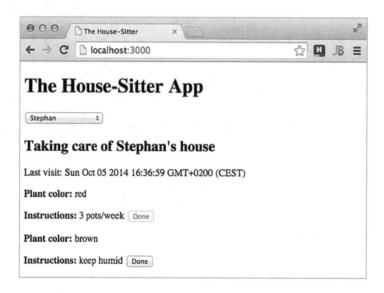

Figure 4.7   The timestamp gets updated onscreen and inside the database by each click on a Done button.

server be lost, Meteor will store the update locally in the browser and resend it once the connection is restored.

4.4.7 *Inserting new data into a collection*

As business grows, new houses are added and new documents must be added to a collection. Generally adding documents is done using the insert() function. Each field of the document must be specified individually, and the value for _id is left out because it's assigned automatically by the database:

```
Collection.insert({field: "value"});
```

Adding a new house to our collection requires a new template as well as another event map to trigger the insertion. In section 4.2.2 you already set up a template called houseForm, which you can extend.

> **NOTE** We haven't discussed routing yet, so all templates are displayed in the same view. Although you could use Session to determine which templates to show, the preferred method involves using a router. Skip ahead to chapter 8 to learn about the principles for using dedicated views for editing and displaying data.

Listing 4.16 shows the houseForm template, which consists of a view for a house document that displays all editable fields inside a form. To keep things simple, let's limit the form to add only a single plant to a house.[3] All input fields will be identified by their ID.

Listing 4.16 Adding new houses using a form

```html
<template name="houseForm">
  <h3>Add a house</h3>
  <form id="houseForm">
    Name <input id="house-name" type="text" placeholder="Name"><br/>
    Plant<br/>
    Color <input id="plant-color" type="text">
    Instructions <input id="plant-instructions" type="text">
    <br/>
    <br/>
    <button id="saveHouse">Save House</button>
  </form>
</template>
```

Next, create an event map for handling the form (listing 4.17). When the button for the form is clicked, the default behavior is to send a form and reload a page. Because you're implementing your own functionality for the button, you must suppress the default behavior by calling the preventDefault() method on the event. Using jQuery, you'll retrieve all values for the input fields and put them in local variables.

---

[3] Don't worry; you'll soon create a more powerful way to add as many plants as you like.

The final line of code does two things. First, it inserts a new document with values from the input fields into the `HousesCollection`. That returns the ID of the new document, which is assigned to the `selectedHouseId` Session variable. That way, the entire page instantly displays the new house in the selection and detail view.

Listing 4.17   Event map for adding a new house

```
Template.houseForm.events({
  'click button#saveHouse': function (evt) {
    evt.preventDefault();
    var houseName = $('input[id=house-name]').val();
    var plantColor = $('input[id=plant-color]').val();
    var plantInstructions = $('input[id=plant-instructions]').val();
    Session.set('selectedHouseId', HousesCollection.insert({
      name: houseName,
      plants: [{
        color: plantColor,
        instructions: plantInstructions
      }]
    }));
    // empty the form
    $('input').val('');
  }
});
```

Prevents sending the form and reloading the page ← `evt.preventDefault();`

Retrieves the input field values using jQuery

Inserts a new document and assigns the return value to the selectedHouseId variable to immediately show the contents of the new document ← `Session.set('selectedHouseId', HousesCollection.insert({`

Empties the form fields ← `$('input').val('');`

This is only a very simple way to add houses that has several shortcomings. The form doesn't allow the user to enter multiple plants for a house. Also, the form is only capable of adding new houses (although you could easily reuse it to allow editing of existing houses as well). In the upcoming section, you'll enhance the example to improve on these shortcomings and refactor some of the code for better efficiency. But first let's put the finishing touches on basic CRUD.

4.4.8   Removing data from a collection

The final step for full CRUD[4] functionality is removing an entry from the database. The relevant function is called `remove()`:

```
Collection.remove(id);
```

Similar to the `update()` method, `delete()` requires a unique ID to know which document to remove. Multiple documents may be deleted only from the server, which we'll look at in a bit when we discuss methods.

---

[4] Create, Read, Update, Delete—a common name for basic operations on persistent data

For the HTML, all you have to do to allow for houses to be deleted is to add a button to the showHouse template. When the button is clicked, you'll identify the house by its ID. There are at least three ways to do this in Meteor:

- If the HTML button had a data-id attribute, you could query its contents in the same way you determined the plant ID.
- If the currently selected house ID is stored inside the Session object, you can use it the same way you did the Done button for updating houses.
- If the template has a data context that provides the ID, you access it directly.

We already covered the first two. This time, the ID is already part of the data context in which the click event takes place. That means you can simplify the way you determine which document to delete and choose the third option. Listing 4.18 shows how to add the button to the template.

> **NOTE** Although it's not needed, you should consider adding a data-id attribute to the delete button to provide some traceability to make debugging easier.

Listing 4.18 Adding a delete button to remove houses from the database

```
<template name="showHouse">
  {{#with house}}
    ...
    <button id="delete">Delete this house</button>      ◁──  Add the button
  {{else}}                                                      just before the
    ...                                                         else tag.
  {{/with}}
</template>
```

There's no event map for the showHouse template yet, so clicking the buttons doesn't do anything. Let's create a new event map in client.js. Listing 4.19 shows the code that essentially performs a Collection.remove(). You'll wrap it inside a confirmation dialog to prevent users from accidentally deleting houses.

Notice that you don't have to capture the event and read out the data-id attribute as you did when you set a plant to a watered state. You can directly access all information contained in the currently selected house document, including _id.

Listing 4.19 Event map for deleting a house

```
Template.showHouse.events({
  'click button#delete': function (evt) {           This is the current data context:
    var id = this._id;                        ◁──   the selected house document
    var deleteConfirmation = confirm('Really delete this house?');   ◁──  Shows a
    if (deleteConfirmation) {                                             confirmation
      HousesCollection.remove(id);   ◁──  Removes the                     dialog before
    }                                     document from the               actually
  }                                       collection on both              removing the
});                                       client and server               document
```

Congratulations, you're now able to perform all basic data operations using Meteor! Roughly 50 lines of HTML code and about 100 lines of JavaScript are all it takes. Take a deep breath and pat yourself on the back.

By now you're familiar with using the `Session` object and various ways to store, manipulate, and retrieve data from a MongoDB database using `Collections`. Although the main functionality for this application is present, you still have some work to do. Depending on your preferences, you could start securing the application now, which would require users and accounts (see chapter 6). A second option would be to add routing capabilities to the application so that the form for adding new houses isn't displayed on the same page as the house details (see chapter 8). But we should address some shortcomings in regard to our application's functionality first: adding and removing a custom number of plants to/from existing and new houses.

In the next chapter, we'll step things up a bit by taking a more reactive approach to overcome the current limitations of our application by leveraging Meteor's core principles of reactivity rather than falling into old habits of performing complex DOM manipulations using jQuery.

4.5   *Summary*

In this chapter, you've learned that

- Reactive data sources are aware of dependent computations.
- Reactive contexts allow functions to be rerun when data sources change.
- `Tracker.autorun()` can turn any function into a reactive computation by providing a reactive context.
- Short-lived data can be stored inside the key-value store of the `Session` object.
- Persistent data is stored in MongoDB `Collections`.
- Meteor automatically publishes all `Collections` to every client unless the `auto-publish` package is removed.
- Both `autopublish` and `insecure` must be removed before putting an application into production.

Fully reactive editing

This chapter covers

- Building reactive forms
- Using reactive data bindings to update views
- Working with unsynchronized, or local, collections
- Displaying collection data within forms and performing updates reactively
- Implementing a simple notifications system

In chapter 4 you created a fully functional yet basic application that allows users to select, view, add, and delete houses. Because you used reactive data sources, you didn't have to manipulate the DOM tree—for example, adding a new `option` element to the drop-down list when you created a new house—Meteor's reactivity took care of it for you.

The most common approach to front-end development is manual DOM manipulation, but it's tedious and error-prone. In most frameworks, data is retrieved from a back end and needs to be inserted into the DOM somehow. If a new database entry is sent to the client, a library like jQuery is used to add a new `li` element or table row. Although this approach is straightforward, it tends to make code overly complex and forces you to explicitly add changes for all occurrences inside a page. Many people associate front-end coding with DOM manipulations, but Meteor allows you to focus on data only and let it perform any changes to views and templates. In this chapter you'll be taking advantage of reactive data bindings that limit the amount of code required and make the application more robust.

This chapter shows you how to enhance the existing application to allow working with more complex data structures. You'll keep all interactions with the DOM at a minimum. In order to do so, you'll take advantage of Meteor's *database everywhere* principle and use a local collection that exists only on the client. That way, you can add and remove any number of plants to a house. Additionally, you'll ensure that unsaved changes won't be discarded by accident by implementing a rudimentary notifications system. By the end of this chapter, you'll be able to create fully reactive front ends powered by reactive data sources.

5.1 The reactive editing workflow

Before you apply some of the advanced Meteor concepts to the houseSitter application, let's revisit the overall flow of information between users and databases (figure 5.1).

When a house is selected, users may change its contents, for example, by adding or removing plants (step 1). Especially when dealing with sensitive data, the application will validate the incoming data in the browser already (step 2). If all data is valid, it's stored inside the local mini-database (step 3). Because the data is still volatile and present only inside the user's browser, it's merely a simulation of the actual saving process. If the user closes her browser at this point, no data is stored on the server although the browser view is already updated (step 4).

After the successful simulation, data is sent to the server with a request to persist it (step 5). Again, validations should occur (step 6) and the actual storing procedure takes place (step 7). Finally, the result of the operation, either an error or a success message, is sent back to the client (step 8). All other users who can currently view the

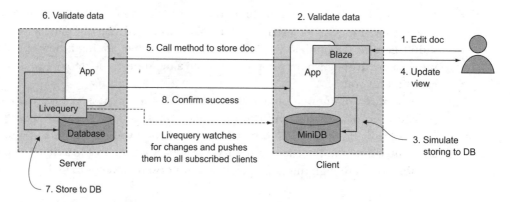

Figure 5.1   The reactive editing workflow

updated document get an instant update of their screen. The *Livequery* component constantly monitors the database for changes and keeps track of all currently subscribed clients.[1]

So far the houseSitter business you built in chapter 4 allows you to take on new clients with only a single plant. You need to be able to serve not only customers with multiple plants but also those with varying numbers of plants. The first improvement for the existing application must be to allow editing of existing documents while also enabling an arbitrary number of plants in each household. The combination of Blaze templates and reactive data sources allows you to implement reactive form editing with just a few lines of code.

Once you introduce reactive editing, you'll have to take into account that the instant updates triggered by Livequery may not always be desirable. There may be times when two people edit the same document, so you need a way to communicate that someone else has changed a document that's currently being edited. You shouldn't discard all unsaved changes because the server holds newer data. All local changes should first be stored in a staging environment, which gives you performance benefits as well as a safety net. You'll also implement a notifications system to highlight changes to the user.

5.2 Reactive front ends vs. DOM manipulation

Most front-end engineers typically think about the DOM first. They consider how and where to put elements or how to serialize data and send it to REST interfaces. jQuery is a handy tool for these tasks, and it's synonymous for many people with front-end development and DOM manipulation.

When you're using different languages and frameworks on the server and the client, you often find yourself faced with the problem of how to map data received from the server to an actual view. If no easy integration is available, there's always jQuery and adding and removing nodes from the DOM. Unfortunately, changing the DOM manually becomes quite messy, even for small tasks, which is why we see a shift toward functional reactive paradigms. Meteor is no exception to this development.

Let's compare the two scenarios side by side. Consider a simple form for adding and removing plants in each of our houses. One button is used to remove an existing plant; another will add another form `fieldset` to allow entering plant details. Scenario A in figure 5.2 shows the associated code when removing a DOM node. A click on a button removes a form's `fieldset` (the parent of the clicked button). It doesn't affect any other occurrences where the plant may be displayed, so in more complex views additional `remove()` operations might be required—for example, when a preview of the house document appears on the same page. Adding a new plant involves a lot more complexity—you need to inject the entire HTML necessary to define a plant

---

[1] We'll discuss subscriptions and publications in more detail in chapter 7.

Scenario A: Manipulating the DOM

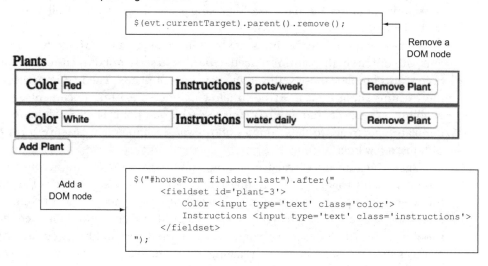

Scenario B: Manipulating the underlying data structure

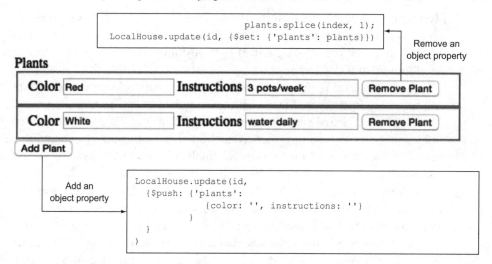

Figure 5.2   Comparing DOM manipulation with reactive data updates

form field. Not only is this line very long; it's also very fragile should you ever decide to adjust the form code by using different classes or adding more fields.

DOM manipulation may be suitable for small front-end hacks, but when writing larger applications it'll be a challenge to maintain that kind of code. Here's where Meteor's seamless integration between front end and back end comes in handy. With

Meteor you can directly work with data and let the framework do all the DOM mapping for you. Changing the data structure will automatically trigger the necessary DOM updates.

Each house is already stored as a document or object inside the database. Why not leave it at that and work with the object rather than worry about the HTML tags? With Meteor you can do this easily so that not only you do not have to worry about mapping content with jQuery, but you also get reactive data binding for free (see the sidebar "Two-way data binding vs. reactivity" for more information on data binding). The HTML form is just a different representational view of the house object. Clicking buttons won't trigger DOM operations but will change an object, as shown in Scenario B in figure 5.2.

As you can see, not only is less code involved, but it also does a much better job at separating data from presentation. As a JavaScript developer you're already familiar with manipulating objects. All that's left is to walk through how Meteor can pass data as an object to the front end.

In this extended example of the houseSitter app, you'll rely on four data sources only:

- `HouseCollection`—A MongoDB collection on the server side used to persist houses
- `Session.get('selectedHouseId')`—Used to keep track of which house is currently selected
- `Session.get('notification')`—Used to store and display notification messages
- `LocalHouse`—A local Minimongo collection that exists only inside the browser and acts as the staging database before changes are sent to the server

The first two were already present in the previous chapter, and you'll add the other two in this chapter. You can also get rid of the button used to track whether flowers have been watered already because you'll focus solely on the management of client or house records. While you're at it, you'll enhance the layout so you use two columns. The contents of the house document will appear on the left and the editing form on the right. Again, you can find the styles used in the code sample accompanying this chapter.

Two-way data binding vs. reactivity

Popular frameworks such as Angular or Ember promote a concept called *two-way data binding*, where changes in the UI can affect the underlying data model, and vice versa. Meteor doesn't rely on such bindings but uses reactivity instead. But what are the actual differences?

Using a traditional server-side language such as PHP or Java, the application retrieves data from a database, renders it into HTML, and sends it to the browser for display. It's possible for the server code to poll the database for changes, re-render,

(continued)

and send an updated view to the browser, using Ajax, for example. If the data is displayed as a form, users can perform as many changes as they like and it won't affect the database content. In fact, form data must be posted first to the server to process and update the data. The server will then store the data in the database, retrieve it, and send an updated view to the browser. Because data flows from a data provider to a consumer, this is sometimes referred to as one-way data binding.

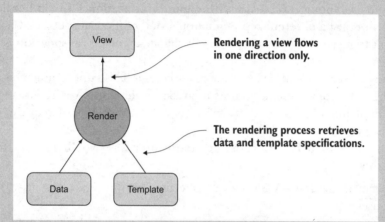

Rendering a view flows in one direction only.

The rendering process retrieves data and template specifications.

One-way data binding

With two-way data binding, the flow is continuous. Every change in a view flows back into the actual data, and vice versa. That means if a form field is updated by a user, the underlying data provider is changed as well. This behavior can be observed if form data is also displayed elsewhere on the site because it would update instantly.

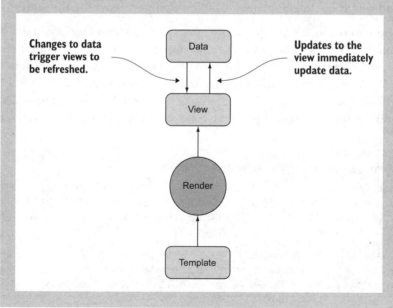

Changes to data trigger views to be refreshed.

Updates to the view immediately update data.

Two-way data binding

(continued)

In practice, these two-way data bindings can have unpredictable consequences, especially when there are multiple instances and each may trigger updates to others.

Although reactivity isn't necessarily related to any data bindings, it can easily be used to monitor events and use computations to automatically perform updates when data is changed. In fact, using a reactive data source is an easy way to implement behavior similar to two-way data binding by using template helpers to show data and using events to update data sources. No code is required to update any views if data changes because it's taken care of by the Blaze engine. If done cleverly, you don't even need to provide any code to send the data back to the server, as you must when using a client-only framework.

If you need more advanced front-end functionality or specifically two-way data bindings, it's possible to combine Meteor with other front-end frameworks such as Angular or Ember by using packages.

5.3 Staging changes in a local collection

In chapter 4 you used two different types of reactive data sources: `Session` and `Collection`. Before you implement any reactive editing, you must decide which to use for holding house data. You could easily use the `Collection` object because all houses are already stored inside it. That way, you could get rid of much of the code and always have the latest editing state inside the database. There are two disadvantages of using a server-side `Collection`:

- Each change—that is, keystroke—must initiate a database write operation, which puts stress on both the network as well as the server. A single client will do quite well, but if you expect thousands of houseSitters to be updating their client's houses you can foresee a lot of load that's best avoided.
- There's no rollback if changes were made accidentally. You still want the user to press a button to persist data to avoid adding complex undo routines.

You could use `Session` to hold the database object, but that would mean you'd have to use a different way to work with data and affect your ability to reuse existing code.

You need an intermediary data storage that holds house data only for the duration of the editing process and hands it over to a `Collection` once the Save button is clicked. To comply with the first point, there's no reason you should send the contents of the staging `Collection` back to the server after each editing step (although you could, if you wanted to build an autosaving variant akin to Google Docs). To avoid any intermediary formats, you can use a special variant of `Collection` as a staging instance: a local or unsynchronized collection. You can see the data flow in figure 5.3.

Local collections have the advantage that they exist only inside the browser's memory. That means they're fast and write operations are cheap. No network

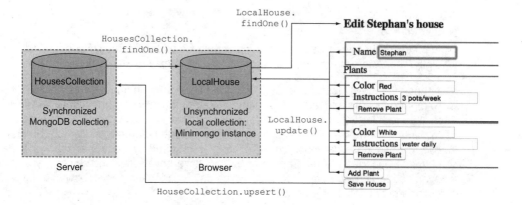

Figure 5.3   The local collection `LocalHouse` is used as a staging environment for house documents.

latency or disk I/O is involved that could slow down these operations. As a bonus, all data is already in exactly the same format as in the persisted MongoDB collection on the server.

> **NOTE**   Using a local staging collection requires you to deal with potential data inconsistencies when server content changes. We'll address this by implementing a notifications system later on.

As a starting point let's use the code for the houseSitter application from the previous chapter and set up a new houseSitter2 app. The only files you're going to change are the client files client.js and templates.html.

When you instantiate a new `Mongo.Collection` without a name or explicitly set the name to `null`, an unsynchronized, or local, collection is created. This can be done in either the server or client environment:

```
LocalHouse = new Mongo.Collection(null);
```

To use the `LocalHouse` collection on the client exclusively, you must add the code to the client.js file. Each client has its own instance of `LocalHouse`, and pushing changes to the server (which in turn will update all clients) will be triggered by clicking the Save button.

You'll also add a default value for `selectedHouseId` to make our code more understandable and a `newHouse` object that defines the structure of a database entry. With the two fields `lastsave` and `status`, you have a better chance of comparing the data available in the staging and server environments. That ability will come in handy later. Listing 5.1 shows the first lines of the updated client.js file.

Listing 5.1 Setting up a local collection

```
LocalHouse = new Mongo.Collection(null);
var newHouse = {
  name: '',
  plants: [],
  lastsave: 'never',
  status: 'unsaved'
  };
Session.setDefault('selectedHouseId', '');
```

Once the collection is set up, selecting a house performs a lookup in the server database and inserts the document for the currently selected ID into the LocalHouse collection. That means we need to revisit the events for the selectHouse template.

So far the only thing the change event on the drop-down list does is set the value for Session, so let's enhance the existing code. Listing 5.2 shows the changes you need to make. When assigning a value to newId things get a little more complex, so we'll look at the code from the inside out. The findOne() operation on the Houses-Collection will return a document based on the currently selected ID. If the empty drop-down option was selected, it can't find a document. In that case, you'll use the newHouse object instead. Either way, after changing the drop-down option you'll have a document.

Because you deal with either an existing doc (which would require using update()) or a new document (which must use insert()), you can use the flexible upsert() method. If it finds an existing document based on its _id, it'll perform an update; otherwise, it'll insert a whole new document. When performing an update upsert() returns how many documents were affected; when inserting a new document it returns an object with two attributes: numberAffected and insertedId. Either way the returned value for insertedId is assigned to newId, which will become the new value for selectedHouseId. If upsert() doesn't need to insert any new documents into the local collection, it means a document with the selected ID is already present and should be used as newId.

Listing 5.2 Adding a house to the local staging collection using the change event

```
Template.selectHouse.events({
  'change #selectHouse': function (evt) {
    var selectedId = evt.currentTarget.value;
    var newId = LocalHouse.upsert(
        selectedId,
        HousesCollection.findOne(selectedId) || newHouse
      ).insertedId;
    if (!newId) newId = selectedId;
    Session.set('selectedHouseId', newId);
  }
});
```

Insert a new doc or update if the _id exists.

If no document was found, set reactiveHouseObject to the newHouse object.

If no insert took place, you can use selectedId directly

Now that you're going to add editing functionality to the form, you need the full house details in two places: the showHouse template and the houseForm. It's more efficient to use a single global helper that can be used in any template instead of creating another helper that returns the house content for the editing template.

Template.registerHelper() allows you to create global helpers, so you'll use it to make {{selectedHouse}} available from all templates in the application (listing 5.3). Note that the helper doesn't perform a database lookup on the server as before; it returns the contents from LocalHouse.

Listing 5.3 Global helper that returns the edit object

```
Template.registerHelper('selectedHouse', function () {
  return LocalHouse.findOne(Session.get('selectedHouseId'));
});
```

Next you can update the showHouse template to use the global helper instead of the template-specific house. Find the {{#with house}} tag and change it as shown in the following listing.

Listing 5.4 Setting the data context to the global selectedHouse helper using {{#with}}

```
<template name="showHouse">
    {{#with selectedHouse}}
        <h2>Taking care of {{name}}'s house</h2>
        ...
    {{/with}}
</template>
```

To conclude the showHouse refactoring, you can remove the code for Template.show-House.helpers completely.

If you use the drop-down list to select a house, its name and plant details should now be shown just like before, only this time they're coming from the local collection, not the server. The houseForm, though, doesn't yet show any data for a selected house because it doesn't yet have a data context. You can either use the same approach as before (adding {{#with selectedHouse}} to the template) or provide the data context directly when including the template in the body. The latter requires adding a single word and not two more lines to the code:

```
{{> houseForm selectedHouse }}
```

For consistency let's stick with the {{#with}} syntax. Also, if you decide later to put templates into separate files, it'll be easier to understand the given data context because it's contained inside the template itself and not inherited from the parent.

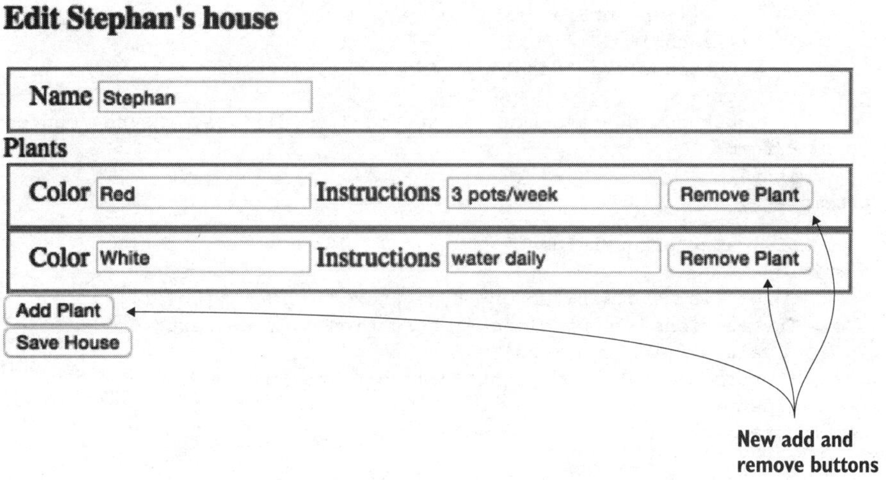

Edit Stephan's house

Figure 5.4   Updated form using `fieldsets` and buttons to add/remove plants

5.4   *Displaying collection data within a form*

Still, no data shows in the input fields, so you must add value attributes to each. Also, you still need to allow for any number of plants to be displayed. Listing 5.5 shows the updated code.

For better visual organization, you'll introduce `fieldsets` around each group of inputs. That way, you can easily keep track of which instructions belong to which plant. In addition, you'll split the templates in the same way you did for the showHouse template. A new `plantFieldset` template will be used for each plant. For removing plants, you'll add buttons to each plant's `fieldset` and place another button for adding new plants just before the Save button of the form (figure 5.4).

Finally, in order to show the existing data inside the input fields, each input gets a new attribute value with an associated expression. As a finishing touch, change the generic "Add a house" heading to mention the current name instead (see following listing).

Listing 5.5   Template code for displaying multiple plants in the HTML form

Set the data context using the global helper.

fieldsets group plant inputs

Existing data is assigned to value attributes.

Change the generic heading to mention the name.

```
<template name="houseForm">
  {{#with selectedHouse}}
    <h3>Edit {{name}}'s house</h3>
    <form id="houseForm">
      <fieldset id="house-name">
          Name <input id="house-name" class="name" type="text"
      placeholder="Name" value="{{name}}"><br/>
      </fieldset>
      <label>Plants</label>
```

```
{{#each plants}}
    {{> plantFieldset}}
{{/each}}
<button class="addPlant">Add Plant</button>
<br/>
<button id="save-house" data-id="{{_id}}">Save House</button>
        </form>
    {{/with}}
</template>

<template name="plantFieldset">
    <fieldset>
        Color <input class="color" type="text" value="{{color}}">
        Instructions <input class="instructions" type="text"
          value="{{instructions}}">
        <button class="removePlant">Remove Plant</button>
    </fieldset>
</template>
```

Buttons for adding and removing plants

Existing data is assigned to value attributes.

Let's revisit the code. You're aiming for reactive data binding, so there must be a way for the application code to map each attribute in the current house object to a unique HTML element. You can verify that this is the case because each data attribute (such as the name and all plant details) are correctly shown. There must also be a way to uniquely tie HTML elements back to the data object, which is missing so far. Apart from the input values each plant `fieldset` looks exactly the same, so you need to enrich it with a unique identifier. You could define `color` as a unique field and add validation code to ensure you never have two plants of the same color, but that wouldn't be a very robust approach. You could even have houses with two plants of the same color, so requiring the `color` attribute to be unique would severely limit future developments. Instead, you can already identify each plant uniquely by its position inside the array. In the next section, we'll introduce a new `index` value that represents a plant's position inside the `plants` array, which enables you to perform reverse mapping.

5.4.1   Adding array index information to an #each loop

At the time this book was written the `{{@index}}` helper did not yet exist[2]. As soon as it's available you can easily access the position of a plant inside an array like that:

```
<template name="plants">
  {{#each plant in plants}}
    Index: {{@index}}
    Plant Color: {{color}}
</template>
```

Until the new helper is available you need to manually implement a solution to get the index of an array element inside an `each` block.

---

[2] The functionality is already available in the development branch, so it should probably be available in Meteor 1.2 and later.

You'll use a global helper called `withIndex`, which will return the `plants` array with each `plant` as an object and enhance it with a new `index` attribute using the `map` function provided by Underscore.js.[3] Using Underscore.js helps you keep the required code to a minimum. Underscore.js ships with Meteor and you don't have to add it manually. Listing 5.6 shows `withIndex`, which takes `list` as an argument. This will be the `plants` array. First, you check if the `plant` object (`v`) equals `null`. If not, you add a new property to the object named `index` with the value of the current array position (`i`). Your new helper takes a list and gives you a new list with exactly the same elements in the same order, with an additional `index` property attached to each object.

Listing 5.6   Using Underscore.js to add an `index` attribute to arrays of objects

```
Template.registerHelper('withIndex', function (list) {
  var withIndex = _.map(list, function (v, i) {          Underscore.js's
    if (v === null) return;                               map function is
    v.index = i;                                          used to iterate
    return v;                                             over a list.
  });
  return withIndex;
});
```

You can pass any array of objects to the `withIndex` function and use `{{index}}` in a template to return the array position of an object inside a loop. That way, you can uniquely identify each cycle and element created by an #each block. In the `houseForm` template, adjust the #each block tag to pass plants to the `withIndex` function as shown in the following listing.

Listing 5.7   Adding an index to plants using template helpers

```
<template name="houseForm">
  ...
  <form id="houseForm">
    ...
    {{#each withIndex plants}}              Adjust this line;
      {{> plantFieldset}}                   the rest remains
    {{/each}}                               as is.
    ...
  </form>
</template>
```

You also need to enhance the `plantFieldset` template to add an `index` for each field (see listing 5.7). You're going to use an attribute, `data-index`, to store it for each input; the `fieldset` itself will use `id` instead.

There's no more need for a compound ID mashed up of house ID and plant color as you did previously, because you can uniquely identify each plant by its position in

---

[3]   Underscore.js is a highly useful library that provides commonly used functions in a simple way. See http://underscorejs.org/.

the `plants` array of the current document by enhancing the template as shown in listing 5.8. You can now have dozens of red plants that share the same name but have different instructions.[4]

> **Listing 5.8   Adding index information to the `plantFieldset` template**

```
<template name="plantFieldset">
  <fieldset>
    Color <input class="color" type="text" value="{{color}}"
     data-index="{{index}}">
    Instructions <input class="instructions" type="text"
     value="{{instructions}}" data-index="{{index}}">
    <button class="removePlant" data-index="{{index}}">Remove Plant</button>
  </fieldset>
</template>
```

Each input element gets a data-index. *(annotation to the left of the code listing)*

At this point both the `showHouse` and the `houseForm` templates will show all plants inside each house. Now let's step it up a notch and implement editing houses with an arbitrary number of plants.

5.5   *Reactive updates using a local collection*

You can edit the document using a safety net so that all your changes remain locally in the browser. Unlike other frameworks, Meteor doesn't differentiate between using the database on a server or locally, so you can reuse everything you learned about CRUD operations in the previous chapter. This time, though, you won't use it to store data back to a server but to edit the contents of a document until you're ready to persist in the central database.

For editing houses, you'll focus on two templates and six events, three in each template. This covers all actions involving only the staging collection. Figure 5.5 gives an overview of which events occur in which templates.

Let's look at the code. You begin with the event map for the `houseForm` template. Editing the document name, adding a new plant, and saving to the remote database are the main functions.

Because all editing events will trigger an `update()` operation, you can reduce the lines of code by introducing a general function to perform updates to `LocalHouse`. As you know, every `update()` of a collection takes two arguments: which objects to update (the document `_id` argument) and how to update it (the `modifier` argument). Let's keep the code lean by using listing 5.9; put that code at the end of your client.js file, and you won't have to touch it again.

---

[4] If you have limited botanical knowledge, it might indeed be useful to require plant colors to remain unique or at least add a location attribute. Otherwise, you shouldn't pursue a career as a professional house-sitter.

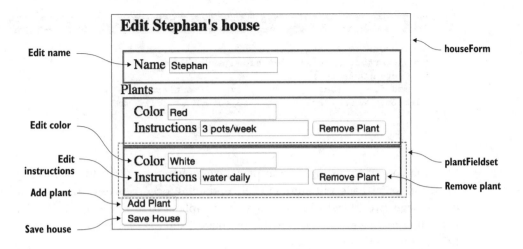

Figure 5.5 Editing a house involves two templates and six events.

Although the _id can easily be retrieved from Session.get("selectedHouseId") you still need to come up with the code required to assemble the modifier for each event.

Listing 5.9 Wrapper function for performing updates to the LocalHouse collection

```
updateLocalHouse = function (id, modifier) {
  LocalHouse.update(
    {
      '_id': id
    },
    modifier
  );
};
```

5.5.1 Event map for the houseForm template

In the previous version of the app, you relied on jQuery to retrieve form values and manually put them into an object to be stored in the collection. This time you can reduce the amount of jQuery involved. Listing 5.10 shows how you can achieve the same goal in a much simpler fashion.

The evt object gives you access to the contents of the input field with an ID of house-name. Whenever a keystroke occurs, you set the name value to the value of the currentTarget property for the caught event and wrap it in the correct $set syntax for updating MongoDB collections. You then call the update() function with both the current document ID and the modifier. To avoid the default browser behavior of reloading the page, you must keep the evt.preventDefault() directive.

Listing 5.10 Event map for updating the house name

```
Template.houseForm.events({
  'keyup input#house-name': function (evt) {
    evt.preventDefault();
    var modifier = {$set: {'name': evt.currentTarget.value}};
    updateLocalHouse(Session.get('selectedHouseId'), modifier);
  },
  //...
});
```

With the code from listing 5.10 in place, each change to the value of the input element for house-name will automatically update all occurrences of the name attribute on the page. Every keystroke will trigger all templates to be partly re-rendered with the new value for name. The rest of the templates, such as the color or instructions fields, won't be rendered again.

Even though the event relates to a button, similar code can be applied to the addPlant event. This time, though, you don't need the $set syntax but, because you're dealing with an array of objects, you need the $push syntax shown in listing 5.11. You can simply insert a new empty plant object with color and instructions as its attributes.

Listing 5.11 Event map for adding a new plant

```
Template.houseForm.events({
  'click button.addPlant': function (evt) {
    evt.preventDefault();
    var newPlant = {color: '', instructions: ''};
    var modifier = {$push: {'plants': newPlant}};
    updateLocalHouse(Session.get('selectedHouseId'), modifier);
  },
  //...
});
```

There's no need to manipulate the DOM in any way—simply changing the underlying data will update your templates. Both editing the name attribute and clicking the button to add a new plant will automatically update the screen. This is reactive data binding in action.

Before we move on to the plantFieldset, let's look at the third event: saving to the remote database (see listing 5.12). To keep track of the last save, each house has a field called lastsave, which you populate with a timestamp.

> **NOTE** Because different clients can have different clock settings, it's not good practice to trust the client to provide an accurate timestamp. Ideally, a timestamp used for database entries should be created by the server. In chapter 7 we'll introduce you to server-side methods that allow you to implement this functionality quite easily.

Again, you're providing a modifier. First you update the local house document and then send it to the remote database. But now you run into a limitation of running code from a client: what happens if you successfully update the local document but persisting the changes in the MongoDB fails? You could (and probably should) work around this by checking return values and catching exceptions. Again, this is something you can accomplish much more easily by using server-side methods, so just keep this limitation in mind. Chapter 7 will give you the necessary tools to deal with these situations more efficiently.

Listing 5.12 Saving the staging document to the database with a timestamp

```
Template.houseForm.events({
  //...
  'click button#save-house': function (evt) {
    evt.preventDefault();
    var id = Session.get('selectedHouseId');
    var modifier = {$set: {'lastsave': new Date()}};
    updateLocalHouse(id, modifier);
    // persist house document in remote db
    HousesCollection.upsert(                    ⟵  Saves the local doc
      {_id: id},                                    on the server
      LocalHouse.findOne(id)
    );
  }
});
```

Three events implemented, three to go. Next up is the plantFieldset template.

5.5.2   *Event map for the plantFieldset template*

Laziness is a virtue for programmers, so let's use only a single event for changes to either the color or instructions attribute of a plant. That way, you'll get updates to all available plant attributes for free, should you ever decide to add, say, a location field. That means you have to determine not only the value of what to insert into the document but also the field name or where to insert it. To uniquely identify a property, you need three pieces of information:

- Current plant index (the position of a plant inside the plants array, such as 0)
- Current plant attribute (the field name inside a document, such as color)
- Updated attribute value (the value for a field, such as blue)

Let's take the following document as an example:

```
{
  name: 'Manuel',
  plants: [
    {color: 'Red', instructions: '3 pots/week'},
    {color: 'Yellow', instructions: 'keep humid'}
  ]
}
```

To change the first `color` attribute for the first plant from `Red` to `Blue`, use the following dot notation:

```
LocalHouse.update(id, {$set: {"plants.0.color": "Blue"}});
```

As you can see in listing 5.13, you first combine the necessary identifiers to access the right element inside the collection. You can obtain the index from the `data-index` attribute of the HTML element, which you defined earlier in this chapter. The `field` name is the same as the `class` attribute of an `input` element. These pieces are concatenated into the dot notation for the currently edited plant and property. Dynamically concatenating field names inside an object or using variables as keys is only possible when using the bracket notation, which is why you must first assign `plantProperty` with the field identifier and then use brackets to assign the new value, which is accessible via `evt.currentTarget.value`.

Listing 5.13   Event map for updating plant properties

```
Template.plantFieldset.events({
  'keyup input.color, keyup input.instructions': function (evt) {
    evt.preventDefault();
    var index = evt.target.getAttribute('data-index');
    var field = evt.target.getAttribute('class');
    var plantProperty = 'plants.' + index + '.' + field;
    var modifier = {$set: {}};
    modifier['$set'][plantProperty] = evt.target.value;
    updateLocalHouse(Session.get('selectedHouseId'), modifier);
  }
});
```

> **Concat the exact identifier for the plant and property.**

> **Assign the new value using bracket notation.**

> **Perform the update as always.**

MongoDB allows you to manipulate data inside a collection in various ways, but unfortunately there's no easy way of removing a single plant object from the `plants` array.[5] But this is exactly what you need the `removePlant` button to do. You'll work around this limitation by first putting all plants in a regular array, splicing it, and then storing the modified `plants` array back into the document.

Because you're in the `plantFieldset` template, the current data context is limited to a single plant object. To read the entire `plants` array, you can perform another lookup in the local collection. The collection is available inside the browser and no network latency would affect the lookup, so you could use the following to get all plants for the currently selected house:

```
LocalHouse.findOne(Session.get('selectedHouseId')).plants
```

---

[5] This limitation in MongoDB is tracked as "A modifier to delete a single value from an array" (https://jira .mongodb.org/browse/SERVER-1014) and dates back to 2010.

Alternatively, you could access the parent data context using the global `Template` object:

```
Template.parentData(1).plants;
```

If you don't put an argument inside the brackets, it defaults to 1, which means the data context one level up is referenced. You can go up as many levels as required and access the data you need by adding its name to the statement. The previous code is equivalent to using `{{../plants}}` within a template.

Once you have all plants from the house document in a regular JavaScript array, you'll use `splice` to extract the element at the position determined by the index associated with the HTML button. The resulting array has one less element and is used inside `modifier`. The following listing shows the event map for removing a plant.

Listing 5.14 Removing plants

```
Template.plantFieldset.events({
  'click button.removePlant': function (evt) {        All plants go into a
    evt.preventDefault();                              regular array.
    var index = evt.target.getAttribute('data-index');
    var plants = Template.parentData(1).plants;     ◀──  Regular arrays can
    plants.splice(index, 1);                        ◀──  use splice to
    var modifier = {$set: {'plants': plants}};           remove an element.

    updateLocalHouse(Session.get('selectedHouseId'), modifier);

  },
  //...
});
```

These are all the events needed to provide full editing of existing houses. Together with the code provided in the `selectHouse` event, this approach is also flexible enough to address the use case of creating new houses; you simply select the empty option from the drop-down.

> **NOTE** We haven't discussed it in detail, but make sure that when removing a house you remove it from both `HousesCollection` as well as `LocalHouse`. Make this simple fix before moving on to the next section.

The application still lacks something in terms of usability. How can you tell whether you've made any changes to the document currently opened in your browser when you return from a lengthy phone call? Or even worse, what happens if a colleague works on the same house as you do simultaneously and saves it without you knowing? You can greatly improve this app with a basic notifications[6] system that provides and save reminders and warnings if there's newer database content.

---

[6] You'll see more efficient ways to implement notifications when we talk about packages in chapter 9.

5.6   *Implementing a simple notifications system*

Any application that allows multiple users to edit the same data simultaneously has to deal with concurrent saves. What happens if you start editing a house and someone saves while you're still editing? Let's assume Manuel and Stephan are both editing the same house document, as shown in figure 5.6. Stephan updates the plants in his home so that the document contains three entries: red, orange, and white. When he's finished, he stores the changes back to the server. Meanwhile, Manuel has started editing Stephan's house as well. He views a local copy with only two plants: red and blue. What should happen with Manuel's view now that the database content has changed? One possibility would be to discard all local changes and reactively update the view with the latest state of the document. Doing so automatically wouldn't be an ideal solution and results in poor user experience; it may frustrate Manuel because it'll feel as if he lost important data. Perhaps his data was even newer than Stephan's.

There are many scenarios where you want to avoid instant updates—for example, when thinking about a simple way to provide fallbacks to cancel an edit, or when documents can only be changed entirely to maintain a certain level of consistency.

Either way, as long as you don't have a means to collaboratively update a document simultaneously and merge updates directly into a document, a better approach is to use notifications to signal that the local copy Manuel is looking at is outdated.

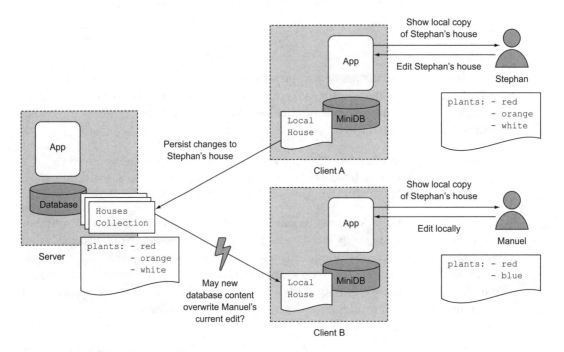

Figure 5.6   Dealing with concurrent edits to the same house

Besides having an area to display notifications, you need a trigger to determine when to show messages and which messages to show, so you'll extend the update() operations on the local document to indicate that a document has been changed by including a status field. Also, you want to avoid overwriting someone else's changes. To do so, you'll implement a notification that appears when remote data is changed by someone else. There are many ways to achieve this—in this chapter, you'll rely on the lastsave attribute to determine whether a document was changed by someone else while editing is still in progress.

A second use case for providing notifications is to prevent a user from accidentally discarding an edited document. So you'll also build in a safety net for the drop-down list so that users won't accidentally switch houses while unsaved changes are present on the page.

5.6.1 Adding a notifications template

All notifications will be displayed at the top of the page. If there are no messages or warnings to show, the notifications area remains invisible. Both the showHouse and the formHouse templates already use a similar approach—if there's no data context, they won't be rendered.

You'll use an additional template called notificationArea that checks whether there's a notification object. If so, it'll use its style and text properties and display a message to the user. The following listing shows the template's code.

Listing 5.15 Using a template for displaying notifications

```
<template name="notificationArea">
  {{#if notification}}
    <p class="{{notification.type}}">{{notification.text}}</p>
  {{/if}}
</template>
```

You can embed this template anywhere you like, in the form template or at the top of the page, by using {{> notificationArea}}.

5.6.2 Adding a status property

Keeping track of the status of a house document is best done by introducing a new status property. There can be three states:

- *The contents of a document in* HouseCollection *and* LocalHouse *are the same*— This requires no notifications. As long as users only look at content and don't use the form to make any updates, there's no need to display any notifications besides the actual document contents.
- LocalHouse *has local or unsaved changes but the remote document hasn't changed*—If there are only local edits, a warning must be displayed that unsaved changes are present on the page and navigating away will discard them.

- *While you were editing the current document, the remote document was changed*—In this scenario the remote database contains newer content than what the user currently sees inside the browser. A warning must tell the user that saving now will overwrite a newer version on the server.

The first state is the initial state when a new house is selected by the user. It doesn't require any additional code, so let's look at the second case: identifying unsaved changes.

To add state, you'll extend the existing modifiers you've used for the Local-House.update() operation. In most cases it's sufficient to add a new key-value pair to the $set statement. Adding plants makes use of the $push operator, so you must add a dedicated $set statement to the modifier. For the color and instructions events, you'll also use bracket notation to add the status to the update modifier. The Save button will set the status to saved, so make sure you set the correct status. The following listing shows which lines must be present inside the event map code.

Listing 5.16 Adding status to the update modifiers

```
Template.houseForm.events({
  'click button#save-house': function (evt) {
    //...
    var modifier = {$set: {'lastsave': new Date(), 'status': 'saved'}};
  },
  'click button.addPlant': function (evt) {
    //...
    var modifier = {$push: {'plants': newPlant}, $set: {'status':
      'unsaved'}};
  },
  'keyup input#house-name': function (evt) {
    //...
    var modifier = {$set: {'name': evt.target.value, 'status': 'unsaved'}};
  }
});

Template.plantFieldset.events({
  'click button.removePlant': function (evt) {
    //...
    var modifier = {$set: {'plants': plants, 'status': 'unsaved'}};
  },
  'keyup input.color, keyup input.instructions': function (evt) {
    //...
    modifier['$set'].status = 'unsaved';
  }
});
```

The Save button sets the status to saved.

$push and $set can be performed inside a single operation.

Adding the status field using bracket notation

Not only will every change to the form contents trigger an update to LocalHouse, but it will also set a status field to unsaved. Only clicking the Save button or selecting another house should reset the current status.

5.6.3 *Using a Session variable to trigger notifications*

You could easily use a helper to determine different states and return the actual display text and style, but in this chapter you'll use a dedicated `Session` variable to trigger messages. Keeping the code separated makes it much simpler to extend the code in the future and only perform updates to a single location. The code presented in listing 5.17 should look familiar by now—it's a simple helper that returns the contents of the `Session` variable named `notification`.

> **Listing 5.17   Helper that displays notifications from a `Session` variable**

```
Template.notificationArea.helpers({
  notification: function () {
    return Session.get('notification');
  }
});
```

The contents for the `Session` variable must be set based on simple conditions. Instead of hooking into the update modifiers, you'll use a computation that checks for certain conditions. If those are met, it'll reactively set the correct notifications content.

   You used `Tracker.autorun` earlier to set up a reactive computation. This time you can limit it to the `houseForm` template because this is the only place where status updates may be triggered. The advantage of using `autorun` inside a template context is that once the template is destroyed the `autorun` function is destroyed as well. We discussed hooking into the `created` callback in chapter 4:

```
Template.houseForm.onCreated(function () {
  this.autorun(function () {
    // do stuff
  })
});
```

Inside the `autorun` you'll check for two conditions to be met:

- Is a house document selected and does its `status` equal `unsaved`? Then let the notification be a save reminder.
- Is the `lastsave` timestamp of the remote doc newer than that of the local staging document? Then let the notification be a warning.

If neither of these conditions is met, you can safely proceed without any notifications. Listing 5.18 shows how to perform the checks in the client.js code. Because the `Session` object can hold entire objects, you store both the `type` as well as the `text` property for the notification via `Session.set()`.

> **Listing 5.18   Setting the notifications inside an autorun**

```
Template.houseForm.onCreated(function () {
  this.autorun(function () {
    if (HousesCollection.findOne(Session.get('selectedHouseId')) &&
      LocalHouse.findOne(Session.get('selectedHouseId')).lastsave <
```

Check if the doc already exists on the server and if it is newer.

```
  HousesCollection.findOne(Session.get('selectedHouseId')).lastsave) {
    Session.set('notification', {
      type: 'warning',
      text: 'This document has been changed inside the database!'
    });
  } else if (LocalHouse.findOne(Session.get('selectedHouseId')) &&
   LocalHouse.findOne(Session.get('selectedHouseId')).status === 'unsaved') {
    Session.set('notification', {
      type: 'reminder',
      text: 'Remember to save your changes'
    });
  } else {
    Session.set('notification', '');
  }
  })
});
```

Check if the local document has an unsaved status.

Open up two browsers and check if the code works as expected (see figure 5.7 for an example). If you open the same house in both and start editing, you'll see a

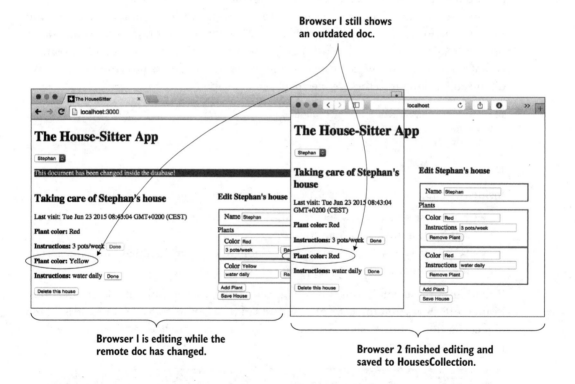

Browser I still shows an outdated doc.

Browser I is editing while the remote doc has changed.

Browser 2 finished editing and saved to HousesCollection.

Figure 5.7   Remote changes trigger a warning message about changed content.

green[7] message text saying that you must remember to save your changes. As soon as you save in one of the browsers, the other will tell you that the document has been changed inside the database on a red background.

You can now build on this rather simple solution. Possible improvements include showing the remote and local documents side by side so that a user can easily see the differences. All that's required is to display the contents from `HousesCollection` in the `showHouse` template and keep the `houseForm` populated with data from `Local-House`. You can even go as far as highlighting the differing fields to give even more guidance. We've covered enough ground now that you should be capable of enhancing the application on your own.

If you want to include information on who changed the document, you must first understand the concept of users and how Meteor handles them. Head over to the next chapter to find out how to deal with users and authentications, and learn how to restrict users to editing only certain fields or documents.

5.7   *Summary*

In this chapter, you learned that

- Local collections are unsynchronized and may be used just like regular databases, even if they exist only inside the browser's memory. That means they aren't affected by network latency or slow disk performance.
- Using reactive data binding between collections and templates removes the need to perform DOM updates manually; simply updating data sources will trigger view updates.
- Reactive data binding can have similar effects as two-way data binding in other frameworks.
- Blaze templates can't return array index positions; a helper function is required.
- `Session` can be used to implement a simple notifications system.

---

[7] Of course the message will only be green if you took the CSS classes from the chapter's code and put them into your styles.css file.

Users, authentications, and permissions

6

This chapter covers

- Enabling user registration via username/ password
- Connecting to an SMTP server to send emails
- Customizing email messages for accounts-related messages
- Adding OAuth authentication via Facebook
- Managing permissions using allow/deny

Once an application is connected to one or more data sources, it's capable of displaying dynamic content. To customize the content different users see, the application needs to know who is requesting data. Most likely some users will be able to add content, but there will be some restrictions on both what data can be accessed and what can be done with it.

For these reasons this chapter introduces the concept of users and accounts. Up until now we've kept things fairly simple and assumed a single type of user: the anonymous guest. Unless the application can identify a guest as a particular user, we can't show user-specific content.

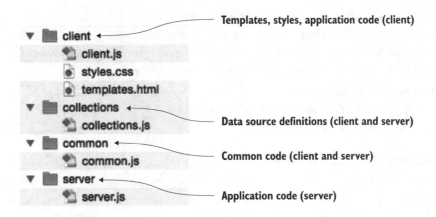

Figure 6.1   Application structure for userApp

The process of identifying a user is called *authentication*. In this chapter we'll discuss how users can sign up to an application and how they can identify themselves using a combination of username and password or log in using an existing service like Facebook, Twitter, or GitHub to verify who they are.

The second main concept of working with accounts, *authorization*, introduces security fundamentals to every application. In its simplest form, logged-in users may be treated differently from anonymous guests. Typically applications require a more granular way to define permissions so the concept of roles such as members and admins becomes important.

In this chapter you'll learn how to add users to any application using Meteor's core functionality for both password authentication and OAuth. Every step, from registering, to editing a user's profile data, to deleting an account, will be discussed. You'll take advantage of what you learned in chapter 4 to use Collections to allow users to exchange messages and apply granular permissions for deleting and viewing these messages.

To explore the user-related functionality, you'll build a small application again. Meteor doesn't require a specific file structure. For this chapter you're going to use the structure shown in figure 6.1.

Begin by creating a new project and setting up the files and folders shown in figure 6.1. Once you've done that, we'll start by addressing the authentication aspect when dealing with users.

6.1   Adding users to an application

Our application should be able to tell who is currently using it. This will be the foundation upon which we can later grant or restrict access and functionality. Fortunately, Meteor makes it easy to add user functionality, and doing so requires hardly any code.

The most common scenario for adding users on the web is to allow visitors to sign up or register themselves. That turns them from guests into users. As the identifier, you'll use an email address or a username, and to verify a user, you'll rely on passwords.

The basic workflow for user management is as follows:

1 User registration or signup
2 Logging in or signing in of existing users
3 Password reset for existing users

6.1.1 *Adding password authentication*

Not every application needs accounts, so the accounts functionality isn't available in a new project. It is, though, part of the core packages of every Meteor installation and can be added quickly using the CLI tool. The following commands will extend an existing application to allow users to sign up, log in, and perform all relevant actions for a basic user workflow:

```
$ meteor add accounts-password
$ meteor add accounts-ui
```

The first command adds the functionality for using passwords. The second adds templates for user actions (registration/login/password reset) and associated styling information. If you don't want any styles applied to the templates because you're going to take care of this yourself, add `accounts-ui-unstyled` instead.

Both commands will ensure that all dependencies are met as well. For example, the `accounts-password` package enables users to reset their passwords. To do so, it requires the `email` module to be able to send the reset link to a user, so it adds it to the application as well. Also, the styles used for the default login mask rely on the LESS preprocessor, so the `less` package is added as well. Meteor will show on the command line detailed messages indicating which packages were added. Inside your project folder you can find information on all packages in the .meteor/packages file.

Once the packages are added, start the Meteor server again.

ADDING USER TEMPLATES

In your client/templates.html file, you can now add the user-related subtemplates. The `accounts-ui` package includes all required templates, and all you need to do is add an inclusion tag anywhere inside the existing templates as shown in listing 6.1.

> **NOTE** For the code in this chapter, we added Bootstrap 3 using `meteor add twbs:bootstrap` to provide a nicer look and feel. Instead of the default `accounts-ui` package we used `ian:accounts-ui-bootstrap-3`, which integrates nicely into Bootstrap 3.

Listing 6.1 Adding `loginButtons`

```
<head>
  <title>Working with users</title>
</head>
```

```
<body>
  <div class="container">
    <div class="navbar">
      {{>loginButtons }}          This includes the actual
    </div>              ◁──┘     user templates.
    <h1>Working with users</h1>
  </div>
</body>
```

Figure 6.2 shows how the login feature is presented to the user. The `loginButtons` template creates an expandable overlay that provides login, signup, and password reset functionality in a single container. When the user clicks Sign In, the dialog opens and provides three buttons. By default users are identified by their email address and a password. Requiring a username or making the email address optional can be configured using `Accounts.ui.config`.

Before we change the default behavior, let's use the login box to sign up the first user.

6.1.2 Registration and password reset

Ideally the signup process for an application should be as simple and quick as possible. That encourages users to register and not cancel the process if multiple steps are involved. Therefore, the default Meteor user registration requires only a minimum of information from the user. Once users are signed up, you can remind them to fill out a profile or answer additional questions.

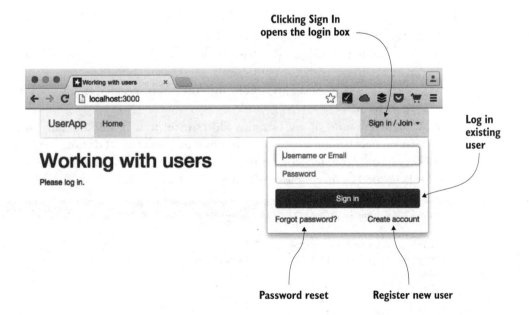

Figure 6.2   Login box

The simplest way to sign up users is to ask for their email address and password. These two parts are sufficient to uniquely identify users and keep their accounts somewhat safe. The accounts-password package requires all passwords to be at least six characters long.

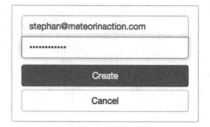

Use the login box to sign up your first user by filling in both fields. Then click the link that says "Create account," just below the Sign In button. Notice how the big Sign In button now shows Create Account as well (figure 6.3)? That's it; you just registered the first user for your application.

Figure 6.3 Using the login box to create an account

THE USERS COLLECTION

Users belong in the long-term memory of the application, so they're stored inside a database collection. Start the Meteor server with meteor run and open Robomongo, or issue meteor mongo in another terminal session in order to access the database. Using a database shell, query the contents of the users collection like this:

```
db.users.find();
```

> **WARNING** There are database users and application users. Application users are stored inside a real Collection, not inside the special Users folder you may see in Robomongo. Database users are needed to connect Meteor with MongoDB, and typically only one user of that type is needed.

When you look at a single user document (see listing 6.2), you see that it now contains four top-level fields:

- _id—Holds the unique database ID for the user, also accessible via Meteor .userId().
- createdAt—A timestamp when the user was created/registered for the application.
- emails—An array of one or more addresses associated with the user. Each email address may belong to only one user and may be verified or not.
- services—An object containing data used by particular login services, such as tokens used by forgot-password links.

Listing 6.2 A single user document stored inside the users collection

```
{
  "_id" : "xcwYNyvMhP8rq6EPp",
  "createdAt" : ISODate("2015-05-22T12:47:33.821Z"),
  "emails" : [
    {
      "address" : "stephan@meteorinaction.com",
      "verified" : false
    }
  ],
```

```
"services" : {
  "password" : {
    "bcrypt" : "$2a$10$OsFJKxSApp68T9elfjKvtXBdBP...SnY"
  },
  "resume" : {
    "loginTokens" : [
      {
        "when" : ISODate("2014-12-26T09:24:51.382Z"),
        "hashedToken" : "sAMzRZMnqWrmXbmOCm7cpKzG5JR5qf...8f9bUTo="
      }
    ]
  }
}
}
```

For each authentication provider, the `services` field holds the information needed to perform authentication. By default, passwords are stored using *bcrypt*, which is also used as the password hash algorithm for BSD and many Linux systems.

There are no restrictions on which fields can be stored inside a user document, so you can extend it as you like. There are two more standard fields that are only filled when needed: `username` and `profile`. Because the signup process doesn't require users to set a `username`, you won't use the field in this example. The `profile` field contains an object, to which the associated user has full read and write access by default. This object is the default storage for things like a real name, biography text, or phone numbers.

To allow users to share social information and protect their identity, you'll require usernames and also make sure all users have a profile that they can fill as they like.

CONFIGURING THE REGISTRATION PROCESS

Because the login box is available only on the client, the corresponding configuration also needs to take place inside the client context. By adjusting the setting for `password-SignupField` for the `Accounts.ui.config` object, you can ask users to provide a username during the registration process. As you can see in table 6.1, each setting has a different requirement as to which fields must be provided during registration.

Table 6.1 Possible values for `passwordSignupFields`

Setting	Username	Email
USERNAME_AND_EMAIL	mandatory	mandatory
USERNAME_AND_OPTIONAL_EMAIL	mandatory	optional
USERNAME_ONLY	mandatory	n/a
EMAIL_ONLY	n/a	mandatory

For this chapter we'll assume each user has a username. An email address isn't important for us—if they don't want to be able to recover their passwords, we won't force users to provide an address. Listing 6.3 shows how to configure our application to ask for both username and an (optional) email address during the registration process.

Listing 6.3   Configuring registration to ask for both username and email

```
Accounts.ui.config({
  passwordSignupFields: 'USERNAME_AND_OPTIONAL_EMAIL'
});
```

Remember that this configuration code belongs in a file that isn't executed on the server or is at least wrapped in a `Meteor.isClient` block. If it isn't, your application will produce errors. Place it in client/client.js.

When the configuration is in place, the login box will show four instead of two fields for creating a new account, as shown in figure 6.4. Because users may decide to not provide us with an email address, they won't be able to reset their password and it becomes important to make sure they enter the password correctly. For this reason, there's also a password verification field that wasn't shown when using a mandatory email address.

Figure 6.4   Creating an account with a mandatory username and an optional email address

If you sign up new users without an email address now, you'll notice that inside the MongoDB collection there is no `emails` field. This is because empty fields aren't created in NoSQL databases. This is different from relational databases like MySQL, where a fixed schema is used. New fields may be added at any time, so there's no need to store empty fields in a document.

EXTENDING THE ACCOUNTS CREATION WITH PROFILE DATA

When you're registering a new user on a web page, the form data is forwarded to the server to process and store inside a MongoDB collection. To extend the default behavior, it's possible to hook into the creation process and add checks or enrich the data stored. This is done using `Accounts.onCreateUser()`, which takes a function as its argument. This function gets called every time a new user is created and enables you to control the content of new user documents. The function itself can make use of two arguments: `options` and `user`.

```
// server.js
Accounts.onCreateUser(function (options, user) {
  user.profile = options.profile;
  return user;
});
```

The `options` object comes from the authentication provider, in this case `accounts-password`. It comes from the client and shouldn't be trusted. By default, `onCreateUser` simply copies `options.profile` to `user.profile` and returns a `user` object representing the newly created user document in the database.

If you want to add profile information to each new user, you need to place your code in the server/server.js file (or inside a `Meteor.isServer` block). Let's keep the default behavior of `onCreateUser` to copy profile data from the authentication provider to the user document. When using passwords, there's no profile data, but when you later add external logins with Facebook or Twitter, you'll be able to use the profile data they pass on. If there's no profile data provided from the signup process, you'll add it as an empty object. Before returning the user document, a new profile property called `rank` will be added to each user, making them a "White belt."[1] The required code is shown in the following listing.

> **Listing 6.4 Adding profile information to new users**

```
// server.js
Accounts.onCreateUser(function (options, user) {
  if (options.profile) {
    user.profile = options.profile;
  }
  else {
    user.profile = {};
  }
  user.profile.rank = 'White belt';
  return user;
});
```

All users who sign up from now on will have a profile field in their user document. Existing users aren't affected by that change because they already went through the `createUser` stage and therefore won't be affected by the updated functionality.

> **TIP** If you want to clear the database, use the command `meteor reset`. This will empty all collections and you can start over with no users.

6.1.3 Setting up email

Especially when an email address is required to sign up, you'll want to ensure that it actually works. For resetting passwords, the Meteor server must be capable of sending out emails to users. If you don't configure the `emails` package, then all messages will be shown on the server console but never actually sent out (see figure 6.5).

As you can see in figure 6.5, Meteor requires the `MAIL_URL` environment variable to hold the connection string for an SMTP server. Using an environment variable is a

---

[1] We'll use the ranking system found in most martial arts here, where practitioners start as white belts and work toward a black belt.

```
● ● ●                                    userApp
=> App running at: http://localhost:3000/
I20141113-10:44:10.289(1)? ====== BEGIN MAIL #0 ======
I20141113-10:44:10.338(1)? (Mail not sent; to enable sending, set the MAIL_URL environment variable.)
I20141113-10:44:10.339(1)? MIME-Version: 1.0
I20141113-10:44:10.339(1)? From: "Meteor Accounts" <no-reply@meteor.com>
I20141113-10:44:10.339(1)? To: stephan@yauh.de
I20141113-10:44:10.339(1)? Subject: How to reset your password on localhost:3000
I20141113-10:44:10.339(1)? Content-Type: text/plain; charset=utf-8
I20141113-10:44:10.340(1)? Content-Transfer-Encoding: quoted-printable
I20141113-10:44:10.340(1)?
I20141113-10:44:10.340(1)? Hello,
I20141113-10:44:10.340(1)?
I20141113-10:44:10.340(1)? To reset your password, simply click the link below.
I20141113-10:44:10.340(1)?
I20141113-10:44:10.341(1)? http://localhost:3000/#/reset-password/LmpvMrBoEOBTlkdamjiomi-WC6luwN3LELCW98Pr6Dr
I20141113-10:44:10.341(1)?
I20141113-10:44:10.341(1)? Thanks.
I20141113-10:44:10.341(1)?
I20141113-10:44:10.341(1)? ====== END MAIL #0 ======
```

Figure 6.5   Unless an email server is configured, Meteor will show emails on the server console.

great way to quickly adjust a configuration value. Most of the time, it provides more transparency to add the mail server configuration to a file, though.

ADDING A MAIL SERVER

The connection details to a mail server are considered highly sensitive. You don't want anyone to find out the credentials for your mail server and start sending spam from your machines. To avoid sharing login details with all users, be sure to configure the mail server not inside a `Meteor.isServer` block but inside a dedicated file within the server folder of your application.

Meteor uses various environment variables for configuration; you can find an overview in chapter 12. All environment variables may be passed directly to the server upon startup or can be set from inside the code using `process.env.<Name of Environment Variable>`. To set `MAIL_URL` to a valid mail server, you'll put the command inside a `Meteor.startup()` function, so it gets executed every time the Meteor server starts. To keep the code clean, you'll use variables to set `username`, `password`, `server`, and `port` instead of writing the SMTP connect string directly. Some characters need to be escaped in a connection string, so each variable is processed by `encodeURIComponent`.

Once you've added the code shown in listing 6.5 to your application, your app will be able to send emails such as password-reset links to all users who provided an email address. Be sure to adjust the variable values to match your own mail server configuration.

Listing 6.5   Configuring an SMTP server in server/smtp.js

```
Meteor.startup(function () {
  smtp = {
    username: 'yourmail@gmail.com',      Adjust these
    password: 'mySecretPassword',        values for your
    server: 'smtp.gmail.com',            SMTP server.
    port: 587
  };
```

```
process.env.MAIL_URL = 'smtp://' +
              encodeURIComponent(smtp.username) + ':' +
              encodeURIComponent(smtp.password) + '@' +
              encodeURIComponent(smtp.server) + ':' +
              smtp.port;
});
```

Now that the application is capable of sending emails, you can encourage users to verify their address upon registration.

> **TIP** Sending mail via SMTP requires the password to be passed in clear text. For better security you can use environment variables instead of storing the password inside a file or alternatively use a local `sendmail` that listens on `smtp://localhost:25` without the need for a password.

SENDING ADDRESS VERIFICATION EMAILS

Again, you'll hook into the `onCreateUser` function to send a verification email as soon as a user registers. The corresponding function is called `sendVerificationEmail`, and it takes two arguments: the user ID and an optional email address:

```
Accounts.sendVerificationEmail(user._id, email);
```

Typically only the first argument is needed, because the address will be part of the user document. But you aren't requiring users to provide an email address, so you should take care that there's no attempt to send emails when the user doesn't have an address. Also, if you hook directly into the creation process, you have to wait for Meteor to create a user document first before you can access it.

The code shown in listing 6.6 first checks if the user provided an email address, then sets a timeout of 2 seconds to wait for the account to be created, and finally sends the verification email.

Listing 6.6 Sending verification emails upon user creation

```
Accounts.onCreateUser(function (options, user) {
    //...
    user.profile.rank = 'White belt';
    if (options.email) {                              ◁─── Only do this if the user
        Meteor.setTimeout(function () {                     provided an address.
            Accounts.sendVerificationEmail(user._id);  ◁── Give Meteor up to
        }, 2 * 1000);                                        2 seconds to create
    }                                                        a user document.
    return user;          Send a verification
});                           email.
```

CUSTOMIZING MAIL MESSAGES

Meteor has default settings for the sender of all accounts-related emails, subjects, and body texts. You can adjust them to hold any text you like. Table 6.2 explains how the settings are accessed inside the `Accounts.emailTemplates` object. Also refer to listing 6.7 to see how they're used.

Table 6.2   Available fields for adjusting accounts-related emails

Field name	Description	Notes
siteName	Name of the application, such as "Meteor in Action App"	Default value: DNS name of the app, such as usersApp.meteor.com
from	RFC5322-compliant sender name and address	Default value: `Meteor Accounts <no-reply@meteor.com>`
resetPassword	Contains three fields; each takes a function: `subject`, `text`, `html`	`text` and `subject` are mandatory, `html` is optional.
enrollAccount	Contains three fields; each takes a function: `subject`, `text`, `html`	`text` and `subject` are mandatory, `html` is optional.
verifyEmail	Contains three fields; each takes a function: `subject`, `text`, `html`	`text` and `subject` are mandatory, `html` is optional.

As you can see, the `accounts-password` package defines three different types of emails it can send. You can trigger them manually by using the corresponding send functions:

```
Accounts.sendResetPasswordEmail()
Accounts.sendEnrollmentEmail()
Accounts.sendVerificationEmail()
```

During user creation, the server sends a verification email. Let's customize the subject and content for this verification email. To keep things simple, you can add the code from listing 6.7 to the existing server/smtp.js file or use a dedicated file server/mailTemplates.js. It must run inside a server environment; otherwise, the browser will throw errors.

Listing 6.7   Customizing the accounts email templates

```
Accounts.emailTemplates.siteName = 'Meteor in Action userApp';
Accounts.emailTemplates.from = 'Stephan <stephan@meteorinaction.com>';

Accounts.emailTemplates.verifyEmail.subject = function (user) {
  return 'Confirm Your Email Address, ' + user.username;
};

Accounts.emailTemplates.verifyEmail.text = function (user, url) {
  return 'Welcome to the Meteor in Action userApp!\n'
  + 'To verify your email address go ahead and follow the link below:\n\n'
  + url;
};

Accounts.emailTemplates.verifyEmail.html = function (user, url) {
  return '<h1>Welcome to the Meteor in Action userApp!</h1>'
  + '<p>To <strong>verify your email address</strong> go ahead and follow the
      link below:</p>'
  + url;
};
```

Adjusting the site name has no effect on the URL users have to click.

Users will see this as the sender of all emails.

Defines the content of the verification email

Even though you can easily define HTML emails, keep in mind that both text and HTML are sent to the recipient. If they set their email client to prefer plain text for displaying content, they won't see the content defined inside the `html` function. Therefore, make sure that you always have the same amount of information in both `text` and `html` templates.

Register as a new user. You'll now receive a customized email with a personal verification link. As you can see, it still points to http://localhost:3000. When deploying your application, you must set the correct URL via an environment variable. If you use `meteor deploy`, it's automatically taken care of. If you use a different method to deploy your application, you have to adjust the `ROOT_URL` to the correct URL by setting the value of the environment variable when starting Meteor like this:

```
$ ROOT_URL='http://www.meteorinaction.com' meteor run
```

Alternatively you can add it to your code and wrap it inside a `startup` block like that:

```
// server.js
Meteor.startup(function () {
  process.env.ROOT_URL = 'http://www.meteorinaction.com';
});
```

6.2 *Authenticating users with OAuth*

Oftentimes usernames and passwords aren't the only option you want to give your users to log into an application. Being able to use an existing account to log into a site lowers the barrier of signing up by not requiring users to type in a single bit of information. Additionally, it simplifies using an application by not having to remember additional usernames or passwords.

Meteor ships with multiple authentication providers that allow users to use a social network instead of a local username. These networks include

- Facebook
- GitHub
- Google
- Meetup
- Meteor Developer Account
- Twitter
- Weibo

All of these are based on OAuth, a complex way to pass authentication data from one site to another. Many community packages are also available that enable other authentication providers such as LinkedIn or Dropbox. The fundamentals of working with OAuth providers are the same for each provider, so we won't discuss each.

6.2.1 *An introduction to OAuth*

The Open Authentication (OAuth) mechanism has become popular among web applications since its beginnings in 2007. The main idea behind it (see figure 6.6) is to

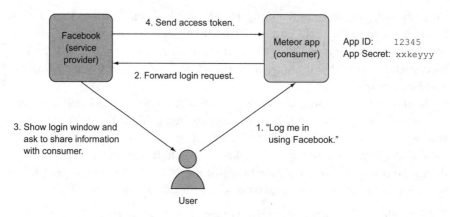

Figure 6.6   OAuth flow using Facebook as the service provider

use a service provider, such as Facebook, to authenticate a user and allow a third-party application to access specific information from the authenticated user (access authorization). This could be simply the username or more sensitive information such as friends or permission to post to the user's wall.

As figure 6.6 shows, there are three main ingredients to every OAuth scenario:

- A service provider, such as Facebook or Twitter
- A consumer, such as your Meteor application
- The user—for example, an existing Facebook user wanting to log into your Meteor application

Many websites can act as a service provider for OAuth. We're going to use Facebook as an example to illustrate the process. Our Meteor application must be connected to Facebook. This is done by creating a new application on Facebook's developer site. To verify our application isn't a malicious script, it will then be able to identify itself using the corresponding *application ID* (App ID) and a *secret key* (App Secret). These are basically the username and password for our Meteor server process. Once both are connected, we can allow users to sign in with their Facebook account.

Instead of entering any credentials in our Meteor app, users can now click a button to log them in via Facebook. Assuming they're already logged in on Facebook, they'll now see a dialog asking them whether they want to share information with the Meteor application. Behind the scenes the Meteor application has forwarded the login request to Facebook as the service provider. If users agree to share their login information with the Meteor application, Facebook generates an access token. This token lets the Meteor app know that users have been authenticated properly and it grants the permissions provided by the users. In the simplest case, Meteor may only have read access to a user's email address. Depending on the configuration settings, we could also request more permissions such as posting to the user's wall.

Not all OAuth providers support the same set of permissions, so they must all be individually configured. The advantage of using OAuth is that the consumer application can talk directly with the service provider to exchange data, if permissions exist. That way, all Facebook friends, recent tweets, or the number of private repos on GitHub can easily be accessed and added to the user's profile.

6.2.2 *Integrating Facebook authentication*

To integrate OAuth authentication via Facebook in a Meteor app, you perform the following steps:

1 Add the `accounts-facebook` package.
2 Create a new Facebook application.
3 Configure the Facebook integration.

ADDING ACCOUNTS-FACEBOOK TO AN APPLICATION

The first step is to add Facebook as the authentication provider for our application. If the application already supports username/password authentication as in section 6.1, it's sufficient to add a single package:

```
$ meteor add accounts-facebook
```

This package won't add any templates to the application. Therefore, if `accounts-facebook` is the only package available in the project, you'll need to manually call all functionality within your templates. Or you can add the `accounts-ui` package, which provides a login box for use with not only password authentication but also for many OAuth services.

All OAuth packages require configuration. Just like users, this configuration is stored inside a MongoDB collection. A collection named `meteor_accounts_login-ServiceConfiguration` will be created as soon as the service is configured. Pending credentials will be stored temporarily as well, which is done in a dedicated collection. This collection is created at server startup already and is called `meteor_OAuth_pendingCredentials`.

There's no need to manually access either of these two collections. Meteor will use these internally only and there's no benefit in querying data from them directly.

CREATING A FACEBOOK APPLICATION

If Meteor can't find a configuration for integration with Facebook, the UI will show a red Configure Facebook Login button instead of the regular login button. Clicking it will bring up a short configuration guide as well as two fields in which you provide the application ID and secret.

You'll need to register yourself as a Facebook developer, which is free of charge but requires you to have a Facebook account. You can create a new Facebook application at https://developers.facebook.com. Under the Apps tab you can add a new application of type Web/WWW. Next you assign an application ID; this can be any name that

**Application name
shown to users**

**Credentials for
OAuth configuration**

**Contact address
for this application**

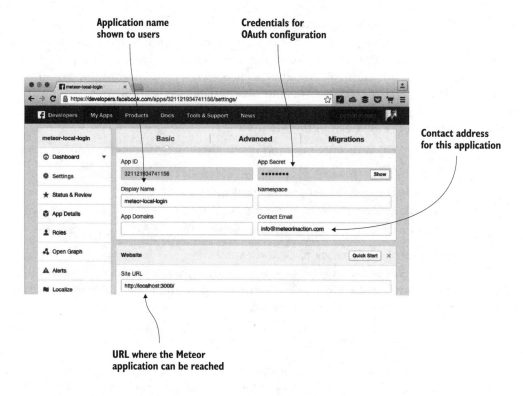

**URL where the Meteor
application can be reached**

Figure 6.7   Settings for a Facebook application used to integrate with Meteor

helps you and your users identify the application. Your users may eventually see the application name, so it's good practice to use the site name or something that closely describes your application. The category for your application and whether it's a test version of another Facebook application don't have any influence on the functionality and can be set to the values that best describe your project.

The site URL for a Facebook application that's used with a local development environment should typically be set to http://localhost:3000. You can take the correct URL setting from the configuration dialog shown by Meteor.

Once you've made these settings, Facebook requires you to set up a contact email for the application before you can activate it. Navigate to the application dashboard on the Facebook Developer site and enter a contact email in the Settings section (see figure 6.7). Finally, you need to activate the application on the Status & Review tab.

An activated Facebook application can be used to authenticate users. The last step to implement logging in via Facebook is to configure the Meteor application.

CONFIGURING
Open the Meteor application in the browser and click the Facebook button to bring up the configuration dialog shown in figure 6.8.

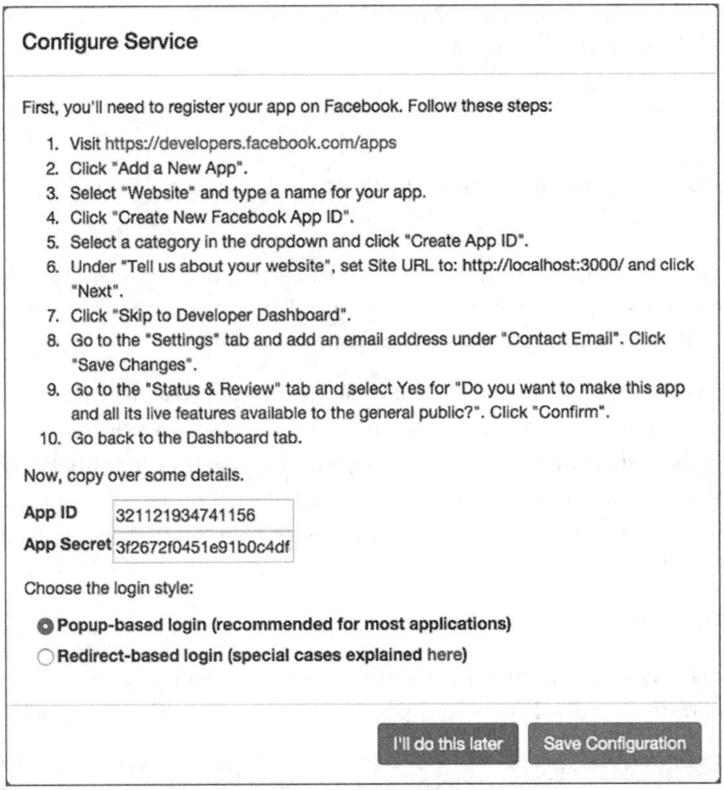

Configure Service

First, you'll need to register your app on Facebook. Follow these steps:

1. Visit https://developers.facebook.com/apps
2. Click "Add a New App".
3. Select "Website" and type a name for your app.
4. Click "Create New Facebook App ID".
5. Select a category in the dropdown and click "Create App ID".
6. Under "Tell us about your website", set Site URL to: http://localhost:3000/ and click "Next".
7. Click "Skip to Developer Dashboard".
8. Go to the "Settings" tab and add an email address under "Contact Email". Click "Save Changes".
9. Go to the "Status & Review" tab and select Yes for "Do you want to make this app and all its live features available to the general public?". Click "Confirm".
10. Go back to the Dashboard tab.

Now, copy over some details.

App ID   321121934741156
App Secret 3f2672f0451e91b0c4df

Choose the login style:

● **Popup-based login (recommended for most applications)**
○ **Redirect-based login (special cases explained here)**

[I'll do this later] [Save Configuration]

Figure 6.8   Configuration dialog for Facebook integration

Besides the basic instructions on how to create a Facebook application, the configuration dialog lets you add the application credentials (App ID and App Secret) as well as a login style. The default is to use a *pop-up–based* dialog, which means the application window will remain when the user logs into Facebook and a new window with the Facebook dialog is opened. In contrast, the *redirect-based* login style will leave the application, redirect the current browser window to Facebook, and reload the entire application once the authentication is successful. Unless you plan on running your application inside a Cordova container on mobile devices,[2] it's preferable to use the pop-up–based login.

Save the configuration and users can start logging in via Facebook. If you've misconfigured the application, you can manually delete the configuration information from the `meteor_accounts_loginServiceConfiguration` collection inside the MongoDB.

---

[2] Refer to chapter 11 on Isobuild to learn more about running Meteor applications on mobile devices.

Open a Mongo shell using either an application such as Robomongo or issue `meteor mongo` on the command line and then use

```
db.getCollection('meteor_accounts_loginServiceConfiguration').remove({service
:'facebook'})
```

If you use `meteor reset` to empty all collections, all login service configurations will also be reset.

> **NOTE** All OAuth configuration is stored inside the application database. Whenever you issue the `meteor reset` command to empty the database, it'll also remove all OAuth configuration data from the database.

As long as no Facebook credentials are available in the database, any user visiting the application will be able to configure it via the browser. To avoid this you can add any OAuth credentials to the application's source code. In case no credentials are configured in the database yet, these will be automatically inserted, just like the fixtures we used in the previous chapters. This requires a package called `service-configuration` to be available:

```
$ meteor add service-configuration
```

Once the package is available, the code shown in listing 6.8 will take care of setting the correct OAuth credentials for Facebook upon the start of your Meteor application.

Listing 6.8 Inserting Facebook OAuth configuration as a fixture in server/server.js

```
if (ServiceConfiguration.configurations.find({
    service: 'facebook'
}).count() === 0) {
  ServiceConfiguration.configurations.insert({
    service: 'facebook',
    appId: 'OAuth-credentials-from-facebook',
    secret: 'OAuth-credentials-from-facebook',
    loginStyle: 'popup'
  });
}
```

ADDING FACEBOOK INFORMATION TO THE USER PROFILE

All users who logged in via Facebook have a new entry in the `services` field in their user document (see listing 6.9). It contains the token used for authentication, but it also includes information such as first and last name, gender, and email. If you want to allow a user to edit this information, it's easiest to copy the data over to the `profile` object inside the user document.

Listing 6.9 The user document when signing up via Facebook

```
{
  "_id" : "nzPMRdhSKx7NJvTGY",
  "createdAt" : ISODate("2015-03-30T21:23:55.475Z"),
```

```
                     "profile" : {
                       "name" : "Stephan Hochhaus"
                     },
                     "services" : {
                       "facebook" : {
                         "accessToken" : "CAAEkDwbZAj.....",
                         "email" : "stephan@meteorinaction.com",
                         "expiresAt" : 1421097429424,
                         "first_name" : "Stephan",
                         "gender" : "male",
                         "id" : "1234567890",
                         "last_name" : "Hochhaus",
                         "link" : "https://www.facebook.com/app_scoped_user_id/123456789/",
                         "locale" : "en_US",
                         "name" : "Stephan Hochhaus"
                       },
                       "resume" : {
                         ...
                       }
                     }
                   }
```

Meteor automatically adds the name property to the profile.

As you can see from listing 6.9, Meteor already copied over the name property from Facebook to the user profile. Hooking again into `Accounts.onCreateUser`, you can copy over data provided by Facebook to the user's profile. You'll copy over first and last name and gender from `user.services.facebook` to `user.profile` so that the user can edit this information inside the Meteor application independently from Facebook.

Listing 6.10 shows how to extend the `onCreateUser` hook to copy over fields from the `facebook.service` to the `profile` field, but only if a user has logged in via Facebook. That way, it can also be merged with the code in listing 6.6 for adding `profile` fields for password authentication.

Listing 6.10　Adding Facebook information to the user profile

```
Accounts.onCreateUser(function (options, user) {
  if (user.services.facebook){
    user.profile.first_name = user.services.facebook.first_name;
    user.profile.last_name = user.services.facebook.last_name;
    user.profile.gender = user.services.facebook.gender;
  }
  return user;
});
```

Even if Facebook has updated information for names or gender, it won't update the settings inside the user's profile object because the `onCreateUser` function will only be called the first time a user logs into the application using Facebook.

6.2.3　*Integrating other OAuth providers*

As mentioned earlier, Meteor comes with multiple packages that allow the integration of social networks as authentication providers. The principles always remain the same.

Before you can configure the external service provider, you must create an application in Twitter, Google, GitHub, or whatever service you plan to integrate. Some of these services require you to set a value for authenticated or callback URLs. As long as an application is under development, this is typically http://localhost:3000. Therefore, it's good practice to create two applications on the service provider: one for the local development environment and another for the live instance of your Meteor application.

USING ALTERNATIVE AUTHENTICATION METHODS IN ONE APPLICATION

Meteor makes it simple to add multiple authentication providers to a single application. But these providers don't share the same data with the consumer, which makes it complicated in many cases to associate alternative login methods to the same user.

Imagine an application is set up to allow authentication via username and password as well as Twitter and Facebook. A user may decide to log in with Twitter one day and with Facebook the next. How could the application tell it's the same user? Possibly if the email address associated with the user's Twitter account matches the one for the Facebook account. Unfortunately, Twitter doesn't expose a user's email address over the authentication API. As a result, Meteor can't connect a Twitter login to a Facebook account. It'll assume both are different users. In a worst-case scenario, users will log in through each of the login methods the application provides and end up having as many accounts as there are login methods.

Of course, it's entirely possible to use multiple authentication providers in the same application and allow users to use them all to identify a single user. To do so you need users to manually connect their profiles to the same account. Unfortunately, this functionality isn't part of the core packages that provide account functionality.

Some community packages are available that save you from creating your own templates and code to allow users to connect multiple social networks to the same account. If you wish to include multiple authentication providers in a single application, take a look at `splendido:accounts-meld` or `bozhao:link-accounts`.

Before adding too many authentication providers to an application, consider which are actually needed. The fact that working with OAuth is so simple with Meteor may lead to overly complicated applications that have little user benefit.

6.3 *Managing user permissions, roles, and groups*

Authenticating users isn't enough—you also need to authorize their actions. Permissions can be used to define what data users can access and what functions they're allowed to use. Administrators should be able to perform all possible actions, whereas regular users can only edit or delete their own data.

To better illustrate how to manage user permissions, let's use a simple messaging application. You can find the source code in this chapter's sample code. It offers limited functionality, which makes it easier to illustrate the main points of Meteor's permission system.

Users can sign up with a username and password. Once they're logged in, the application shows a list of users, each of which can be selected by clicking them. Once a user is clicked, the ID will be assigned to a Session variable and a second template will display basic profile data and allow users to view and leave messages. Only the owner of the message board should be allowed to delete messages.

All functionality implemented in this sample application is based on the contents of chapters 3 (working with templates) and 4 (working with data) with some references to the beginning of this chapter in regard to user accounts.

As highlighted in previous chapters already, Meteor uses a package called insecure for every new application. This allows the client and every user, authenticated or not, to save or remove data from the database. The first step in adding security to an application is to remove the package using the following:

```
$ meteor remove insecure
```

The result of removing the insecure package is that no user is able to write to the database anymore. Viewing data is possible because the autopublish package is still available. We'll talk about removing it in the next chapter. First we'll concentrate on restricting access for users.

The simplest form of managing user permissions in Meteor is by using the allow/ deny function for any collection.

6.3.1 Managing permissions with allow/deny

Meteor trusts all code executed on the server by default. All client code isn't considered safe to use, especially with the insecure package removed. Any inserts, updates, or removes to a database collection from the browser result in an *Access denied* message.

> **NOTE** Allow and deny only affect write operations to the database. Reading from a collection can be controlled using Publications and Subscriptions.

Each collection exposes an allow function and a deny function that can limit or grant permissions to users. Listing 6.11 shows the syntax, which is the same for both allow and deny. The code must run in the server environment, but it's safe to also run it inside the client. Therefore, it can be put in the same file where collections are defined, because it removes redundancy. If you prefer, you can also put it in a server-only file. Either way, a client may not change the server code and work around permissions, even if you send this code to the browser.

Listing 6.11 Using allow for a Messages collection

```
// collections.js
MessagesCollection = new Mongo.Collection('messages');
MessagesCollection.allow({
  insert: function (userId, doc) {
    return true;
  },
```

```
      update: function (userId, doc) {
        return true;
      },
      remove: function (userId, doc) {
        return true;
      }
    });
```

Multiple allow and deny rules may be defined; sometimes they'll overlap. Meteor first executes all deny callbacks to determine if an action is forbidden. If any of the deny callbacks returns true, then the user won't be able to carry out the associated action, even if there is an allow rule that returns true. If there are multiple allow rules, only one has to match and return true to allow a user to carry out an action.

> **NOTE**   The allow and deny callbacks affect only direct writes to the database and not Meteor method calls. Methods will be discussed in full detail in the next chapter.

You can use MessagesCollection.allow to enable sending messages without the insecure package and also restrict the deletion of messages to a user by the recipient only.

SENDING MESSAGES TO A USER

By selecting a user, you make it possible for every logged-in user to write a message to their site. Each message document contains five fields:

- _id—A unique ID for the message document
- sender—The user ID from the author of a message
- recipient—The user ID of the recipient of a message
- message—The actual message text
- timestamp—The creation date of the message

It's impossible to create a new message document from the browser unless an allow callback returns true. Only logged-in users should be able to send a message, so we need to return true when the user trying to insert a new document has a user ID (see listing 6.12). Guests don't have a user ID and therefore their value for userId would return false.

> **Listing 6.12   Allowing logged-in users to insert new messages**

```
MessagesCollection.allow({
  insert: function (userId, doc) {
    return userId;
  }
});
```

Be aware that this grants permission to users to insert whatever they like into the database. The only restriction is that the user is logged in and writes to the messages collection. New fields are added on the fly—for example, in case a user wants to add an additional field called `messageSubtext`. To prevent users from adding new fields to a document, you can use a deny rule that checks whether all defined fields are provided and that none is missing. Listing 6.13 shows how the Underscore.js library that is part of Meteor can be used to extract all document fields to an array. Using a second array that contains all valid field names, you can verify that no mandatory fields are missing and no additional fields are coming from the client. When inserting data, the `_id` field will be added by the database automatically. Because it's not sent by the client, it's not part of the `validFields` array for the insert method.

> **Listing 6.13 deny inserts with missing or additional fields**

```
MessagesCollection.deny({
  insert: function (userId, doc) {
    var fieldsInDoc = _.keys(doc);
    var validFields = ['sender', 'recipient', 'timestamp', 'message'];
    if (_.difference(fieldsInDoc, validFields).length > 0) {
      console.log('additional fields found');
      return true;
    } else {
      console.log('all fields good');
      return false
    }
  }
});
```

Using Underscore.js to put all document field names into an array

Check for additional or missing fields.

Although you've effectively ensured that only known fields are provided for a new user document, you have no control over the contents of these fields. A user might send a string as the sender, an object or array, or even a binary BLOB.

Using allow/deny rules isn't too complicated, but they should be used only for relatively simple tasks; otherwise, maintaining the growing complexity will become complicated. The more rules you add to an application, the harder it becomes to tell which cases will be denied and which will be allowed.

> **NOTE** For better control over database operations, consider using Meteor methods instead of allow/deny rules. Chapter 7 will provide a thorough introduction.

REMOVING MESSAGES FROM A WHITEBOARD

In case a recipient doesn't like the contents of a message, she should be able to delete the message. But not everybody should be allowed to remove messages—only the recipient should be able to do so.

You can't set a deny rule that globally denies all remove operations and add one allow rule for the recipient. Remember that it takes only a single deny rule to return `true` to prevent any other allow rule from execution. Therefore, you'll work with a single deny rule that checks whether the user requesting to remove a message is the same as the recipient. The deny rule in listing 6.14 returns `true` if the `userId` for the currently logged-in user is different from the user ID in the `recipient` field of the message document.

Listing 6.14   Deny message removal for everyone but the recipient

```
MessagesCollection.deny({
  remove: function (userId, doc) {
    return doc.recipient !== userId;
  }
});
```

The deny code eventually runs on the server side of the application, even if you placed the code inside a file that can be accessed on both client and server. The `userId` parameter is provided by the `accounts` packages directly, and it's determined and passed to the `remove` function on the server. It isn't possible to change this value from the browser console to fake another user's ID.

DELETING A USER ACCOUNT

The users collection is special in several ways. For one, by default users can edit only the content of the profile field. Even if no dedicated allow rules are available, new users can still sign up and create a new user document. Deleting a user, even if it's his own account, isn't possible once the `insecure` package is removed. But using a simple allow rule on the `users` collection enables the removal of accounts (see following listing).

Listing 6.15   Enabling users to remove their account

```
Meteor.users.allow({
  remove: function (userId, doc) {
    return doc._id === userId;
  }
});
```

> **TIP**   When you need more control over user authorization, take a look at the roles packages `alanning:roles` or `nicolaslopezj:roles`. They allow you to implement user groups with much greater transparency than allow and deny rules alone.

6.4   Summary

In this chapter, you've learned that

- Meteor ships with several accounts package that enable user registration and login.
- Connecting to an SMTP server can be done via an environment variable or inside the code.
- System email messages can be adjusted via their own `Template` objects.
- OAuth integration is a core feature that requires little effort to implement.
- Simple database permissions can be implemented using `allow` and `deny`.
- For more complex permission settings, `allow` and `deny` should be replaced by Meteor methods.

Exchanging data 7

In the early stages of development, it may often be helpful to have the contents of the server database available on the client as well. The increased convenience comes at the price of both performance and security, though. If the idea is to build low-latency and high-performance applications for the web, you must refrain from replicating the entire database on each client. Additionally, sharing all data probably includes sensitive information that should be viewed only by its owner. As a result, you must get rid of the automatic data publication and regain control over all database content.

This chapter introduces two key concepts to working with Meteor: publications and methods (see figure 7.1).

Using Meteor's publications and subscriptions you can control not only how much data is sent to each client but also which fields are available to which user. In this chapter you'll learn how to set up data publications on the server that'll allow your application to easily hold thousands of database documents while sending only small subsets to the clients. That way, you can effectively address many performance issues that might arise.

In chapter 6 we discussed allow/deny rules for securing write operations to the database. Methods, Meteor's remote procedure calls, are a powerful alternative to these simple rules. Methods may run on the server or the client. You'll use them to secure all write operations to the database by properly validating all content received from the client. Their use isn't limited to database operations, though—they can also be used for other actions like sending emails.

Throughout this chapter you'll be enhancing an application so that it becomes robust enough to be deployed to the internet. The application you'll use will store workout data to cover the following aspects:

- Manually defining publications and subscriptions
- Limiting data sent to a client by using parameterized subscriptions
- Aggregating data
- Restricting data only to a particular user
- Securing database writes with methods

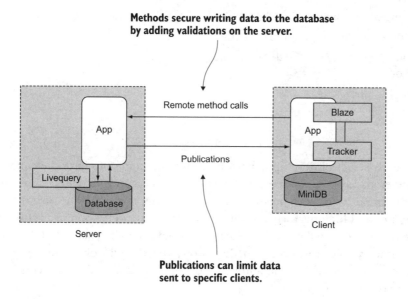

Figure 7.1   Publications and methods give developers full control when dealing with data.

The workout tracker is very simple; all code is put into five files. You'll use a fixtures.js file to populate the collection with random workout data—look at the sample code for this chapter to see how it works:

```
├── client
│   ├── workoutTracker.html
│   └── workoutTracker.js
├── collections
│   └── Workouts.js
└── server
    ├── fixtures.js
    └── publications.js
```

7.1 Publications and subscriptions

Up to this point, Meteor has automatically published all collection data to all clients using the autopublish package. This package isn't suitable for production environments because it doesn't limit the amount of data sent to a client. What works well for a few database entries during development doesn't scale well with hundreds or thousands of documents. Also, it doesn't provide any access restrictions—every client may access all data. In this section, you'll learn ways to send data to the client in an efficient and secure way.

You're going to use an application that stores workouts such as running or biking and presents them to a user in a simple table. All workouts will be stored inside a single collection and contain the date when they happened and their distance as well. You'll create a lot of sample workout documents at startup and show all of them in one table at first. Because you don't want the client to load all the data at once, you'll then limit the number of workouts loaded to the client and also add a button to fetch more data on each click. Eventually you'll add an aggregated view of the whole data. For that, you'll add up the distance of the workouts of each month. The aggregated data in the client will also be updated reactively. When a new document is added to the workouts collection, the count for the affected month will reactively show the updated sum.

7.1.1 publish() and subscribe()

Publications and subscriptions always come in pairs. Although Collections are typically declared on both the server and the client, publications exists only on the server. They can retrieve data from a database using the Collection.find() method just like a template helper. In figure 7.2 you can see an example where the publication retrieves three documents from the database. Those documents are then published under the same name as the collection: workouts.

On the client a Meteor.subscribe() call initiates a request to the server to send data for the workouts collection. Notice that it doesn't request the content from the database but from the server—more precisely, the result for Collection.find(). In this case the result is just three documents. The client receives these documents and puts them into a local collection of the same name. Although the Collection object

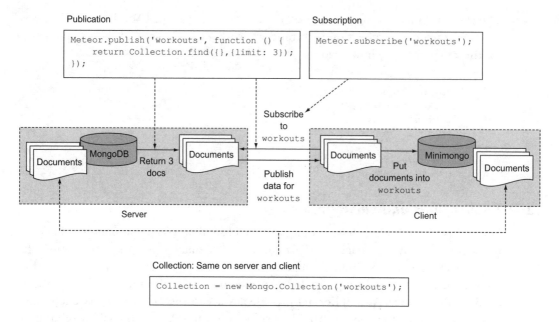

Figure 7.2   An overview of publications and subscriptions

has the same name on the server and client, it may hold different data, depending on context and publication settings.

REMOVING AUTOPUBLISH

Because you'll manually decide what content to send to clients, you must remove the autopublish package. Adding and removing packages with Meteor is done via the CLI tool. Here's how you get rid of the autopublish package:

```
$ meteor remove autopublish
```

Once the package is removed and the Meteor server is started, the client will have no data available anymore. Even though the client still knows about all available collections, no data is transferred from the server-side MongoDB to the browser's Minimongo instance. If you were to query for documents with any collection, you wouldn't get any results back.

SETTING UP A PUBLICATION

In order to display the data you need from the workouts collection inside the MongoDB, you have to provide a *pub/sub pair.* First you'll set up a simple publication that sends all workout documents to all clients that subscribe to that publication. Because all publications live in the server scope, you'll put them in a new publications.js file within the server folder. The following listing shows how to set up the publication.

Listing 7.1 A simple server-side publication

You name a publication in order to subscribe to it, as you'll see later on.

```
Meteor.publish('workouts', function () {
  return WorkoutsCollection.find({});
});
```

Publications can return data just like template helpers.

NOTE Publications are one-way streets that send data from the server to the client. To send data from the client back to the server, you must provide a secure method to insert and update data. We'll look at this topic later in the chapter.

Setting up a publication won't have any effect on the client at this point. It must specifically ask for the data via a subscription.

7.1.2 Global subscriptions

On the client you must add a subscription. Inside the workoutTracker.js file, add the following line at the top:

```
Meteor.subscribe("workouts");
```

Once you subscribe to the publication, you'll see that all the data that's available on the server-side MongoDB is also available through the Minimongo on the client. You can check inside a browser console by using the same code as inside the publication:

```
WorkoutsCollection.find({})
```

Calling `Meteor.subscribe()` returns an object with a `stop()` and a `ready()` method. `stop()` can be used to terminate a subscription, and `ready()` is `true` if the server has marked the publication as ready. It's a reactive data source just like `Collection` or `Session`.

This is basically what the `autopublish` package gave you for free for all collections. Next you'll start to control the data that's published to the client by limiting the number of documents going to the client.

Using servers as clients

There are scenarios when two Meteor servers should exchange information. Technically, one server becomes the client of the other. The `subscribe()` method works only inside the client context, but there's a way one server can subscribe to the data of another using a Distributed Data Protocol (DDP) connection.

You can connect to another server using `DDP.connect()`. It takes the URL of the remote server as the only argument. Once successfully connected, it'll return an object that allows you to use `subscribe()` (to access published data), `call()` (to invoke methods), `methods()` (to define client-side methods), and a few more functions.

(continued)

Connecting one server to another and acting as a client takes only three lines of code. First, the server-to-server connection is defined; a connection to http://192.168.2.201:3000 will be established. To receive the published data, you need to declare a collection. This time it'll take not only a name as its argument but also how to connect to the master. Hence, `server2` will be the second argument. Finally, the server may subscribe to `remoteData`. Again there's a slight variation because you need to call the `subscribe()` method on the remote server rather than the local Meteor instance:

```
var server2 = DDP.connect('http://191.168.2.201:3000/');
var RemoteCollection = new Mongo.Collection('remoteData', server2);
server2.subscribe('remoteData');
```

7.1.3   *Template-level subscriptions*

Subscriptions using the `Meteor.subscribe` function are greedy. Regardless of whether a user views the subscription data, the function will register a subscription with the server and trigger data transfers. As soon as a user hits the front page of your application, all subscriptions will be made and data will be loaded, even if the user never looks at it. You can avoid such global subscriptions by binding them to templates, using Meteor's template-level subscriptions.

When you use a template-level subscription, the subscription is initiated when the template is created. When the template is destroyed, the subscription is also terminated. That way, you can limit the actual data transfers between client and server. You also don't need to worry about which route[1] requires which data; you can pass this relation directly to the template that requires that data. Each `Template` instance has its own `subscribe` function, which uses the same syntax as `Meteor.subscribe`. In the `onCreated` callback of a template, you can access the current template instance via `this`:

```
Template.workoutList.onCreated(function () {
  this.subscribe("workouts");
});
```

Whenever the `workoutList` template is created, Meteor will automatically set up a subscription to the workouts publication. To determine whether the subscription is ready, you can use the `Template.subscriptionsReady` helper. It returns `true` if all subscriptions of a template are ready and can be used to show a loading indicator for the template itself, as shown in the following listing.

---

[1] We'll discuss route-based subscriptions in the next chapter.

Listing 7.2   Using a template-level subscription with a loading indicator

```
// workoutTracker.html
<template name="workoutList">
  {{#if Template.subscriptionsReady}}          ◁——  Returns true if all template
    <ul>                                                 subscriptions are ready
    {{#each workouts}}
      <li>{{workoutAt}}</li>          ◁——  Displays
    {{/each}}                                workout details
    </ul>
  {{else}}                            ┌ Lets users know
    loading workouts...        ◁——┤ that data is
  {{/if}}                            └ being loaded
</template>

// workoutTracker.js
Template.workoutList.onCreated(function () {
  this.subscribe('workouts');          ◁——  Sets up the
});                                            subscription

Template.workoutList.helpers({
  workouts: function () {
    return WorkoutsCollection.find({}, {     ◁——  Returns all workouts,
      sort: {                                      newest first
        workoutAt: -1
      }
    });
  }
});
```

Using template-level subscriptions gives you more control over when and where to load data. By avoiding global subscriptions, you also decrease the required traffic when initially loading a Meteor application. Especially when you're rendering multiple templates on the same page, there's no need to wait until all data is available—each template can use its own loading indicator.

In the rest of this chapter, we'll use the global `Meteor.subscribe` because the examples are rather simple. For more complex applications, you can use the same syntax and place your subscriptions in the `onCreated` callback of a template. Their behavior is exactly the same, except they differ in lifespan:

- `Meteor.subscribe` is set up when the client loads your application and is terminated when the client closes the connection.
- `Template.subscribe` is set up when the associated template is created and is terminated when the template is destroyed.

7.1.4   *Parameterizing subscriptions*

For performance reasons, you never want the entire database content to be sent over the network. Besides taking a long time to transfer, too much information may be confusing to users. Therefore you'll publish only the 10 newest documents of the workouts collection initially. Users can choose to request more documents if they want to see older records as well. Obviously you need to adjust the existing publication code.

It must support both limits and take an argument to dynamically determine an offset to allow sending a second or third set of 10 documents. Let's take it step by step.

The first thing you'll do is tell the publication the limit you want to set for the workout query. You can add parameters to the subscription call that'll be available as parameters inside the server-side publication function. This way, you can set options for the publication; the client tells the server what to do.

> **WARNING** Whenever you're dealing with data coming from the client, you must validate it before using it.

The publication takes an `options` argument that first needs to be checked. Instead of adding your own validation, you can use Meteor's `check()` function.

VALIDATING DATA VIA CHECK()

With the `check()` function, you can match input values against known patterns. To limit the subscription, you expect the user to provide a number and nothing else. `check()` uses a simple syntax with two arguments—the value itself and the pattern it should be checked against:

```
check(value, pattern);
```

To ensure that the provided parameter contains only a number, you use `check (options, Number)`; inside the publication. In our example, you're dealing with an object, so you have to check a pattern for every parameter of the object:

```
check(options,
  {
    limit: Number
  }
);
```

You'll use `check()` again when we discuss methods.

DYNAMIC SUBSCRIPTIONS

Listing 7.3 shows the code from the server's publications.js file.

Listing 7.3   Adding parameters to a publication

```
Meteor.publish('workouts', function(options){          ◁┐ The publication takes
  check(options,                                          │ an options object as
    {                                                     │ a parameter.
      limit: Number
    }
  );
  var qry = {};
  var qryOptions = {
    limit: options.limit,
    sort: {workoutAt: 1}                   ◁─── Sort all
  }                                             database entries
                                                by timestamp to
  return WorkoutsCollection.find(qry, qryOptions);   ◁─── ensure the limit
});                                                       starts from the
                                                          newest.
```

Sort all database entries by timestamp to ensure the limit starts from the newest.

Using the limit query options from MongoDB returns only a limited number of documents.

Every client can now subscribe to this publication and set a limit. The check() function expects an option object and will throw an error unless one is passed by the subscription. You have to create the subscription for the client that subscribes to the data provided by this publication. You'll do this inside the client folder's workoutTracker.js file because the subscription is available only in the browser. You'll use Session to keep track of the currently used limit (see the following listing).

Listing 7.4 Subscribing to a publication with parameters

```
Session.setDefault('limit', 10);          For the limit parameter of the subscription,
                                          you want to use a Session variable with a
                                          default value of 10.
// Subscriptions
Tracker.autorun(function(computation){          Autorun creates a reactive
  Meteor.subscribe('workouts', {                context that renews the
    limit: Session.get('limit')                 subscription if the limit changes.
  });
});                                       The Session object is passed
                                          as the value for limit.
```

When the application first starts, the Session variable limit is set to 10 because it doesn't have any other value. This is what setDefault does and it ensures that limit will always have a value.

The reason you need to put the subscription inside a Tracker.autorun is to create a reactive context. Once the Session variable limit changes, the subscription to workouts gets rerun with the updated limit value. This means whenever the limit value changes, triggered by an event or directly from the JavaScript console, the subscription is updated automatically. Then the new data from the publication is added to the client's Minimongo and also rendered in the template.

To allow for a more convenient way to increase the number of documents to show, you can add a button with a click handler that adds 10 to the current limit value in the Session object (see following listing).

Listing 7.5 Adding an event handler to increase the limit by 10

```
Template.workoutList.events({
  'click button.show-more': function(evt, tpl){
    var newLimit = Session.get('limit') + 10;     Changing the limit in the reactive
    Session.set('limit', newLimit);               Session variable updates the
  }                                               subscription automatically.
});
```

As you can see, it's not too difficult to remove the autopublish package and take control over the data that's available on the client. With reactive variables, it's also very easy to modify a subscription and the data that's available. The same approach you used for limiting the amount of documents can easily be used for filtering and sorting.

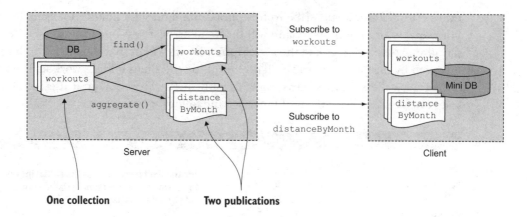

Figure 7.3 Using two publications from a single database collection

Before you proceed to the next section, try to add a second button that provides a value of -1 or 1 to sort all documents in ascending or descending order.

7.1.5 *Publishing aggregated data to a client-only collection*

Imagine you run three times a week, four weeks a month. Then you're not only incredibly fit, but you also need to look at 12 different entries to understand how many miles you covered in a single month. That makes quickly comparing stats a pain. This is when data aggregation comes in. Instead of showing all the fine details, you sometimes need a summary of large amounts of data to make sense of it. Let's extend the application so you can say for sure that you ran farther in June than in January.

If you had all workout documents available on the client, aggregating could be an easy task. By iterating over each document and adding the distance for each month, you'd be all set. Unfortunately, this approach has multiple downsides. One is you'd have to pass a lot of data over the wire. If you wanted to aggregate the data of the last 10 years, you'd end up sending thousands of documents over the network. Another downside is that the computation takes quite some time, and this would slow down the user's UI, resulting in poor user experience. Therefore, you need to aggregate the data on the server and publish the aggregate as well. Figure 7.3 shows the client subscribing to both publications. Whereas workouts uses the find() method, distanceByMonth will use MongoDB's aggregation framework.

> **Data aggregation with MongoDB**
>
> If you're familiar with SQL, you're probably already thinking about doing a SELECT with a COUNT(*) and a GROUP BY, but that won't work in the NoSQL world. MongoDB itself is built to handle large datasets and give analytical insight, so it also offers a way to aggregate data, just not using GROUP BY. You're going to use the *aggregation pipeline*

(continued)

to compare the distances between all months of the year. Minimongo, the client implementation in the browser, doesn't support using the aggregation pipeline, but this is okay as you'll see.

The approach you'll take involves creating a publication that doesn't send data directly from a `Collection` but creates the aggregated data inside itself and returns this to all subscribers. This data is stored inside a collection that exists only on the client. It's not persistent in the server-side MongoDB because it'd leave you with redundant data.

At first, you'll create a new publication named `distanceByMonth`. It doesn't have a corresponding collection inside the database. Where you previously put a `find()` operation on a database collection, the second argument to `publish()` will now hold the aggregation.

The aggregation framework for MongoDB isn't supported out of the box. Several community packages are available that provide aggregation capabilities so you can easily add it yourself. You'll fall back to the core MongoDB driver, then define the actual pipeline, run the aggregation so that it doesn't block any other processes, and finally mark the subscription as `ready`.

Any publication can send status messages to its subscribers, indicating that content has changed or that it's done with sending all available content. When publishing a database collection directly, these status messages are automatically managed by Meteor. When using a custom publication they must be called explicitly.

- `added(collection, docId, fields)`—When a new document is created, the first argument is the collection, followed by the document ID. The third argument contains all fields of the document (excluding the `_id` field).
- `changed(collection, docId, fields)`—For changed documents, again the collection name and ID are passed as the first argument, followed by an object that contains all updated fields (fields with a value of `undefined` have been deleted from the document).
- `removed(collection, docId)`—This takes two arguments: the collection name and the document ID that was removed.
- `ready()`—This takes no arguments and informs the client that all available data has been sent.

Listing 7.6 gives you the full code, which we'll go through bit by bit. To use the MongoDB core driver you must use `MongoInternals`, which is defined as part of the `mongo` package included with each new Meteor project. A reference to the default database used by Meteor is stored inside `db`. Because you're using the core MongoDB driver, you can use all functions, including `aggregate()`. The `pipeline` variable contains an array with details about the actual aggregation. The MongoDB aggregation pipeline consists of stages. Each stage transforms the documents as they pass through the pipeline. First, all matching documents are determined. In this scenario, all documents match because we haven't defined any restrictions. Next, all resulting documents, or rather the specified field contents, are grouped together. All workouts are grouped by month and are given a new _id that represents the month (1 = January, 2 = February, etc.).

MongoDB isn't reactive by itself and calling it would result in a synchronous call that would block all other server requests until the aggregation is finished. This is why you need a way to unblock the aggregation and receive a callback once it's done while maintaining the full Meteor context. Asynchronous calls to external components should always be wrapped inside Meteor.bindEnvironment().

> **NOTE** This aggregation operates on the fly, meaning that every subscription will trigger the aggregation on database contents. If you notice that the processing takes a long time, it may be a better option to write the aggregated data to a dedicated collection.

Using the Underscore library, all months' results are added to the subscription distanceByMonth. Finally, the publish() function signals the client that the subscription is ready.

Listing 7.6 Aggregation inside a publication

```
Meteor.publish('distanceByMonth', function(){           Because there's no official support
  var subscription = this;                                 for aggregation from Meteor, use
                                                                    the core Mongo driver.
  var db = MongoInternals.defaultRemoteCollectionDriver().mongo.db;    ◁┘

  var pipeline = [                    ◁┐  The aggregation settings create
    {                                     documents with the _id field equal to
      $group: {                           the month of the workoutAt field and
        _id: { $month: '$workoutAt' },    the sum of all distances of this month.
        distance: { $sum: '$distance' }
      }
    }
  ];                                      ◁┐  Create the
                                             aggregation.
  db.collection('workouts').aggregate(   ◁┘
    pipeline,
    Meteor.bindEnvironment(             ◁┐  Because you can't use asynchronous
      function(err, result){               code in a publication, use
        console.log('result', result);     Meteor.bindEnvironment.
        _.each(result, function(r){
          subscription.added('distanceByMonth', r._id, {distance:
            r.distance});                ◁┐
        })                                  Add the data to
      }                                     this subscription.
    )
  )

  subscription.ready();      ◁┐  The subscription is
});                             ready to send the
                                data to the client.
```

On the client side, you create a collection available only on the client that takes this data. Create this collection inside the client folder in the workoutTracker.js file:

```
DistanceByMonth = new Mongo.Collection('distanceByMonth');
```

This looks and behaves exactly like any other collection, but the data comes from your custom publication and not the server-side MongoDB. You can use the data inside this collection as you normally would. You can create a new template and helper to display the data from the aggregation publication. Refer to the sample code for more details.

One downside of this approach is that this data isn't reactive because the aggregation framework is just a dumb data source. That means if someone added a new workout for the month of April with an 8-mile distance, the aggregated data on the client for April wouldn't be increased by 8 automatically. When the page is reloaded the subscription would be initialized again so that the screen would update correctly. This is definitely not how things are supposed to be inside a Meteor application where the client should be reactive. Next, you'll see how to improve the publication to make this aggregated publication reactive again.

7.1.6 *Turning an aggregation publication into a reactive data source*

Unlike a normal `Collection.find()`, the aggregation publication isn't reactive. Nevertheless, you want a client's aggregated data to update reactively when data changes—just like adding a workout would update the limited list automatically. What's missing to turn the aggregation into a reactive data source is an *observer* that monitors the workout collection and performs an action if a new workout is added.

Every collection cursor available—for example, the returned cursor from calling `WorkoutsCollection.find()`—has the ability to observe the documents that were added, deleted, or changed inside the collection. Which documents are observed depends on the query that's used by the `Collection.find()` method.

By limiting the query for a `find()`, you can keep an eye only on workouts with a type of `jogging` and react if a new document is added, changed, or removed. At a later point, we could add a different action for workouts of type `chess` or `aerobics`. The function you'll use for monitoring updates to a data source is `observeChanges()`.

There are three cases that you can observe; each has an associated callback with one or more attributes. The associated callbacks are similar to those used for setting the publication status, but they don't require that you pass a collection name as an argument:

- `added(docId, fields)`—When a new document is created, the first argument is the document ID, and the second contains all fields of the document (excluding the `_id` field).
- `changed(docId, fields)`—For changed documents, again the ID is passed as the first argument, and the second contains only the updated fields (fields with a value of `undefined` have been deleted from the document).
- `removed(docId)`—This takes a single argument: the ID of the document that was removed from the collection.

NOTE   Although they have the same names, the added, changed, and removed functions in a publication use a slightly different syntax.

The following listing shows the syntax of using all three callbacks on a watched `WorkoutsCollection` query.

Listing 7.7   Observing changes in a collection

```
WorkoutsCollection
  .find( query )
  .observeChanges({
    added: function(id, fields){
      // do something if a document was added matching the query
    },
    changed: function(id, fields){
      // do something if a document of the query changed
    },
    removed: function(id){
      // do something if a document of the query was removed
    }
  });
```

You know how to aggregate data in a publication as well as how to create a callback if a document is added to a collection. That's all you need to make the aggregation publication reactive. The trick is to create an object within the publication that keeps track of all the aggregated data via `observeChanges()`. In this example `workoutHandle` is used to watch the collection and observe if a new document is added. If so, you can update the total distance of the month in the object that keeps track of the aggregated data. The newly updated data is then sent down to the client, telling it that the subscription has changed (see the following listing).

Listing 7.8   Using `observeChanges` to update aggregated data

```
Meteor.publish('distanceByMonth', function () {
  var subscription = this;
  var initiated = false;
  var distances = {};


  // existing aggregation code

  var workoutHandle = WorkoutsCollection
    .find()
    .observeChanges({
      added: function (id, fields) {
        if (!initiated) return;
        idByMonth = new Date(fields.workoutAt).getMonth() + 1;


        distances[idByMonth] += fields.distance;
```

You need this because the very first documents from the initial subscription shouldn't affect the added callback.

This object keeps track of all distances for each month.

Create the ID of the document. The +1 comes from the month starting at index 0.

Update the distance for the month since a new workout was added.

```
        subscription.changed('distanceByMonth',
          idByMonth, {
            distance: distances[idByMonth]
          }
        )
      }
    });

  subscription.ready();
});
```

Inform the client that the subscription was changed.

Now whenever a new workout is added to `Workouts`, the object that tracks the aggregated data (`workoutHandle`) is updated and sends the change to the client. Go to your browser and add a new workout through the console. You'll see that the aggregated data updates accordingly.

One last but very important thing to do is to clean up the publication accordingly. The observe methods will run endlessly if you don't stop them. The right moment to stop the observation of the collection is when the client subscription stops:

```
subscription.onStop(function(){
  workoutHandle.stop();
});
```

The subscription (or this) has an onStop callback that's fired whenever the client subscription is closed.

The handle that's returned from the observerChanges() function is used to stop observing.

Whenever the client stops the subscription, observing will be stopped as well.

NOTE If you want to publish a single document, you still have to use `collection.find({_id: options._id})` and not `findOne()`. This is because a publication must return a cursor whereas `findOne()` returns the actual result as an object.

7.1.7 Limiting data visibility by user ID

You can now control the data that's sent to the client and make sure that not every workout is sent to it. Still, you need to find a way to decide how many documents a user can see and that he sees only his own workouts and not the ones from other users (see listing 7.9). For this, you'll add the accounts packages we looked at earlier in this chapter. In a publication you can access the `userId` of the currently logged-in user by using `this.userId`, which is null if the user isn't logged in.

Listing 7.9 Sending only the data a user is allowed to see

```
Meteor.publish('workouts', function (options) {
  check(options, {
    limit: Number,
    sorting: Number
  });
```

```
    var qry = {
      userId: this.userId         ◄─┐  Query for all workouts that
    };                               │  belong to the currently
    var qryOptions = {               │  logged-in user
      limit: options.limit,
      sort: {
        workoutAt: options.sorting
      }
    }

    return WorkoutsCollection.find(qry, qryOptions);
});
```

It's important to store the reference to the user inside the workout document. If you do this, it's as simple as adding { userId: this.userId } to the query in the Workouts-Collection.find(qry...) function. Also note that if you log in or out, the data changes reactively.

The aggregated data is a little bit more complicated to adjust because you need to match the aggregation itself as well as the query that you want to observe (see the following listing).

Listing 7.10 Aggregation of a user's documents

```
Meteor.publish('distanceByMonth', function () {
  var subscription = this;
  var initiated = false;
  var distances = {};
  var userId = this.userId;
  var db = MongoInternals.defaultRemoteCollectionDriver().mongo.db;
  var pipeline = [{
    $match: {
      userId: userId         ◄─┐  The aggregation should only
    }                          │  be done over documents
  }, {                         │  that match the userId.
    $group: {
      _id: {
        $month: '$workoutAt'
      },
      distance: {
        $sum: '$distance'
      }
    }
  }];

  db.collection('workouts').aggregate(
    pipeline,
    Meteor.bindEnvironment(
      function (err, result) {
        console.log('result', result);
        _.each(result, function (r) {
          distances[r._id] = r.distance;
          subscription.added('distanceByMonth', r._id, {
            distance: r.distance
          });
```

```
        })
      }
    )
  )

  var workoutHandle = WorkoutsCollection
    .find({
      userId: userId
    })
    .observeChanges({
      added: function (id, fields) {
        if (!initiated) return;

        idByMonth = new Date(fields.workoutAt).getMonth() + 1;

        distances[idByMonth] += fields.distance;

        subscription.changed('distanceByMonth',
          idByMonth, {
            distance: distances[idByMonth]
          }
        )
      }
    });

  initiated = true;
  subscription.onStop(function () {
    workoutHandle.stop();
  });
  subscription.ready();
});
```

> ◁ In this publication there should be only the documents with the logged-in userId observed.

There's not much to do to update the aggregation publication so that it depends on the user. Only the aggregated documents with the correct `userId` should be counted in. Lastly, the documents that should be observed have to be found by the query `{userId: this.userId}`.

7.2   Meteor methods

Meteor makes sending data from clients to the server very easy. But on the web you can never trust the data that comes from a client. You can never be certain that there isn't a malicious hacker on the other end trying to access or modify sensitive data. Therefore, everything coming from a client must be validated before processing. Using the browser's console, every validation could be bypassed. This applies to all web applications, regardless of whether they're written in Java or JavaScript.

The solution is to implement a safeguard on the server side that deals with all write actions. Meteor uses a concept similar to remote procedure calls (RPCs) that can be called from the client and are executed on the client and afterward on the server, too. These are known as *methods*. Not only do they help secure applications but they're also capable of making apps more user friendly using latency compensation.

Storing data inside a database takes a relatively long time, depending on network connections and write speeds. Figure 7.4 illustrates how methods are used to apply

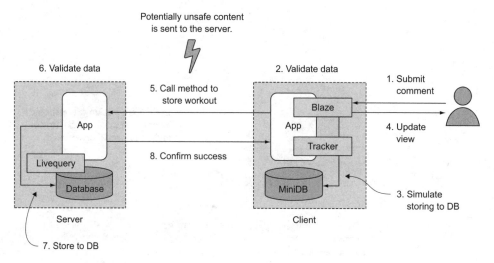

Figure 7.4   User-generated content must always be validated on the server because it may be possible to bypass the code executed on the client.

security and increase the perceived speed of write operations. First, a user submits a new workout. An event handler receives the data and passes it to a client method. This method will perform data validation to check whether the distance entered is valid. If all checks are passed, it simulates storing data to the database by adding it to the local Minimongo instance and updates the screen for the user. This happens in a fraction of a second, because all events take place in the memory of the local computer or mobile device. But now the data is sent to the server, where the same method will be executed. Some server-specific checks might be added as well, such as making sure the user ID is correct. If all validations pass, data is stored in the database and success is confirmed to the client.

Methods can be used not only for database operations but also for anything else that needs to take place on the server, such as sending emails or triggering processes.

In this section you'll replace the default `insecure` package (which lets anybody access every database document) with methods that allow for a fine-grained level of security. Users will be able to add their own workouts to the collection. For this, you'll use a method call to send the write actions instead of direct inserts and updates.

7.2.1   *Removing the insecure package*

Just as the `autopublish` functionality was provided in form of a package, there's a package called `insecure` that allows a client to initiate writes to the server-side database. As the name suggests, it isn't intended for production environments but rather to speed up the development process. To remove the package from your application, stop the Meteor server and issue the following command:

```
$ meteor remove insecure
```

Figure 7.5 When the `insecure` package is removed, access is denied in the browser for any write operation.

Having the ability to update and insert data from the browser console is useful during development, so it's up to you whether you prefer to remove the `insecure` package early on in a project or leverage its power for quicker development. Either way, a production application should never be deployed with `insecure` still active.

Once the `insecure` package is removed and the server is started again, any attempt to update, insert, or remove a document from the client will result in an error message in the console (see figure 7.5).

> **NOTE** Read access to data is defined using publications, so removing the `insecure` package doesn't protect any sensitive data. It simply prohibits the client from writing to the server-side database directly.

7.2.2 *Using methods to write data to collections*

The place to put methods depends on what you want to do. If you put a method inside the server folder you can still call it from the client, but the method is processed only on the server and not on the client. If the method is shared between the server and the client, the process is similar to the `Collection.insert()` functionality. This means a method call is processed on the client immediately. Then if all goes well it's also processed on the server, and if something goes wrong here, the function is reverted on the client. This way, you gain the latency compensation with methods too.

> **TIP** If a method is executed on the client, it's running as a simulation. You can check by using `this.isSimulation()` inside a method context to determine whether the code is used to trigger a remote method or runs as a stub. It returns `true` if the method is running on the client, but simulations can also be used on the server.

You now want users to be able to add workouts themselves by adding a simple form. If the form is submitted, you want to extract the data from the form and use it in a method call. In the method, you want to make sure that the data is allowed and valid and that it comes from a logged-in user—a guest shouldn't be able to add workouts. Finally, you create a new workout in the method.

`Meteor.call()` takes one mandatory argument: the method name. Additionally, you can add as many arguments as you like and they'll be available in the method. The last argument you provide is a callback function to deal with the results returned by the method (see listing 7.11). The callback itself takes two arguments: error and result. The value for error remains undefined as long as the method finishes as expected. result contains the return value of the method—in this case, the document ID for the newly inserted workout.

Listing 7.11 A method call from the client

```
Template.addWorkout.events({
  'submit form': function (evt, tpl) {
    evt.preventDefault();


    var distance = parseInt(tpl.$('input[name="distance"]').val());


    Meteor.call('CreateWorkout', {
      distance: distance
    }, function (error, result) {
      if (error) return alert('Error: ' + error.error);
    });
  }
});
```

Listen to the submit form event as usual.

The default behavior of a form submit should be prevented because it would reload the page.

Use jQuery to extract the data from the distance input field and make it an integer.

The method is called by its name and additional parameters.

The method has a callback that's called if an error happens or a result was returned from the server.

A method always has a name and can have as many parameters as you like. This way, you can use a method to send data from the client to the server. Next, you must define the method; its purpose is to create a workout. Let's put it into a new file in a methods folder. It should be available on the client and the server as well, which allows you to take advantage of latency compensation (see the following listing).

Listing 7.12 Using a method to create a new document

```
Meteor.methods({
  'CreateWorkout': function(data) {
    check(data, {
      distance: Number
    });

    var distance = data.distance;
    if(distance <= 0 || distance > 45){
      throw new Meteor.Error('Invalid distance');
    }

    if(!this.userId){
      throw new Meteor.Error('You have to login');
    }
```

Creating a method follows the scheme of helpers: a method function that takes a key-value object as a parameter.

The key of the object is the name of the method.

Use check to make sure that only data is used in a method that you allow.

Do a vaildation on the distance.

If the validation fails, throw a new Meteor.Error. It's like a normal JavaScript error but is automatically populated to the client.

The userId of the currently logged-in user is accessed via this in a method.

```
    data.workoutAt = new Date();          Add some data to
    data.type = 'jogging';                the document you
    data.userId = this.userId;            want to create.

    return WorkoutsCollection.insert(data);    ◁──  You can be sure now that
  }                                                 the data that goes into
});                                                 the collection is saved.
```

If you look at the method, you'll see that the `data` parameter is what's finally passed to the `WorkoutsCollection.insert` method. Because of this, it's really important to make sure that you know exactly what's inside the data object that's coming from the client. If you didn't make any security checks, a user could add any data inside your `WorkoutsCollection` collection. We'll use the `check()` function again and look at it in a little more detail.

USING AUDIT-ARGUMENT-CHECKS TO VALIDATE ALL USER INPUT

Each argument sent to a method should be checked before processing it. The more form fields are used, the harder it is to keep track of whether every user input has been checked yet. Meteor ships with a package called `audit-argument-checks`, which checks that every argument was indeed checked before it was used. Add it to your project via this command:

```
$ meteor add audit-argument-checks
```

Every time the client sends an argument to the server for processing, `audit-argument-checks` will ensure that it's checked first. You need to add checks to all methods. If there's no check in place, a method will still execute but you'll see an exception on the server, as shown in the following listing.

> **Listing 7.13 Console message for unchecked values in methods**

```
Exception while invoking method 'CreateWorkout' Error: Did not check() all
    arguments during call to 'CreateWorkout'
    at _.extend.throwUnlessAllArgumentsHaveBeenChecked (packages/check/
    match.js:352)
    at Object.Match._failIfArgumentsAreNotAllChecked (packages/check/
    match.js:108)
    at maybeAuditArgumentChecks (packages/ddp/livedata_server.js:1596)
    at packages/ddp/livedata_server.js:648
    at _.extend.withValue (packages/meteor/dynamics_nodejs.js:56)
    at packages/ddp/livedata_server.js:647
    at _.extend.withValue (packages/meteor/dynamics_nodejs.js:56)
    at _.extend.protocol_handlers.method (packages/ddp/
    livedata_server.js:646)
    at packages/ddp/livedata_server.js:546
```

Depending on what you expect arguments to be, you need to use different checks. Although `Match.Any` will accept any value from the client, others are stricter. Table 7.1 lists the available pattern matches for checking variable content.

Table 7.1   Match patterns for checking variable content

Pattern	Matches
`Match.Any`	Matches any value.
`String, Number, Boolean, undefined, null`	Matches a primitive of the given type.
`Match.Integer`	Matches a signed 32-bit integer. Doesn't match Infinity, -Infinity, or NaN.
`[pattern]`	A one-element array matches an array of elements, each of which match pattern. For example, `[Number]` matches a (possibly empty) array of numbers; `[Match.Any]` matches any array.
`{key1: pattern1, key2: pattern2, ...}`	Matches an object with the given keys, with values matching the given patterns. If any pattern is a `Match.Optional`, that key doesn't need to exist in the object. The value may not contain any keys not listed in the pattern. The value must be a plain object with no special prototype.
`Match.ObjectIncluding({key1: pattern1, key2: pattern2, ...})`	Matches an object with the given keys; the value may also have other keys with arbitrary values.
`Object`	Matches any plain object with any keys; equivalent to `Match.ObjectIncluding({})`.
`Match.Optional(pattern)`	Matches either `undefined` or something that matches `pattern`. If used in an object this matches only if the key isn't set as opposed to the value being set to `undefined`.
Any constructor function (e.g., `Date`)	Matches any element that's an instance of that type.
`Match.Where(condition)`	Calls the function `condition` with the value as the argument. If `condition` returns `true`, this matches. If `condition` throws a `Match.Error` or returns `false`, this fails. If `condition` throws any other error, that error is thrown from the call to check.

7.3   Summary

In this chapter, you've learned that

- Pub/sub is Meteor's way to get data from the server to a client.
- To secure applications, `autopublish` and `insecure` must be removed; publications and methods should take their place.

- Publications may return data from a database or publish customized data.
- Publications can securely limit the published data by document fields such as a user/owner ID.
- Subscriptions can either be made globally for the entire application or scoped to individual templates.
- Writing to the database via server-side methods is secure and more flexible than using allow/deny patterns.
- The `audit-argument-checks` package helps to ensure all data provided by a client is validated before it's used.

Routing using Iron.Router

This chapter covers

- Adding routing capabilities to Meteor applications
- Creating layouts
- Improving code structure using `Iron.Router`
- Extending `Iron.Router` with controllers, hooks, and plug-ins
- Creating server-side routes and APIs

As your application grows in size and complexity, you'll have to deal with lots of subscriptions, publications, collections, and templates. You need a way to organize all these things as well as specify what to render and what data context should be available in the rendered templates.

One good approach to handling this complexity is to use *routes*. This means you decide what to subscribe to and what to render and you specify the data context, depending on unique URLs. The router handles all those tasks. The most commonly used package with Meteor is `Iron.Router`.

`Iron.Router` is a community package maintained by Chris Mather and Tom Coleman. Tom wrote one of the first routers for Meteor, called `meteor-router`, and

Chris also started a routing project called `meteor-mini-pages`. Luckily for the Meteor community, they combined their efforts and developed a single router, which eventually became the `Iron.Router` package.

The Meteor Development Group (MDG) had a router on its own roadmap once but decided that it wasn't necessary for them to build one, even though routing is a crucial aspect of every web framework. The reason was that the community efforts in building a router were so good that a router developed by MDG wasn't needed.

8.1   Routing in web applications

If you click a link on a normal website, the URL changes in the browser. The browser then requests the resource from the server that belongs to the new URL. The first thing the web server does after it receives a request with a given route is go through a dictionary of all the routes it knows. If the route of the request matches a known route in the dictionary, the defined action is performed. At the end of each action, the response is created and sent back to the browser, which renders the HTML it received for the new route. The router typically handles all of this functionality (figure 8.1).

Let's say you're on a community website and see a list of profiles. One of them is from Manuel. If you click the *Manuel* link, the URL of the browser changes and a request is sent to the server. The server performs the actions defined for the route to generate the HTML needed for Manuel's profile. At the end, the response is sent back.

With Meteor, you create client-side web applications. This means if you click a link, there's no request back to the server for a different HTML document. In a web application, if you click a link the view is changed directly in the browser, without the need for a new HTTP request to the server. This means that technically you don't need any

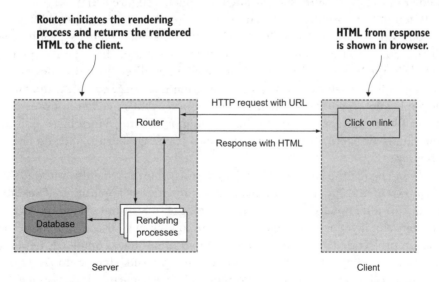

Figure 8.1   The client's HTTP request is handled by a server-side router that responds with HTML.

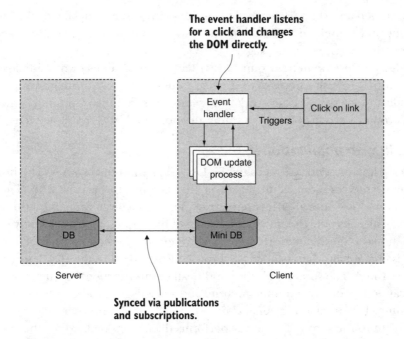

Figure 8.2   A client-side web application can handle the DOM manipulation in an event handler.

routes because you can link the functions that change the DOM directly on the event handler of a click event on specific anchor elements (figure 8.2).

When links to profiles are listed on a website, the process is quite different from the one on a static website. If you click the link for Manuel's profile, the URL doesn't change at all, but instead the event is handled by a JavaScript function directly in the browser. The DOM could be changed directly on the click and show a loading indicator—for example, a simple string like Loading.... At the same time, the application fetches some data from the server that's needed in order to render the profile. In Meteor, you do this by updating or creating a new subscription. If the new data is available on the client, the DOM is changed again and the new profile is rendered.

If you change the current HTML based on click events like this without changing the browser's URL, it affects the maintainability of your application. The URL combined with a dictionary of routes that your application understands is a very good starting point if you want to figure out where to look in your code. Suppose you want to join a project that's creating a complex application that's completely new to you. If you click a profile of the community website and the URL changes to */profiles/manuel*, you can start looking at the defined routes and see what action is performed. You can use the URL as a first hint where to look for relevant code, which is very important.

The main reason why you should always use URLs even for a client-side application is the architecture of the web itself. Its URLs define every resource you can reach in the web. URLs enable you to share content with your friends. If your community application will consist of only one URL, you can never share an interesting profile with anyone. But if you perform actions like filtering or sorting of tables, it would be good to reflect this in the URL as well. Consider a special and very important filter and sorting combination of a large data set that you need to access very often. If you can access this exact data set with a URL, you can easily bookmark it and reach it much faster than you would if you had to set up the configuration every time you wanted to access it.

URLs are important not only for humans browsing through the web but for applications as well. If a search engine crawls a website, it always tries to understand the content of the given document that relates to a specific URL. If a user then types search phrases into the search bar, the search engine will try to present the best matching URL as a response. If your application has only one URL for all the content it contains, a search engine can't properly redirect visitors to the exact view that would be relevant to the search phrase of the user.

Because routes are so important for Meteor applications, `Iron.Router` implements a router. The router is available on both the client and the server sides. On the client side, the router helps you set up new subscriptions but also end old ones based on a given URL. In addition, it takes care of rendering the specified template based on the current URL (figure 8.3). As you'll see in this chapter, `Iron.Router` has even more capabilities.

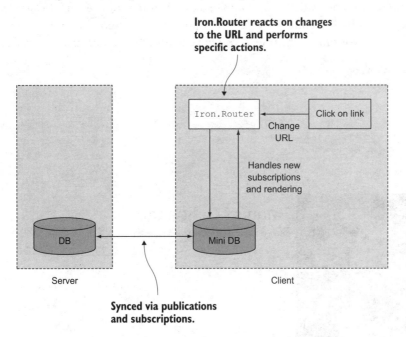

Figure 8.3 `Iron.Router` **listens for URL changes and performs actions defined for a route.**

You can also use `Iron.Router` to react as a normal server-side router. This means you can create REST interfaces with a Meteor application. The main use case of `Iron.Router` is client-side routing, and this is what we'll focus on in this chapter. But we'll take a look at server-side routing at the end of this chapter, too.

8.2   Client-side routing

In this section we'll show you how to use `Iron.Router` to implement client-side routing. The router component will run exclusively on the client and let you navigate around without having to contact the server.

You'll be building a community application where you can see users' profiles and comment on their profile pages. An important aspect of an application like this (and for nearly any web application) is to have URLs that are sharable. Think of your profile page on our new community website. Without your unique URL, you couldn't share it with anyone or even access it yourself.

At the end of this chapter you'll have built an application that can contain an unlimited number of profile pages, each with a unique and sharable URL. Each profile will have a dedicated URL that shows the contents, as shown in figure 8.4. Our application will have multiple routes not only for static pages but also for dynamic pages that require data in order to render the templates.

8.2.1   Adding Iron.Router

Meteor doesn't come with a router as a core feature, but as mentioned earlier, `Iron.Router` is a high-quality package developed by the Meteor community that's well maintained. For your Meteor project, you have to add `Iron.Router` as a package first:

```
$ meteor add iron:router
```

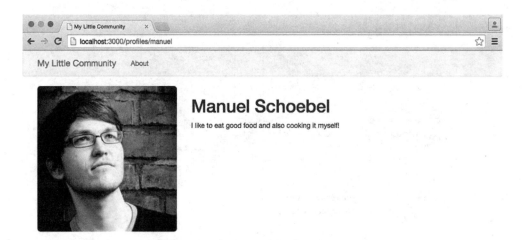

Figure 8.4   A simple profile page of a single-page community application

Once you've added Iron.Router you get access to the Router object in your application in both the client and server environments. Therefore, you can use it to perform server-side routing as well. We'll get back to using Router on the server in a bit.

Create a router folder just at the root of your application folder. Inside this folder you'll put all router-related files, beginning with the routes.js file that contains all route definitions (figure 8.5).

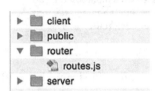

Figure 8.5 Iron.Router works on both the client and the server, so putting a routes.js file somewhere outside the client or server folder makes it accessible in all environments.

You'll use the routes.js file to define all the routes the application should contain. It's a good practice to have every route of your application in a single file to allow for a quicker overview.

8.2.2 Creating your first routes

Our next goal is to set up two basic routes. One is the standard *home* route, which should be rendered at the root of your application. This route relates to the path /. The second route is a simple *about* page that should be rendered when users access the /about URL (see figure 8.6).

> **NOTE** To reduce the complexity of the code we won't show any of the bootstrap markup. The code download for this chapter contains all the relevant bootstrap code in order to achieve a more polished look. To add the Bootstrap CSS-Framework, you have to add the twbs:bootstrap package.

The file structure you'll use for the first step is shown in figure 8.7.

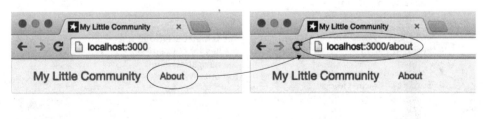

Figure 8.6 Clicking the About link in the top navigation changes the URL to /about.

Figure 8.7 To create two simple routes, you must define the routes and the templates that should be rendered for each route.

The home.html file (see listing 8.1) contains the template that should be rendered if a user is on the root path, /. Navigating to the /about page should bring up a static site with further information about the application. For this you'll use an about template that's stored in the static folder. The index.html file contains some general templates as well as the <head> element for the application.

Listing 8.1 Initial templates for the community application

```
// index.html
<head>
  <title>My Little Community</title>
</head>

<template name="header">
  <nav>
    <ul>
      <li><a href="/">My Little Community</a>
      </li>
      <li><a href="/about">About</a>
      </li>
    </ul>
  </nav>
</template>

// home.html
<template name="home">
  {{> header}}

  <h1>Home</h1>
</template>

// about.html
<template name="about">
  {{> header}}

  <h1>About</h1>
</template>
```

The header template contains the navigation so it can be included in other templates.

The templates include the header template so the navigation is on top of every view.

There's nothing too fancy about the templates yet. The navigation inside the header template contains two anchor elements. One links to the root path <a href="/">My Little Community</a> and the other links to the about page <a href="/about">About</a>.

Next you want to add those routes to the `Iron.Router` and render the appropriate template using the code from the following listing.

Listing 8.2 Setting up different routes

The specified template is rendered.

```
// routes.js
Router.route('/', function(){
  this.render('home');
});

Router.route('/about', function(){
  this.render('about');
});
```

Defines a path and associates it with a function to call if the URL matches this path

The `Router` object has a `route` function that takes two parameters—the path and the associated function. The function is called if the URL changes and the path matches the specified one. Inside the scope of the function that's called, you have access to the current instance of the so-called `RouteController` object via `this`. With the help of the `RouteController` you can, for example, render a template to a specific location into the DOM. In this case, because you have nothing else defined, the template specified with the string parameter of the `this.render('templateName')` function will be rendered simply inside the `<body>` element.

8.2.3 *Defining a layout depending on a route*

For the entire application you want to maintain a consistent layout—for example, by keeping the main navigation on top. Therefore, you can set a default layout for all routes. Alternatively, some routes may require different layouts. The front page shows multiple images side by side whereas a profile page uses a single, bigger profile image instead.

SINGLE LAYOUT

In our previous example, we included the navigation at the top of the application in every rendered template (see figure 8.8).

A more effective way to reuse the header template is to use a layout template for each route and alter only a part of the layout based on the current route. This is especially useful if layouts grow more complex or multiple layouts must be used within a single application.

As you can see in figure 8.9, for both routes the `masterLayout` template should be rendered so that it always has the `header` template on top. The dynamic part is changed depending on the current route. If the current path is /, the dynamic part of the layout should be replaced with the template called `home`, and if the path changes to /about, the dynamic part of the layout has to be exchanged with the template called `about`.

In the layout template you use the `{{> yield}}` template helper that's defined by the `Iron.Router` package. With `{{> yield}}`, you can specify exactly where the

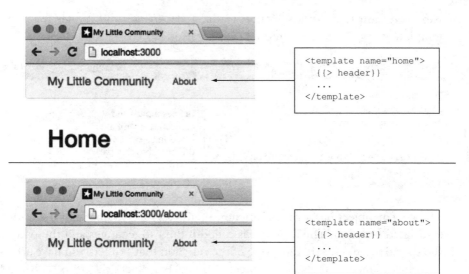

Figure 8.8   Reusing templates for each route without using a layout

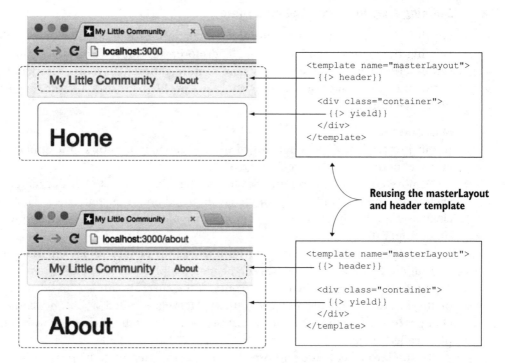

Reusing the masterLayout and header template

Figure 8.9   `{{> yield}}` is a dynamic area that's replaced with the template that should be rendered for the current route.

template for the route should be rendered; it's a placeholder for content. This is what's called a *region*.

Remember to consolidate the code from your view templates to the masterLayout template, as shown in the following listing.

```
// masterLayout.html
<template name="masterLayout">
  {{> header}}

  <div class="container">
    {{> yield}}
  </div>
</template>

// home.html
<template name="home">
  <h1>Home</h1>
</template>
```

To specify which layout should be used for each route, you must set it inside the Router object via the configure() function. To keep the configuration separate from route definitions, put the following content inside a new file router/config.js:

```
Router.configure({
  layoutTemplate: 'masterLayout'
});
```

USING MULTIPLE LAYOUTS

Instead of a single layout template for all routes, you need two layouts to differentiate the profile page from the front page. First let's look at the old masterLayout and the new profileLayout (figure 8.10).

As you can see, the profile layout has two columns. The column on the left renders the profile picture and the right column contains profile information. You still have one main content region that's specified with the {{> yield}} template helper. The second region on the left needs a name so it can be referenced later in the route function. For that, you can use a named yield like this: {{> yield "name"}}.

In the route function you can specify which layout should be used. If you don't specify a layout, the one set by the configure function is used. If it hasn't been configured, the template is directly rendered into the <body> (see the following listing).

```
Router.route('/profiles/manuel', function () {      Sets a layout
  this.layout('profileLayout');
  this.render('profileDetail');                     The layout template is used to render
});                                                 the specified profileDetail template.
```

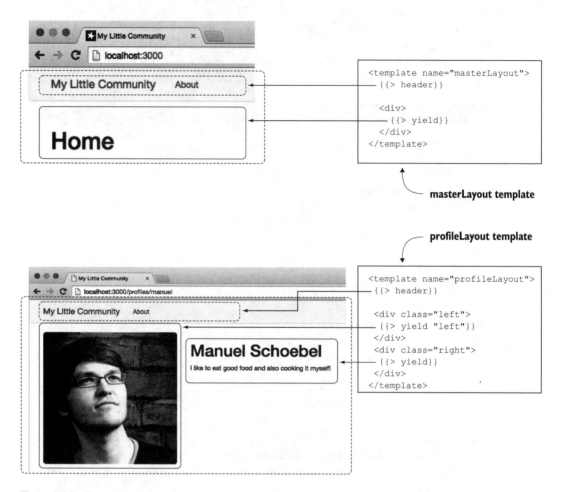

Figure 8.10   The second layout for the profile pages should be used on routes for profiles.

DEFINING THE CONTENT TEMPLATE FOR NAMED REGIONS

If you have named regions like the previous example—{{> yield "left"}}—you want to define which template should be rendered there. You can do so in one of several ways.

The easiest approach is inside the template itself. Iron.Router uses a template helper named contentFor that lets you define content for specific regions (see listing 8.5). Anything outside this block is rendered to the main region.

> **Listing 8.5   Rendering a template inside a named yield with template helpers**

```
// profileDetail.html
<template name="profileDetail">
  {{#contentFor 'left'}}          ◁——  The block contents are
    <img src="...">                     rendered to the region
  {{/contentFor}}                       called left.
```

```
                                                                    | This is rendered
   <h1>Manuel Schoebel</h1>                                         | into the main yield.
   <p>I like to eat good food and also cooking it myself!</p>
</template>
```

You can also use `contentFor` as a partial and specify which template to render:

```
{{> contentFor region='left' template="profileImage"}}
```

The most flexible way to define contents for a region is inside the route definition. The `render()` function has a to option that can be used to specify the region in which you want to render templates and data (see the following listing).

Listing 8.6 Rendering a template inside a named yield using JavaScript

```
// profileDetail.html                                      Setting the template
<template name="profileDetail">                            and region using a
  {{> contentFor region='left' template="profileImage"}}  ◁── template helper

  <h1>Manuel Schoebel</h1>                                 | This is rendered
  <p>I like to eat good food and also cooking it myself!</p>| into the main yield.
</template>

<template name="profileImage">                         ◁─┐
  <img src="...">                                          │
</template>                                                 │  The option "to"
                                                            │  specifies where to
// routes.js                                                │  render a given
Router.route('/profiles/manuel', function () {             │  template.
  this.layout('profileLayout');                            │
  this.render('profileImage', {to: 'left'});            ◁──┘
  this.render('profileDetail');
});
```

You defined the route for a specific profile in a static way because you used the route `/profiles/manuel`. Of course, you want to have only one route for profile detail pages, as you'll see next.

8.2.4 Setting the data context depending on a route

On the home route of our application, you want to have multiple profiles with links to their details page. The profile detail page should have a template that renders the data of the individual profile that's specified through the URL. That means the route `/profiles/stephan` should render the profile detail template with Stephan's profile data. The route `/profiles/manuel` should render the profile detail template as well, only with Manuel's profile data (figure 8.11).

Figure 8.11 shows the core functionality you'll implement in this chapter. You'll need a list of profiles on the home route, a *more...* link that redirects to the profile URL, and a dynamic route that displays detailed profiles.

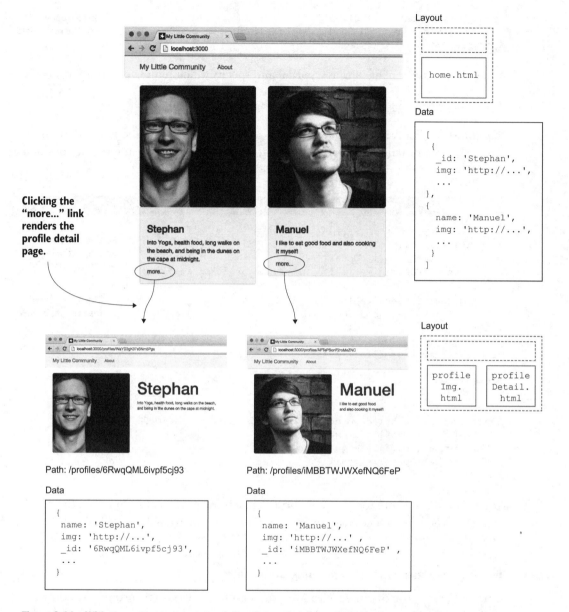

Figure 8.11   With `Iron.Router` you can define the rendered template, the layout, and the data context.

The data context of the home route has to be a set of profiles that should be rendered. On the profile's detail page you only require a single user's data as the context for the `profileDetail` template. Because the URL defines the data context, you'll use `Iron.Router` to set it.

To make things easier, let's assume that the `autopublish` package is still active so that all profile data is available on the client. You also need all profile data to be available inside `ProfilesCollection`. Refer back to chapter 7 to learn how to set up publications and subscriptions that limit the data on the client.

The relevant logic is located in the routes.js file (see listing 8.7). You now have three routes: home or `/`, `/about`, and a dynamic `/profiles` route that accepts a user ID as a URL parameter to determine which profile to display. The `/about` route stays the same, but the other two require updating.

The home route now sets the data context of the home template. It returns an object that contains all profiles available on the client and makes them accessible via `profiles`. This makes it possible to access all profiles inside `{{#each profiles}}...{{/each}}` within the home template. There's no need to define a template helper that returns data; `Iron.Router` can take care of it entirely.

Listing 8.7 Setting the data context with `Iron.Router`

```
// routes.js
Router.route('/', function(){                    Profiles are accessible
  this.render('home', {                          via {{profiles}} in the
    data: function(){                             home template.
      return {profiles: ProfilesCollection.find()};
    }
  });
});

Router.route('/about', function(){               Set the data
  this.render('about');                          context of
});                                              the rendered
                                                 template.
Router.route('/profiles/:_id', function(){
  profile = ProfilesCollection.findOne({_id: this.params._id});
  this.layout('profileLayout');
  this.render('profileDetailLeft', {
    to: 'left',
    data: function(){
      return profile;
    }
  });
  this.render('profileDetail', {
    data: function(){
      return profile;
    }
  });
});
```

Colons indicate path variables.

Access path variables via this.params.key.

Set the data context of the rendered template.

Data is directly accessible, for example, via {{name}} in the profile templates.

In case of the profile's detail page, you expect the path to be /profiles/:_id. The leading : (colon) signifies that `_id` is a variable, which is read from the URL. Its content is accessible through the `params` attribute of the current route controller instance. You access the current value from the URL with `this.params._id`. This way, you can identify which document to retrieve from the database. Let's take a closer look at the data option.

8.2.5   Data subscriptions with Iron.Router

You've seen that multiple aspects depend on the current route: the layout that should be used, the templates that should be rendered, and the data that you want to look at. Typically the autopublish package won't be available within a package, so you must be able to dynamically subscribe to data depending on the current route.

On the home path of the social community, say you'd like to show some random profiles, limited to a maximum of 10. This involves subscribing to the data. But instead of being subscribed to this data all the time, you want to be subscribed to it only for the home route. If you navigate to a profile's detail page, you don't need to have all the data of the 10 profiles available anymore.

At first you'll remove the autopublish package from the application. On the server you'll create a publication that includes a slight delay to simulate network latency. The following listing shows the publication code for the server.

Listing 8.8   Publishing the profiles collection with a one-second delay

```
// publications.js
Meteor.publish('profiles', function () {
  profiles = Meteor.wrapAsync(function (cb) {      ← This code simulates
    Meteor.setTimeout(function () {                  waiting time.
      cb(null, ProfilesCollection.find({}, {       ← Here the actual query to the
        limit: 10                                      MongoDB happens and the result
      }));           ←  Limit the publication         is stored in the profiles variable.
    }, 1000);           to 10 profiles.
  })();

  return profiles;     ← The collection cursor from the
});                       MongoDB query is returned from
                          the publication.
```

Next you need the client to subscribe to this publication. Let's start with the home route. Instead of using a simple this.render() call, you'll pass an object as the second route argument. The result will be the same, but the syntax is different (see following listing).

Listing 8.9   Defining a route's behavior by options only

```
Router.route('/', {                 The template option specifies
  template: 'home',       ←         which template to render.
  data: function() {                                          Data context is set
    return {                                       ←          using the data option.
      profiles: ProfilesCollection.find({}, {limit: 10});   ←  Return 10 profiles
    }                                                           from the
  }                                                            ProfilesCollection.
});
```

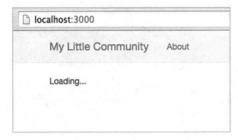

Figure 8.12 Iron.Router automatically renders a loading indicator when using `waitOn`.

As you can see, by using options instead of a `route` function you save some lines of code and it works perfectly fine for this simple use case.

While you wait for data you want the application to render a loading indicator. `Iron.Router` comes with a `waitOn` option that you can use to define all required subscriptions (listing 8.10). A loading template is automatically shown when you use the `waitOn` option. It's possible to change the default loading template via the `loadingTemplate` option. You can do so either in the route's options or globally for the entire application in the global router configuration.

Listing 8.10 Subscribing based on a route

```
Router.route('/', {
  waitOn: function () {
    return Meteor.subscribe('profiles');        ◁──  If waiting for multiple
  },                                                  subscriptions, you can
  template: 'home',                                   also use an array.
  data: function () {
    return {
      profiles: ProfilesCollection.find({}, {
        limit: 10
      })
    };
  }
});
```

When the `home` route is requested, you'll see a loading indicator, as shown in figure 8.12. Once the subscription is ready, the `home` template will be rendered with the correct data.

The same technique is used to display individual profiles. To tell the application which profile to display you must also include the requested profile ID. As mentioned earlier, you can pass it to the subscription using `this.params._id`. Without using the `render()` function, the route looks like the following listing.

Listing 8.11 Waiting on individual profile subscriptions

```
Router.route('/profiles/:_id', {
  layoutTemplate: 'profileLayout',
  waitOn: function() {
    return Meteor.subscribe('profile', this.params._id);
  },
```

```
  template: 'profileDetail',
  yieldTemplates: {
    'profileDetailLeft': {
      to: 'left'
    }
  },
  data: function() {
    return ProfilesCollection.findOne({
      _id: this.params._id
    });
  }
});
```

These are the fundamental building blocks you need to create single-page applications. Iron.Router not only helps you organize your code but also lets you accurately define which templates should be rendered, which subscriptions are required, and what data should be available in the templates' data context.

Ready to step it up a bit? Let's look at some more advanced use cases.

8.3 Advanced routing methods

For the rest of this chapter, we'll look at advanced techniques that are useful and commonly used in applications. They're related to

- *Maintainability*—Using named routes for easier reference and organizing code in controllers and plug-ins
- *Appearance*—Highlighting active links with different classes
- *Performance*—Loading external libraries for specific routes only
- *Functionality*—Using hooks to add view counters and prevent anonymous users from accessing routes

8.3.1 Using named routes and link helpers

It's good practice not to hard-code any links in an application, such as the href attribute of an anchor element. If a route changes, you'd have to edit all hard-coded occurrences manually, so it's much better to rely on route names and use a helper to generate the link path. As with templates you can give a name to a route and use it to reference the router. The name of a route is one of its options in the route definition. To link to a named route, you'll use the pathFor template helper.

Listing 8.12 shows how to link to named routes. A profile page requires a profile's ID to properly display its contents. In that case the route named profile must fill a variable called _id and the {{pathFor}} template helper must have access to it. It's possible to set the data context through Iron.Router or use the {{#with}} block helper to pass a value for _id. Listing 8.12 uses Iron.Router to set the context.

Listing 8.12   Using named routes

```
// routes.js
Router.route('/', { name: 'home' });
Router.route('/about', 'about', { name: 'about' });
Router.route('/profiles/:_id', { name: 'profile.details' });

// index.html
<template name="header">
  <nav>
  ...
    <ul>
      <li><a href="{{pathFor 'home'}}">My Little Community</a></li>
      <li><a href="{{pathFor 'about'}}">About</a></li>
    </ul>
  </nav>
</template>

// profilePreview.html
<template name="profilePreview">
  <img src="{{profileImg}}">
  <div>
    <h3>{{name}}</h3>
    <p>{{profileText}}</p>
    <a href="{{pathFor 'profile.details'}}">more...</a>
  </div>
</template>
```

Links to /

Links to /about

The profile route requires :_id and inherits the data context of the profilePreview template.

When {{pathFor}} is used, it returns a relative URL, making it work equally well in different deployment environments. If you need an absolute URL, you should use {{urlFor}} instead. A third option is {{#linkTo}}, which you've used earlier in this chapter as well. It renders the anchor element and allows for content to be included between its tags—for example, when providing a link text (see following listing).

Listing 8.13   Using the `linkTo` block helper to render anchor elements

```
{{#linkTo route='about'}}About{{/linkTo}}

// renders to
<a href=""/about">About</a>

{{#linkTo route='home' class='navbar-brand'}}
   My Little Community
{{/linkTo}}

// renders to
<a class="navbar-brand" href="/">
   My Little Community
</a>
```

Any attribute you add to a {{#linkTo}} block helper will be rendered to the anchor element, too. That way, you can add attributes such as class, data-*, or id.

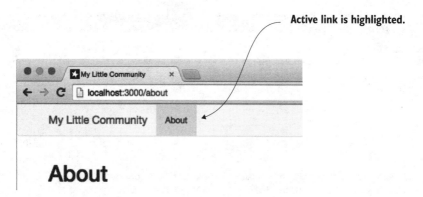

Active link is highlighted.

Figure 8.13   An active navigation item has a CSS class active and a highlighted UI.

8.3.2   *Working with active routes for better navigation links*

To let users know which part of an application they're currently dealing with, you should highlight the link associated with the current route. This way, users can directly see where they are on the application (figure 8.13).

For this functionality, you need a global template helper that can be used in any template and for any navigational link. The purpose of the global helper is to check whether or not the currently active route matches the route of the link. To be able to tell which route is currently active, you'll take advantage of Iron.Router's named routes feature:

```
Router.route("/about", {name: "about"});
```

Every route can have an optional name, which makes it easier to reference it. Listing 8.14 defines a template helper that determines the name for the current route and returns it to the template. In the HTML file it's then possible to implement a simple check and set the CSS class for the li element to active for the current route.

Listing 8.14   A global template helper that highlights an active link

```
// helpers.js
Template.registerHelper("isActiveRoute", function(routeName) {
  if (Router.current().route.getName() === routeName) {
    return 'active';
  }
});
```
Returns active if the name of the currently active route equals routeName

```
// index.html
<nav>
  <ul>
    <li class="{{isActiveRoute 'about'}}">
      {{#linkTo route="about"}}About{{/linkTo}}
    </li>
  </ul>
</nav>
```
The template helper takes a string of the route name to check as a parameter.

The linkTo helper creates the actual link tag for the about route.

You can use this template helper on every navigational link where you want to set the `active` class depending on the current route name. You can also use this helper for anything else that needs to check the name of the currently active route.

8.3.3 *Waiting for external libraries to load*

Meteor loads every JavaScript to the client with the initial page request. If your application contains a lot of external JavaScript libraries, it's a good idea to not put everything into the main application folder because doing so will increase the amount of data to be transferred when first accessing the page. The resulting load time will be longer than for a statically rendered page. If you use external libraries that aren't required by the initial page, it's better to split them from the initial loading request.

Iron.Router makes it possible to load an external library based on a route. When adding a map or date picker, the library must be loaded before rendering, which can also be achieved with `Router`.

A package called `wait-on-lib` provides the necessary functionality:

```
$ meteor add manuelschoebel:wait-on-lib
```

This package enables you to use an object called `IRLibloader`, which can be used in a `waitOn` function named `Iron.Router` just like you do with a `Meteor.subscription`. Let's say you want to load the jquery.fittext.js library only for the /profiles/:_id URL. Once loaded, it'll make text sizes flexible. The library itself is located in the public folder as public/jquery.fittext.js.[1]

With the `wait-on-lib` package, the `waitOn` function is used as shown in listing 8.15. You define a full URL or a filename; `wait-on-lib` will look for the file inside the public folder.

Listing 8.15   Waiting for external libraries to load

```
// router.js
Router.route('/profiles/:_id', {
  // ...
  waitOn: function() {
    return [
      Meteor.subscribe('profile', this.params._id),    ◁  You can subscribe to
                                                           publications as you
                                                           would normally do.
      IRLibLoader.load("/jquery.fittext.js")   ◁  IRLibLoader behaves like a
    ];                                            subscription and includes
  },                                              a loading indicator.
  //...
});
```

---

[1] Everything inside the public folder is served as is. This means even if a JavaScript file is located in public, it won't be minified by Meteor, even when running with the `--production` flag.

Even though Meteor is loaded as one complete application, it's still possible to load libraries you don't need for every visit of the application separately in order to reduce the data that has to be transferred on an initial page load.

8.3.4   *Organizing routes as controllers*

Until now you've added all of a route's functionality directly in the `route()` method. If you did this in a large application, the routes.js file would quickly become too large to comfortably manage, and you'd lose the ability to get a quick overview of an application's route at a glance. As a means to better organize your code, `Iron.Router` introduces the concept of controllers (see the accompanying sidebar).

Introducing routing controllers

Many web frameworks build on the MVC principle, which consists of *models*, *views*, and controllers. Therefore the term *controller* comes with a lot of associations. Meteor doesn't rely on the MVC pattern, which means that some of these assumptions may not be accurate. So what is a controller in the `Iron.Router` context?

A routing controller is the blueprint for commonly shared routing instructions. Each route can build on these default settings and extend them as required. Technically the routing controller is an object that stores state information when changing URLs. Controllers offer two main benefits when applications grow larger:

- Inheritance—Routing controllers may build on each other to model an application's behavior, enforcing the *Don't repeat yourself* principle (DRY).
- Organization—Separating route logic into different files helps maintain a better overview of the actual routing and business logic.

By default, all of the routing functions like `route()` and `render()` rely on the default `RouteController` object.

You can specify a controller for each route and put it into its own file. That way, you can remove all logic from the routes.js file and split it across multiple files, similar to how you deal with templates.

Let's say that you want to use a controller for the home route. It should wait for a subscription to the `profiles` collection and set the data context so that all available profiles are shown inside the `home` template.

To specify a controller for this route, you can set it explicitly as a string or a controller object. The controller itself typically has the same name as the route, suffixed by the word `Controller`. To organize your code, place each controller in a dedicated file. For the `HomeController` you need to define the `waitOn`, `template`, and `data` attributes as shown in listing 8.16.

Listing 8.16 Using an `Iron.Router` controller

```
// routes.js
Router.route('/', { controller: 'HomeController' });

// homeController.js
HomeController = RouteController.extend({
  waitOn: function () {
    return Meteor.subscribe('profiles');
  },
  template: 'home',
  data: function () {
    return {
      profiles: ProfilesCollection.find({}, {
        limit: 10
      })
    };
  }
});
```

> Using controllers makes the routes.js file much more readable.

> Every controller extends the default RouteController object.

`RouteController` can have the same attributes as `route()`. This means you can also create your own custom `action` function or specify a `layoutTemplate`. Splitting your routes into separate controllers leaves a clean and short routes.js file (see following listing).

Listing 8.17 Routes declaration using controllers

```
Router.route('/', { controller: 'HomeController' });
Router.route('/about', 'about');
Router.route('/profiles/:_id', { controller: 'ProfileController' });
```

> Basic routes don't need controllers.

If you're using named routes, you don't even have to specify a controller anymore. If you have a route named `home`, then `Iron.Router` automatically looks for a controller called `homeController` or `HomeController`: The following works just like the code in listing 8.17:

```
Router.route('/', { name: 'home' });
Router.route('/about', { name: 'about' });
Router.route('/profiles/:_id', { name: 'profile.details',
                         controller: 'ProfileController'});
```

> If needed you can pass both a name and a controller ID to the route.

8.3.5 *Extending the route process using hooks*

A hook is basically a function that can be added to the routing process. One of the most common requirements for using route hooks is to prevent anonymous users from accessing internal routes. Another use case is tracking some statistics or count views, like the number of times a certain profile has been viewed. To track each view, you can use an `onRun` hook. This hook runs exactly once regardless of whether a computation invalidates and a rerun takes place. Therefore, `onRun` is the perfect hook to use to increase the view count.

Iron.Router hooks

For every hook you can create one function or an array of multiple functions that will all be called.

onRun—Called when the route runs for the first time. It runs only once!

onRerun—Called every time a computation is invalidated.

onBeforeAction—Called before an action or route function runs. If there are multiple functions, you have to make sure that next is called because this doesn't happen automatically with onBeforeActions. If you want the next onBeforeAction to be called, you have to call this.next.

onAfterAction—Called after the action or route function runs.

onStop—If a route stops—for example, a new route is run—this hook is called.

In listing 8.18, you add an onRun hook to the ProfileController. Now whenever the route is accessed, an update to the ProfilesCollection is made, increasing the views field by 1 for the current profile _id.

> **Listing 8.18   Adding a hook to a `RouteController`**

```
// ProfileController.js
ProfileController = RouteController.extend({
  layoutTemplate: 'profileLayout',
  template: 'profileDetail',
  yieldTemplates: {
    'profileDetailLeft': {to: 'left'}
  },
  onRun: function() {                        On every run of this
    ProfilesCollection.update({              route, the views attribute
      _id: this.params._id                   is increased by 1.
    }, {
      $inc: {
        views: 1
      }
    });               Use next() to
    this.next();      continue routing.
  },
...
});
```

Now every view of a profile is counted, and you can add it within the data context of a profile via {{views}}.

In our community application, there are several routes only members should be able to access. This can be implemented with the onBeforeHook just as easily. See listing 8.19 for the code. Within the onBeforeAction hook, you perform a check for the current user ID. If there's no user ID available, you redirect the request to show a membersOnly template. In combination with a data publication that checks for a user ID, this will be enough to prevent users from seeing content they aren't authorized for.

Listing 8.19 Requiring a logged-in user for a specific route

```
// profileController.js
ProfileController = RouteController.extend({
  // ...
  onBeforeAction: function() {
    if (!Meteor.userId()) {
      this.render('membersonly');
    } else {
      this.next();
    }
  },
//...
});
```

You can make these hooks reusable by putting them into controllers or wrapping them into plug-ins.

8.3.6 Creating an Iron.Router plug-in

If you create hooks that you want to use for multiple applications or share with the community, creating Iron.Router plug-ins is the way to go. These plug-ins enable portable functionality that's easy to share and use in applications or packages. Let's turn the hook that requires users to be logged in into a plug-in.

Each Iron.Router plug-in can be added as part of the configuration. You can include it for all or just for specific routes. Because you already have an onBefore-Action hook in the /profiles route, you can remove the code from here and place it inside a new router/plugins/membersOnly.js file. Creating a plug-in is similar to the way you define template helpers. Plug-ins take two parameters: router and options. Instead of simply reading the parameters passed to a plug-in, use a lookupOption function to access all configuration options available to Iron.Router. You could use the function to access layoutTemplate the same way you use it here to access the setting for membersOnlyTpl. As you can see in listing 8.20, most of the code for a plug-in is fairly similar to an actual route.

To use a plug-in, you don't call it from a specific route or controller but instead set it in the router configuration file router/config.js (see listing 8.20). A plug-in is loaded via Router.plugin('name', options). The options object contains two settings: membersOnlyTpl defines which template to render when an anonymous user tries to access a route that requires a user ID, and only contains an array of the routes affected. You have a single route, /profile, that should be protected. If most of your routes require a plug-in, then you can use except rather than only to define all routes that don't require a logged-in user.

Listing 8.20   Creating a reusable `Iron.Router` plug-in

**The plug-in is named
membersOnly.**

**It runs as an
onBeforeAction
hook.**

```
// membersOnly.js
Iron.Router.plugins.membersOnly = function(router, options) {
  router.onBeforeAction(function() {
    if (!Meteor.userId()) {
      this.render(this.lookupOption('membersOnlyTpl'));
    } else {
      this.next();
    }
  }, options);
}
```

**Continue if there
is a user ID.**

**this.lookupOption may also
access options set in the
global Router.configure()
settings.**

**Template that should
be rendered in case the
user isn't logged in**

```
// config.js
Router.plugin('membersOnly', {
  membersOnlyTpl: 'membersonly',
  only: ['profile.details']
});
```

**The plug-in is applied only
to the profile.details route.**

Keep in mind that this plug-in checks for a user ID only on the client side. Any malicious user can fake a user ID, so it isn't sufficient to rely on routing functionality as the only security measure. A combination of a router with a publication that checks for a user ID on the server side should be used to secure your application for production. Even if users could get to the layout and templates of a single profile, they still couldn't access any data if it's not published to the client in the first place.

8.4   *Server-side routing with a REST API*

If you need an API for non-Meteor clients, you can't take advantage of DDP, so you may need a traditional HTTP interface. For an automated process, you might want to allow scripts to look up usernames based on their ID. Then all routing takes place on the server because you're dealing with a dumb client that knows only a single URL. There's no point in first sending all JavaScript over the wire if all the client needs is a single name string.

Implementing server-side routing requires passing the `where` option to the `route()` function. You use this option to limit the route to the server only. Providing an HTTP interface effectively bypasses most of Meteor's functionality, so you'll rely on the basic Node.js functionality with both `request` and `response` objects (see listing 8.21). Instead of defining all headers and using `response.write()`, you shorten the code to use only `response.end()`. In the `response.end()` function, you perform a database lookup with the given ID and return the `name` attribute (figure 8.14).

Figure 8.14 When provided with a valid ID, the API responds with the name of a member.

Listing 8.21 Simple server-side route

```
Router.route('/api/profiles/name/:_id', function() {        Node.js request object
  var request = this.request;
  var response = this.response;                       Node.js response object

  response.end(ProfilesCollection.findOne({
    _id: this.params._id                              This route should run
  }).name);                                           only on the server and
}, {                                                  not on the client.
  where: 'server'
})
```

If you make a request with a query string and message as the key, the server will respond with the value.

For more advanced APIs, it's even possible to use the route() function to determine whether a GET, POST, or PUT request was received. For more RESTful routes, take a look at listing 8.22. It defines a GET method for /api/find/profiles that returns all database entries from the profiles collection and a POST method for /api/insert/profile to create new profiles via an API. Remember when using this for your own API to secure the API endpoints—for example, by requiring a login system.

Listing 8.22 RESTful routes

```
// routes.js                                       These are server-
Router.route('/api/find/profiles', {               only routes.
    where: 'server'
  })
  .get(function() {                                 Defines what to do
    this.response.statusCode = 200;                 with GET requests
    this.response.setHeader("Content-Type", "application/json");
    this.response.setHeader("Access-Control-Allow-Origin", "*");
    this.response.setHeader("Access-Control-Allow-Headers",
            "Origin, X-Requested-With, Content-Type, Accept");
    this.response.end(JSON.stringify(
      ProfilesCollection.find().fetch())            All REST responses
    );                                              should be JSON.
  })
```

```
Router.route('/api/insert/profile', {
    where: 'server'
})
.post(function() {
    this.response.statusCode = 200;
    this.response.setHeader("Content-Type", "application/json");
    this.response.setHeader("Access-Control-Allow-Origin", "*");
    this.response.setHeader("Access-Control-Allow-Headers",
            "Origin, X-Requested-With, Content-Type, Accept");
    // returns ID for new profile
    this.response.end(JSON.stringify(
        ProfilesCollection.insert(this.request.body)
    ));
})
```

These are server-only routes.

Defines what to do with POST requests

All REST responses should be JSON.

TIP   If you need to build a REST interface, instead of using `Iron.Router` directly you should also look into using either the `nimble:restivus` or `simple:rest` package, which both offer a simpler approach for creating routes and endpoints.

`Iron.Router` is an extremely versatile and highly configurable router that's tailored to the Meteor platform. It enables applications to react on specific route requests and can also be used to greatly improve your code structures.

8.5   Summary

In this chapter, you've learned that

- URLs enable applications to be accessible and shareable.
- `Iron.Router` is the de facto standard for routing in Meteor.
- Templates, subscriptions, and the data context can be defined using routes.
- Routing functionality can be structured and grouped by using named routes, controllers, hooks, and plug-ins.
- Routes can be created for the client and the server.

The package system

One of the most powerful aspects of Meteor is its active ecosystem of packages. Throughout this book we've taken advantage of packages to extend applications' functionality without having to write more than a few lines of code (for example, using `twbs:bootstrap` or `iron:router`) or to remove unwanted features (for example, using `autopublish` and `insecure`). This chapter takes a closer look at what types of packages can be used by Meteor and how they work together.

The more parts are involved in a system, the more complicated it can be to take into account all dependencies. When you're using a third-party library, it's important to work against a known set of API calls. In the worst case, libraries change their API between versions, which results in updates to small parts and breaks the entire functionality of an app. Package managers can be used to identify dependencies between the various parts that an application comprises. Their job also includes keeping possible incompatibilities to a minimum so that changing any part won't result in a hopelessly broken chunk of code.

When you're finished with this chapter, you'll be able to use existing packages and create your own, which allows you to structure your Meteor applications in even more efficient ways.

9.1   *The foundation of all applications*

All applications you build with Meteor, even the simplest "Hello World" example, already rely on dozens of packages. These packages are what compose Meteor—without them, all that's left is plain Node.js. Although you could certainly write amazing applications that way, the packages system makes it much easier and quicker to achieve results, much like standing on the shoulders of a giant. It's like accessing the DOM with vanilla JavaScript instead of jQuery—it works, but it requires a lot more effort, which could better be spent enhancing other functionality.

Applications consist of both business logic and a number of underlying packages that provide functionality (see figure 9.1).

Packages can be categorized into three types:

- Isopacks, which are Meteor's own package format
- Cordova packages, which provide mobile functionality
- NPM packages, which are Node.js packaged modules

Isopacks are Meteor's own package format, which we'll focus on in this chapter. We'll also look at how to integrate npm modules as packages. If you want to find out more

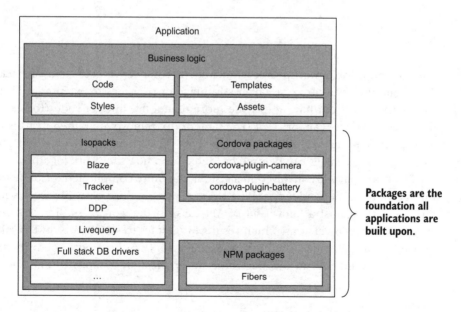

Figure 9.1   Packages are the foundation for all business logic in a Meteor application.

about using Cordova packages, you can skip ahead to chapter 11, where we discuss mobile applications and packages in more detail.

9.2   Using Isopacks

Because of their isomorphic nature, Meteor packages are called Isopacks. In contrast to npm modules, they aren't limited to the server, but they can include server, browser, and even mobile code. They provide a single command and architecture-specific functionality hidden from the user. For example, an HTTP.get() function can be called anywhere in the code. Technically, it requires different implementation on the server and the browser. Therefore, the http package, which provides the HTTP functionality, uses XMLHttpRequest in the browser environment and in the Node.js context falls back to http.request.

Isopacks aren't limited to JavaScript code; they can also include styles and templates (for example, including a login dialog as in accounts-ui) and even static assets such as images or fonts. There are packages that can also change the build process, such as supporting CoffeeScript or LESS styles. We'll take a closer look at those when we discuss Isobuild (chapter 11).

9.2.1   Version Solver and semantic versioning

Isopacks rarely stand on their own; usually they have dependencies on other packages. This avoids repeated code but requires a sophisticated way to determine which packages play well together. *Meteor Version Solver* is an optimizing constraint solver for package dependencies. It goes beyond simply resolving constraints because it doesn't find *a* possible solution but aims for *the best* solution.

Any update to a working application bears the risk of breaking existing functionality. Adding a new package is no different, which is why Version Solver tries to maintain the existing package versions when new packages are included. If that's not possible, it checks for a solution that involves only changing direct dependencies and thus preferring backward-compatible upgrades over new versions with updated APIs. Favoring certain solutions over others is what makes Version Solver an *optimized* constraint solver.

All Isopacks follow the semantic versioning scheme to enable the Version Solver to determine whether breaking changes will be introduced by a package. All packages that provide a public API for other packages use a version consisting of three parts:

```
MAJOR.MINOR.PATCH
```

Semantic versioning

For version numbers you have to use semantic versioning. This basically means you always have three numbers separated by a dot—for example, version: "1.2.3".

The first number is the major version number. You increase this number if the package changes significantly and contains incompatible API changes. This signals to the

(continued)

developer using the package "If I update from version 1.*x.x* to 2.*x.x*, I have to be sure to adjust my codebase using new API methods."

The second number is increased if new functionality is added but no breaking changes are expected. This way, the developer using the package knows that he can update from version 1.2.*x* to 1.3.*x*, knowing that his app will still run. He can decide if the new functionality is useful for him and use it if necessary.

The third number is increased for patches that fixes bugs but don't break any APIs. Developers using the package nearly always want to update to this kind of version because the package is more stable but doesn't break anything in their app.

You can read more about semantic versioning at http://semver.org/.

When dealing with package constraints, developers can now take one of several approaches:

- A package requires an exact version.
- A package requires a minimum version.
- A package requires either an exact version or a minimum version.

This gives Version Solver various options to determine the optimal package combination. When a package requires a minimum version of 2.0.0, any version that starts with a 2 will be a valid choice because all releases share the same feature set. But if a package requires a minimum of 2.2.0, then only higher version numbers will be acceptable choices because it's possible to introduce new features when increasing a minor version as long as existing functionality and APIs are still available. Packages that require any 2.*x.y* version may work with 3.*x.y* versions, but Version Solver won't consider higher (or lower) major version numbers for resolving constraints. You'll learn more about defining required versions when we show you how to write your own package in a bit.

It's important to remember that unlike Node.js Meteor supports only a single version of a package per application. It's not possible to have different versions of a package like `jquery` or `http` installed. Although it could work on the server, this approach would lead to unpredictable behavior on the client side. As a consequence, the constraint resolver must always return one package version that satisfies all requirements.

9.2.2 *Finding packages*

The Meteor Development Group (MDG) runs a public package server that holds all available Isopacks. This package server is a DDP service that's accessible at packages.meteor.com. It's possible to build your own client, but the preferred method to search for packages is via the CLI tool. A more convenient way is to use the web interface at https://atmospherejs.com. The package server contains both core packages that are created by the MDG as well as community packages contributed by other organizations or individuals.

TYPES OF ISOPACKS

Isopacks have a two-level namespace. Most packages have a prefix such as `twbs` or `iron` that identifies the maintainer. These are the *community packages*. Isopacks that have no prefix are provided by the MDG and are considered *core packages*.

The core packages are the ones that are created and maintained by the MDG itself. If you create a new Meteor project, you'll add a lot of Meteor core packages immediately, although there are only three packages explicitly added and the rest come in as dependencies from those three:

- `meteor-platform`—A collection of nearly 50 packaged libraries, including Tracker, Blaze, Minimongo, and jQuery. To see all packages that are included by `meteor-platform` you can run `meteor show meteor-platform`.
- `autopublish`—Automatic publications for all collections.
- `insecure`—Allow database writes from the client.

To see all packages that are maintained by the MDG, you can search them with the CLI tool. Make sure that you don't forget the dot at the end of the search command to show all packages:

```
$ meteor search --maintainer=mdg .
```

You can add core packages with `$ meteor add package`.

The fact that a package has a prefix doesn't tell anything about its stability or acceptance; it's merely an indicator of who is responsible for handling issues that may arise.

> **NOTE** Some packages have an `mrt:` prefix, which indicates that they've been automatically migrated to the new packaging system that was introduced in Meteor 0.9.0. They may not be actively maintained anymore. Be careful when using those.

SEARCHING PACKAGES VIA THE CLI TOOL

Using the `meteor` CLI tool, you can directly access the package repository and perform a search. By using the `search` command, you can look for any string inside a package name—for example, `ddp`:

```
$ meteor search ddp
```

The search returns the 10 packages shown in figure 9.2.

As you can see, the result set lists multiple packages, one of them a core package named `ddp`. The other packages are community packages starting with the organization names of the package creators.

The `search` command only lists a short line that summarizes what a package does. To see more details about an individual package, use the `show` command. The output includes the contents of the package's readme file as well as a list of available versions (see figure 9.3).

Core package

Community package

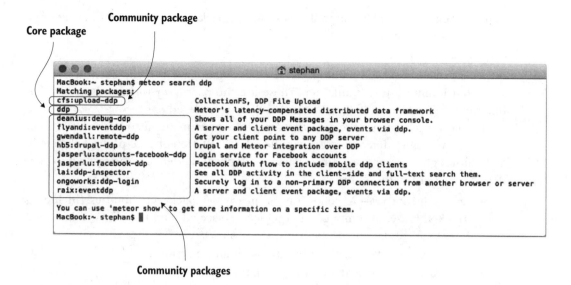

```
● ● ●                            ⌂ stephan
MacBook:~ stephan$ meteor search ddp
Matching packages:
cfs:upload-ddp                  CollectionFS, DDP File Upload
ddp                             Meteor's latency-compensated distributed data framework
deanius:debug-ddp               Shows all of your DDP Messages in your browser console.
flyandi:eventddp                A server and client event package, events via ddp.
gwendall:remote-ddp             Get your client point to any DDP server
hb5:drupal-ddp                  Drupal and Meteor integration over DDP
jasperlu:accounts-facebook-ddp  Login service for Facebook accounts
jasperlu:facebook-ddp           Facebook OAuth flow to include mobile ddp clients
lai:ddp-inspector               See all DDP activity in the client-side and full-text search them.
ongoworks:ddp-login             Securely log in to a non-primary DDP connection from another browser or server
raix:eventddp                   A server and client event package, events via ddp.

You can use 'meteor show' to get more information on a specific item.
MacBook:~ stephan$ ▉
```

Community packages

Figure 9.2   Searching the packages repository for ddp using the CLI tool

```
MacBook:~ stephan$ meteor show ddp
Package: ddp@1.1.0
Maintainers: mdg
Exports: DDP, DDPServer (server)

DDP (Distributed Data Protocol) is the stateful websocket protocol
that Meteor uses to communicate between the client and the server. For
more information about DDP, see the [DDP project
page](https://www.meteor.com/ddp) or the [DDP
specification](https://github.com/meteor/meteor/blob/devel/packages/ddp/DDP.md).

This package is used by nearly every Meteor application and provides a
full implementation of DDP in JavaScript. API documentation is on the
[main Meteor documentation page](http://docs.meteor.com/), under
"Publish and subscribe", "Methods", and "Server connections". Note in
particular that clients can use
[`DDP.connect`](http://docs.meteor.com/#ddp_connect) to open a DDP
connection to any DDP service on the Internet.

Recent versions:
  1.0.11  October 28th, 2014     installed
  1.0.12  December 9th, 2014     installed
  1.0.13  December 19th, 2014    installed
  1.0.14  January 20th, 2015     installed
  1.1.0   March 17th, 2015       installed

Older and pre-release versions of ddp have been hidden. To see all 54 versions, run
'meteor show --show-all ddp'.
MacBook:~ stephan$ ▉
```

Figure 9.3   The meteor show command shows a package's readme content and available versions.

SEARCHING PACKAGES ON ATMOSPHEREJS.COM

Atmospherejs.com is a client for the Meteor packages server built by Percolate Studio. It sports a unique UI to search for packages. Unlike the CLI tool, it not only searches for matching package names but also searches within the contents of the readme files. Therefore, a search for ddp on atmospherejs.com returns 23 instead of 10 results (see figure 9.4).

Using the web interface also has a significant advantage: each package has a popularity indicator that's calculated based on how often a package is updated and how many users download it. Additionally, it's possible to "star" packages to show their usefulness. Especially with a large number of packages doing similar things, this popularity indicator can be a great help when deciding between two (or more) alternatives. Also, each package's details page has two links: one to the associated GitHub repository and another for reporting bugs.

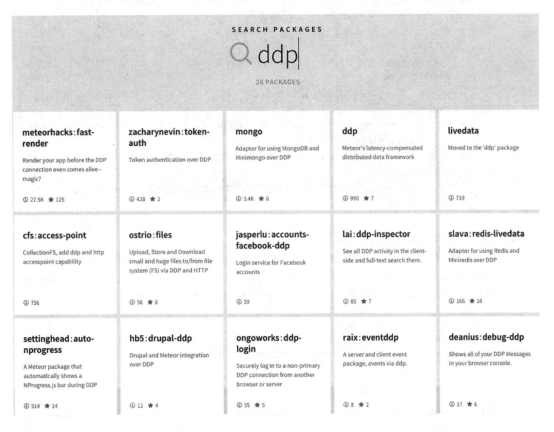

Figure 9.4 Searching atmospherejs.com for ddp

Popular Meteor packages

Thousands of packages are available for the Meteor platform, which makes it hard to discover new packages. But some packages became quite popular in a short period of time and should be known by all Meteor developers:

- `alanning:roles`—Offers role-based authorization.
- `aldeed:autoform`—Lets you easily create forms with automatic insert and update, as well as provide automatic reactive validation.
- `aldeed:collection2`—Provides automatic validation of insert and update operations on the client and server.
- `bengott:avatar`—Provides a consolidated user avatar template (Twitter, Facebook, Gravatar, etc.).
- `cfs:standard-packages`—Contains a file management system for Meteor.
- `ecwyne:polymer-elements`—Lets you add Polymer elements to Meteor.
- `Iron:Router`—Enables you to add routing to an application.
- `meteoric:ionic`—Provides a port of the Ionic UI components for Meteor without the need for Angular.
- `meteorsteam:meteor-postgres`—Allows you to use PostgreSQL databases with Meteor.
- `msavin:mongol`—Offers a convenient way to inspect collection contents during development.
- `numtel:mysql`—Adds MySQL support with reactive SELECT subscriptions to your application.
- `ongoworks:security`—Implements logical security for client-originated MongoDB collection operations.
- `splendido:accounts-meld`—Links accounts from different OAuth providers to the same user.
- `tap:i18n`—Adds support for localizing/internationalizing applications.

9.2.3   *Adding and removing Isopacks*

In this book you've added and removed packages several times, so we'll now focus on dealing with specific versions. Adding a package at its latest and greatest version is done using `meteor add`. To add Twitter Bootstrap, use the following:

```
$ meteor add twbs:bootstrap
```

If you want to use a specific version such as v3.3.2, you can use the `@=` operator:

```
$ meteor add twbs:bootstrap@=3.3.2
```

Check in the .meteor/packages file. You'll now see that not only is the name of the package listed but also the version constraint (see figure 9.5). Even if there's a newer version it'll never be considered for this project because v3.3.2 is pinned.

```
MacBook:packagesApp stephan$ meteor add twbs:bootstrap@=3.3.2

Changes to your project's package version selections:

twbs:bootstrap  added, version 3.3.2


twbs:bootstrap: Bootstrap (official): the most popular HTML/CSS/JS framework
for responsive, mobile first projects
MacBook:packagesApp stephan$ cat .meteor/packages
# Meteor packages used by this project, one per line.
# Check this file (and the other files in this directory) into your repository.
#
# 'meteor add' and 'meteor remove' will edit this file for you,
# but you can also edit it by hand.

meteor-platform
autopublish
insecure
twbs:bootstrap@=3.3.2
MacBook:packagesApp stephan$ ▌
```

Figure 9.5   Adding a specific package version to a project

Unfortunately, this leaves very few choices for Version Solver, and adding a specific version should only be done in rare cases—for example, when you're trying to resolve issues with certain package combinations. Otherwise, it's usually best to define a minimum version instead.

To define a minimum version, use @:

```
$ meteor add twbs:bootstrap@3.3.2
```

This code tells Version Solver to always use Twitter Bootstrap in version 3 but never below 3.3.2.

The Twitter Bootstrap package is a rather simple package; it doesn't introduce additional dependencies when it's added to a project. If you use more complex Isopacks such as `Iron:Router`, a number of dependencies will be added to the project as well. Those are transitive dependencies, meaning they're explicitly added by the developer but a package demanded them to be added. Identifying and resolving these dependencies is the job of the package manager. Meteor handles these transitive dependencies behind the scenes.

Removing a package doesn't require any version information—it's sufficient to use the package name:

```
$ meteor remove twbs:bootstrap
```

If a package brought in transitive dependencies, removing it will also remove all packages that aren't required by the remaining Isopacks directly or as dependencies.

9.2.4   *Updating packages*

Every time you issue the update command in a project folder, Version Solver automatically determines whether it's necessary to update any of the packages. Although Version Solver acts conservatively when adding new packages and tries to avoid any updates, the update command tells it to aim for the newest available versions:

```
$ meteor update
```

The default behavior of the update command will also look for a newer Meteor release and update core packages, which may be unwanted when, for example, you're fixing a bug. By providing a package name to the command, you can limit its actions to a single package. To update all community packages in a project, use the --packages-only switch:

```
$ meteor update --packages-only
```

Because all core packages are tied to a Meteor release, they won't be updated by this command.

9.3   *Using npm packages*

Meteor is built on top of Node.js, so it's possible to use all packages for Node.js as well. npm manages those packages. Its repository contains more than 100,000 packages. A huge community of JavaScript developers has created packages for almost any use case and it's simple to integrate them into Meteor projects as well.

There are two ways to add an npm package to a project. The first is to wrap it into a Meteor package, which is usually the better approach. Most npm packages are designed to work only within the server context, so they don't follow the isomorphic nature of Isopacks. The second approach is to use the meteorhacks:npm package, which allows you to use a packages.json similar to plain Node.js projects.

Writing an isomorphic wrapper for an npm module is quite advanced and goes beyond the scope of this book, so we'll focus on bringing in modules directly. Let's start by adding the required Meteor package:

```
$ meteor add meteorhacks:npm
```

The package enhances Meteor applications so that npm modules can be used directly. Because the package needs to perform some configuration tasks before it can add modules, the project must be run using the meteor run command after you add meteorhacks:npm. As a result, a new folder named *packages* will be added to the project. It contains an npm-container package that will take care of adding npm modules.

To specify which module you want to add to a project, you'll use a packages.json file. This file is also created when first running a Meteor project with the npm package added, and it's located at the root of the application folder. As shown in listing 9.1, all modules that should be added to the application are listed as keys and the required versions as values. We're using the gravatar module as an example.

Listing 9.1   Adding npm packages via packages.json

```
{
  "gravatar": "1.1.1"
}
```

Adjust the contents of the packages.json file and restart Meteor, and the npm module will be added automatically. Because npm doesn't provide client functionality, modules are required from server-side code only using Meteor.npmRequire(). Once a module is loaded, it can be used in the same way you would in a plain Node.js application. Refer to a module's documentation to learn more. For the gravatar module, you can get the URL for a user's avatar image by calling gravatar.url(email), with email being a valid email address of a Gravatar account (see following listing).

Listing 9.2   Using the gravatar npm module from a Meteor method

```
Meteor.methods({
  getGravatar: function(email){
    var gravatar = Meteor.npmRequire('gravatar');
    var url = gravatar.url(email);
    return url;
  }
});
```

This method can be called from anywhere in the code using this familiar syntax:

```
Meteor.call('getGravatar', 'mail@example.org', function(err, res) {
  return res;
});
```

9.4   Creating an Isopack

All functionality that should be reusable across different applications should be implemented as a package to achieve maximum portability. Also, for structuring a single application it's good practice to think of different features as components. This helps maintain a clean separation of concerns and is one of the cornerstones of scalability. A large codebase greatly benefits from being split across packages.

Creating packages involves multiple steps. Meteor doesn't yet support private package repositories, so all packages must either be published publicly or used locally within a packages folder inside a project. This is also where package development usually starts. Before publishing to the official packages repository, you must test each package. The tinytest package is specifically designed for unit-testing packages.

To illustrate the process of creating Isopacks, we'll show you how to take the notification functionality introduced in chapter 5 and wrap it into a package that lets you easily create errors, warnings, or success messages using a single line.

9.4.1 *Creating a package*

Each package has a maintainer that's identified by the prefix. Meteor developers can either use their own username or that of an organization (allowing multiple people to work on the same package). If you're a registered Meteor developer, you should use your username as a prefix when creating a new package. In case you haven't yet registered for an account, you can do so on the meteor.com site.

You have two options when deciding where to locate a new package: inside an existing application or outside. If you choose to create a new package inside an existing application, you must still add it via the `meteor add` command. The cleanest solution is to create new packages outside of any application context. Therefore, you should create the new package outside of your current application.

The syntax to create a new package is as follows:

```
$ meteor create --package <prefix>:<name>
```

You're going to create a new `notifications` package with a `meteorinaction` prefix, as shown in figure 9.6. The command creates a boilerplate file structure, including a README.md file.

This basic structure assumes that all code goes inside a single JavaScript file; all unit tests in a dedicated *-tests.js file; and metadata, such as the package name, version, and dependencies, in the package.js file. As with regular Meteor projects there's no need to keep the given structure; the only mandatory file is package.js, so let's start there.

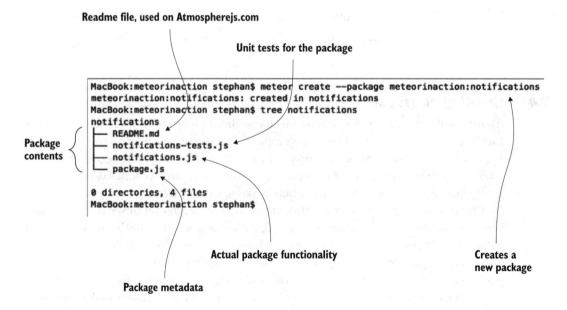

Figure 9.6 Creating a `notifications` **package using** `meteor create --package`

9.4.2 *Declaring package metadata*

The package.js file contains three important blocks:

- `Package.describe()`—The name and description of the package and the link to a Git repository
- `Package.onUse()`—The definition of the actual package, which Meteor API version to use, which files are used, and so forth
- `Package.onTest()`—The test definition for the package

Using these blocks allows for fine-grained control over tasks such as declaring the load order of files. All settings within this file can have an effect on whether or not a package can be used within a Meteor project. The key ingredients are semantic versioning numbers, as explained in the previous section.

If a package relies on npm packages, a fourth block may be used: `Npm.depends()`. For packages that use npm packages, you don't have to add the `meteorhacks:npm` package.

PACKAGE.DESCRIBE

The `describe` block determines the actual name of a package. Regardless of the path name, the setting for the `name` value takes precedence. The following properties are set inside the description:

- name—A unique name for the package, using a Meteor developer account/organization as a prefix.
- version—A version number in the `major.minor.patch` format. When you use a hyphen, you can add prerelease information after the patch, such as `1.1.0-rc1`.
- summary—A single line to be displayed when using the `meteor search` command.
- git—The URL to a Git repository containing the source code for the package.
- documentation—The documentation file you want to use; it must be set to `null` if no documentation should be used.
- debugOnly—If set to `true`, this option will prevent the package from being included in `build` bundles.

PACKAGE.ONUSE

This block is the essence of a package—without it, a package wouldn't accomplish anything. `Package.onUse()` takes a single function as its argument. It holds the package control `api` object that keeps track of dependencies and exports.

The first setting via `api.versionsFrom()` should be the Meteor API version a package is built against. This release version will set the baseline for the versions required for all dependencies that are part of the platform. If a package requires other packages, those are listed in the `api.use()` declaration. Typically all packages must include a version declaration like `templating@1.0.11`. Because the templating package is part of the Meteor core release and we already set a baseline using `api.versionsFrom()`, we can omit the version string. All community packages must include a version constraint. This can be in the form of either `package@=1.0.0` (to require exactly version

1.0.0) or `package@1.0.0` (to require at least version 1.0.0). It's even possible to use a combination such as this:

```
api.use('package@1.0.0 || =2.0.1');
```

In this example, Version Solver would try to include exactly version 2.0.1. If that isn't possible, it'd fall back to any 1.x.y release of the package.

If a package depends on multiple other packages, these are provided as an array. The second argument to `api.use` specifies the architecture—that is, `server`, `client`, `web.browser`, or `web.cordova`. Even though packages are isomorphic, this allows for a leaner build output. If a package is required only on the server, the build process won't include it with the browser bundle, thus reducing the size of what needs to be sent via the network.

To access package functionality from the business logic, you export a global to be used anywhere inside the code via `api.export()`. Again, it's possible to specify in which context this global is available. For displaying notifications, you expose a `Notification` global that works only within the client.

When you're using multiple source files, `api.addFiles()` takes an array with all names listed; otherwise, a single string is sufficient. In contrast to Meteor applications, not all files are loaded automatically but only those listed here. The order in which they're passed to `addFiles` also specifies their load order.

The `meteorinaction:notifications` package uses three files: a JavaScript, an HTML, and a CSS file. The full `onUse()` definition is shown in the following listing.

Listing 9.3   Defining the `notifications` package

```
Package.onUse(function (api) {
  api.versionsFrom('1.1.0.2');
  api.use([
          'templating',
          'ui'
        ],
        'client'
       );
  api.export(
          'Notification',
          'client'
         );
  api.addFiles([
          'notifications.html',
          'notifications.js',
          'notifications.css'
        ],
        'client'
       );
});
```

PACKAGE.ONTEST

By default, all packages are tested using the `tinytest` package; therefore, it's the first dependency to be declared inside the `onTest()` block. The package under test must be declared as a dependency as well, even if it's the current package. As you can see in the following listing, the overall syntax is similar to `Package.onUse()`.

> **Listing 9.4   Defining unit tests for the `notifications` package**

```
Package.onTest(function(api) {
  api.use('tinytest');
  api.use('meteorinaction:notifications');
  api.addFiles('notifications-tests.js', 'client');
});
```

Now we have all metadata definitions in place and we can implement package functionality.

> **Depending on npm packages**
>
> If a package requires functionality from an npm package, the dependency is declared using the following:
>
> ```
> Npm.depends({package: 'version'})
> ```
>
> This code will make an npm package available to the application. To use its functionality instead of using the plain Node.js syntax for `require`, simply prefix it with `Npm`:
>
> ```
> Package = Npm.require('package');
> ```

9.4.3   Adding package functionality

The `notifications` package consists of three files:

- Styles
- Templates
- JavaScript code

In the styles file you define three classes: `error`, `success`, and `warning`. Each has a different `background-color` and `color` attribute to differentiate between the types of error. You can copy over the template code from chapter 5 into the notifications.html file, as in listing 9.5. You'll enhance it slightly to use a button to dismiss a notification.

> **Listing 9.5   Template code for the `notifications` package**

```
<template name="notificationArea">
  {{#with notification}}
  <p class="{{type}}">{{text}}</p>
  <button>{{buttonText}}</button>
  {{/with}}
</template>
```

All notifications will be stored inside a `Session` variable. Therefore, we need a template helper to display the contents of `Session.get('notify')`. Again you can reuse the code from chapter 5. You also need an event to clear the variable contents when the user clicks the button (see following listing).

Listing 9.6 Template helpers and events for the `notifications` package

```
Template.notificationArea.helpers({
  notification: function () {
    return Session.get('notify');
  }
});

Template.notificationArea.events({
  'click button': function () {
    Session.set('notify', '');
  }
});
```

Before you can use the package, you must expose its functionality via the `Notification` global you declared in the package.js file. You'll add four functions to set and clear messages:

- `setSuccess`
- `setWarning`
- `setError`
- `clear`

Each of these sets the contents of the `Session` object to a different value (see following listing).

Listing 9.7 Exposing package functionality via the `Notifications` global

```
Notification = {
  setError: function (text) {
    Session.set('notify', {
      type: 'error',
      text: text,
      buttonText: 'Oh, no.'
    });
  },
  setWarning: function (text) {
    Session.set('notify', {
      type: 'warning',
      text: text,
      buttonText: 'Good to know...'
    });
  },
  setSuccess: function (text) {
    Session.set('notify', {
      type: 'success',
      text: text,
      buttonText: 'Cool!'
    });
  }
```

```
  },
  clear: function () {
    Session.set('notify', '');
  }
};
```

That's it—you now have a fully functional package. But before you can use it in a project, you need to add it just like any other package:

```
$ meteor add meteorinaction:notifications
```

Meteor expects local packages to be available in a packages directory within your project. But what if you created the package outside of an application? You can always create a link in the filesystem, but that won't work well across different workstations. It's better to specify the location of local packages via the environment variable `PACKAGE_DIRS`.

In this case, the package exists in /Users/Stephan/code/packages/notifications, with the packages directory being the one we need for our app. Therefore, we're going to set `PACKAGE_DIRS` to /Users/Stephan/code/packages/. It'll find the `notifications` package automatically. You can either export the variable globally using `$ export PACKAGE_DIRS=/Users/Stephan/code/packages` (Linux and Mac) or `C:\>set PACKAGE _DIRS=c:\code\packages` (Windows) or set it directly when calling any `meteor` commands (if you're on Windows be sure to adjust the path):

```
$ PACKAGE_DIRS=/Users/stephan/code/packages meteor add
meteorinaction:notifications
```

> **NOTE** Remember that if you set the environment variable when calling `meteor` you must also do it for each `meteor run` command so that the package location can be resolved.

If you experience problems adding a package, check that it's there and has the correct name declared inside the package.js file.

Before we take a look at unit-testing packages, let's perform a quick manual test. Add the `notificationArea` template to your app and set a message using the `Notifications` global. To keep things simple, you can use the default Meteor app and extend the button click, as shown in listing 9.8. Figure 9.7 shows the result.

> **Listing 9.8　Adding a notification via the** `notifications` **package**

```
Template.gravatar.events({
  'click button': function (evt, tpl) {
    // ...
    Meteor.call('getGravatar', email, function (err, res) {
        // ...
        Session.set('gravatarUrl', res);
        Notification.setSuccess('I found a gravatar image!');
      }
    });
  }
});
```

Clicking this button
removes the notification

{{> notificationArea}}

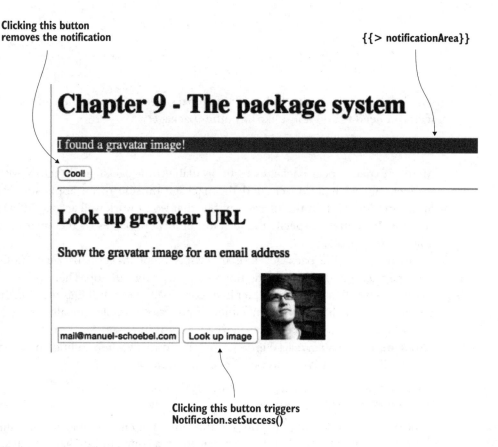

Figure 9.7   **Using the** notifications **package**

Now that you know the package works, you'll implement unit tests to make sure that core functions won't break when you upgrade the package in the future.

9.4.4   *Testing Isopacks using tinytest*

The tinytest package is designed to make testing packages as simple as possible. It comes with a nice web interface that presents all test results at a glance, making it easy to run and analyze tests. Running package tests is again done using the meteor CLI tool:

```
$ meteor test-packages
```

This code will start a Meteor application on localhost:3000 where you can see all the results of all tests (figure 9.8).

The tests rerun automatically if you change any of the tests, just like a regular Meteor application. If you want to develop your application and also have the tiny-

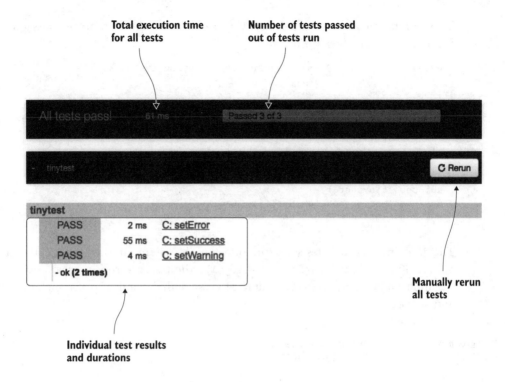

Figure 9.8 The test reporter for `tinytest`

test reporter running at the same time, you can specify a different port for the test reporter:

```
$ meteor test-packages --port 4000
```

This way, you can have the test reporter running on http://localhost:4000 and your normal Meteor application on http://localhost:3000. A simple unit test with `tinytest` as the `notifications` package is shown in the following listing.

Listing 9.9 Testing `Notification.setError` **with** `tinytest`

```
Tinytest.add('setError', function (test) {          First you add a test with
  var msgText = 'An error message';                 a name to tinytest.
  Notification.setError(msgText);
  test.equal(Session.get('notify').text, msgText);    Tinytest exposes different test
  test.equal(Session.get('notify').type, 'error');    functions such as equal.
});
```

If you want to structure your tests even more, you can use a hyphen in the name of your test. That way, you can group tests and get a better overview in the test reporter.

To group all messaging-related tests you use Msg and then group by messaging type (success/warning/error) like this:

```
Tinytest.add('Msg - Error - setError', function(test) {
  //...
});
```

This allows you to fold and expand groups of tests, which becomes especially important for larger packages (figure 9.9).

Let's revisit the test setup defined in package.js:

```
Package.onTest(function(api) {
  api.use('tinytest');
  api.use('meteorinaction:notifications');
  api.addFiles('notifications-tests.js', 'client');
});
```

The last line declares tests to run only on the client. If you change the line to api.addFiles('notifications-tests.js'); the tests are run in every environment the application is targeted to be built for. In case of the default app, this includes client and server.

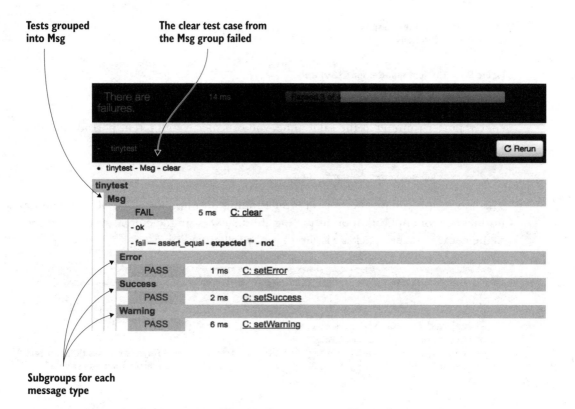

Figure 9.9   Using groups to structure the output of tinytest reports

If the notifications tests are run on the server side, they'll all fail because the `Notification` global is only exported to be available on the client. The web report will show all tests, regardless of the platform they ran in. Each test is prefixed by either an `S` or a `C` to indicate whether it ran on the server or the client (see figure 9.10).

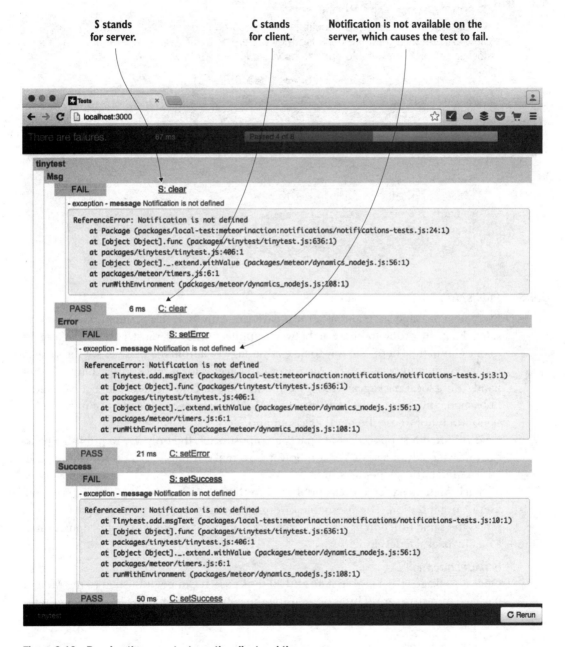

Figure 9.10 Running the same tests on the client and the server

You can also specify a single test that should run on the server and on the client, too. You should use `tinytest` to unit-test your packages, especially if you want to publish your packages to let others use them too.

A concise `tinytest` API reference

Unfortunately the `tinytest` package isn't documented very well, but most API calls are straightforward to use because they adhere to basic testing operations. The following is a list of available operations you can use when writing unit tests:

- `test.equal(actual, expected, message, not)`
- `test.notEqual(actual, expected, message)`
- `test.instanceOf(obj, class)`
- `test.matches(actual, regexp, message)`
- `test.isTrue(actual, msg)`
- `test.isFalse(actual, msg)`
- `test.isNull(actual, msg)`
- `test.isNotNull(actual, msg)`
- `test.isUndefined(actual, msg)`
- `test.isNaN(actual, msg)`
- `test.length(obj, expected_length, msg)`

9.4.5 *Publishing*

Every new package starts out as a local package. Although this is fine, it has its downsides. First, in order to share it between applications you must copy and paste its folder manually. There's no way to take advantage of automatic updates via the `meteor update` command because Version Solver can't access local repositories. On the other hand, using local packages is the only option to keep code private. Once a package is published, anyone may use it within their Meteor projects, so it's important to understand when not to use the `publish` command.

Until Meteor supports private package repositories, the only way to publish a package and take advantage of Version Solver is to make it public. To do so, you need to have a Meteor developer account.

Each Meteor package that's published to the Meteor repository is connected to a user or organization. The username or organization is always part of the package and serves the same function as a namespace. You can use it to build up your reputation as a quality package developer.

INITIAL PUBLICATION

Once a package is in a usable state and all tests pass, it can be published to the Meteor package infrastructure. This is done using the `publish` command. New packages must also include the `--create` flag:

```
$ meteor publish --create
```

All subsequent updates to a package can be done using `meteor publish`. After you publish your package, you can add it to any Meteor application with the `meteor add authorname:packagename` CLI command.

> **Publication errors**
>
> When you're publishing packages, there are not many things that can possibly go wrong. One of the most common errors is trying to publish the same or even an older version of an existing package.
>
> Some users have reported issues when publishing packages that are located in an actual Meteor project under the packages hierarchy. Should you encounter issues with publishing packages, try moving them out of an existing project context.

After you publish a package, it'll be visible via the `meteor search` command and also on atmospherejs.com. Remember to include a useful readme file to explain how to use the package. To enable atmospherejs.com to show the contents of the readme file, you also need to configure a valid Git repository in the package.js file.

UPDATING

Updating a package basically requires two steps. First, increment the version number in your package.js file. Then, publish the update using the `meteor publish` command inside the package folder. In contrast to the initial `publish` command, there's no need to use the `--create` flag.

UNPUBLISHING

There's no way to remove a package that was released. The reason for this is that you can't know if someone is already using your package—deleting the package would break every app using the package.

The only thing that comes close to unpublishing or deleting is to hide a package from the `search` and `show` commands. You can do so by setting a package to `unmigrated`. Issue the following command inside the root folder of a package to exclude it from all searches on the public repository:

```
$ meteor admin set-unmigrated
```

9.5 Summary

In this chapter, you've learned that

- Meteor applications take advantage of a powerful packages system that combines Isopacks, npm packages, and Cordova plug-ins.
- The public packages repository is hosted by Meteor and can be accessed via `meteor search` or at http://atmospherejs.com, where you can explore packages.
- All packages rely on semantic versioning to allow Version Solver to identify the optimal combination of package versions for a project.

- Creating packages helps to better structure an application.
- `tinytest` is the unit-testing library specifically for testing Isopack functionality.
- Anyone with a Meteor developer account can publish packages to the public repository.
- Once a package is published, it can't be deleted but it can be set to an invisible state.

Advanced server methods

This chapter covers

- Understanding the difference between synchronous and asynchronous functions
- Using asynchronous functions
- Integrating external APIs
- Uploading files

Even though Meteor is an isomorphic platform, some things can only be done in certain environments. This chapter introduces you to some advanced concepts on the server. With Node.js running in the background, it's time to take a closer look at the event loop and the right way to work with asynchronous code. This is especially useful if you plan to have your application communicate with external APIs.

While we're looking into server specifics, we'll also discuss a simple way to upload files to the server. The code in this chapter should run on the server unless stated otherwise.

10.1 Reintroducing Node.js

The foundation of the Meteor stack is Node.js (see figure 10.1). Technically, it's a server implementation of the V8 JavaScript engine that can also be found in the

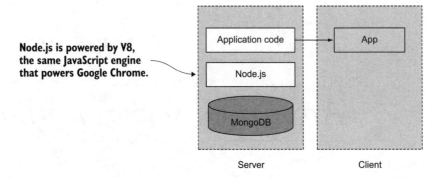

Node.js is powered by V8, the same JavaScript engine that powers Google Chrome.

Figure 10.1   Node.js is the server engine for all Meteor applications.

Google Chrome browser. Therefore, it comes as no surprise that Node.js shows the same characteristics as a browser. It's because of two reasons:

- Node.js is event driven.
- Node.js uses nonblocking I/O.

These two characteristics make Node.js stand out from other server technology such as PHP or Rails that typically execute code in a linear or synchronous way. But even if Node.js is by nature nonblocking, you can still write blocking code.

JavaScript was designed for an environment where actions could take a long time—like querying additional data from a server over a 56k modem connection. It doesn't block the execution of all other actions just because it waits for a return value. Imagine phoning a call center and being put on hold. Would you wait and listen to the music playing or would you do other things like rearranging your desk, walking around, or browsing the web? If you do anything else while waiting, then your call doesn't block other activities and can be considered *asynchronous.*

Callbacks are usually used in JavaScript to get back to a task once a result is available. If call centers were powered by JavaScript, instead of making you wait they'd offer you a callback once an agent was free to talk to you. Most of the time they don't, though, probably because it's hard to keep track of large numbers of callbacks.

10.1.1 *Synchronous code*

Even though Meteor builds on top of the Node.js single-threaded event loop architecture (remember the pizza example from chapter 1?), the general programming style in its methods is synchronous rather than the asynchronous callback style typical of Node.js. The linear execution model is easier to follow and understand, especially on the server. This means that one function is processed after another and then the return value is returned. Meteor retains the scalability of Node.js and combines it with a simplified way of writing code (see following listing).

Listing 10.1 Blocking synchronous code in methods

```
addSync = function(a, b){                    ◁      Synchronous function
  return a + b;                                     that adds two values
}

blockFor3s = function(value) {
  var waitUntil = new Date().getTime() + 3000;
  while(new Date().getTime() < waitUntil) {};
  return value;
}                                                   Block the CPU
Meteor.methods({                                    for 3 seconds.
  'blockingMethod': function(value){
    console.log('Method.blockingMethod called');    Synchronous
    var returnValue = 0;                             addition
    resultComputation = blockFor3s(value);    ◁
    returnValue = addSync(resultComputation, 1);  ◁
    return returnValue;                             The result is returned after
  }                                          ◁      both functions complete.
});
```

Listing 10.1 uses a simple method that processes two synchronous functions and returns the result value. The way the `blockFor3s` function is called requires the server's full attention until it completes, effectively blocking the CPU for all other requests. They have to wait until the blocking function completes. You can test this easily if you open two browsers and call the method in both via the console using the following:

```
Meteor.call('blockingMethod', 1);
```

You'll notice that the first browser causes the method to run and the console.log is printed out in the terminal. If you call the method within 3 seconds on the second browser, it's not called immediately. There's no console message printed out to the terminal. Once the first method call is finished, the second method call is executed and the console.log is finally printed out to the console. If you call the method four times as quickly as you can and pass values from 1 to 4, the result will be the same as shown in figure 10.2. The method pauses for 3 seconds between each request.

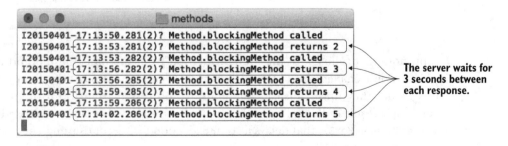

Figure 10.2 Calling the `nonBlocking` **method will result in a pause of 3 seconds between each response.**

Now imagine hundreds of users making requests to an application that needs to run a method that can't be run in parallel. Like a traffic jam, these requests would pile up and leave the app unresponsive and users unhappy. As long as you're inside the event loop you need to allow methods to give way to others in order to avoid having a single user lock the entire application with a long-running request. The answer lies in using asynchronous code.

10.1.2 *Asynchronous code*

To prevent single operations from blocking the execution of all other activities, you should offload long-running tasks into another process. Processing-intense tasks could be executed on another CPU of the same machine or on a remote server. To accomplish this, Node.js typically uses callbacks. This means you call a function and register another function that should be executed once the long-running and blocking function is done. That second function is the callback. That way, the CPU isn't blocked and it can continue processing other requests while waiting for the result of the long-running function (see figure 10.3).

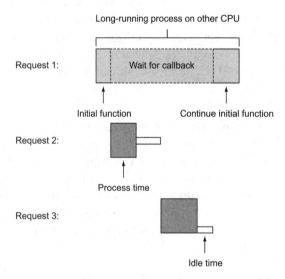

Figure 10.3   While request 1 is waiting for another process to finish, two other requests are handled.

Simply adding a callback to the Meteor method from the blocking method in listing 10.1 won't change the observed behavior, because methods don't wait on callbacks before they finish. Instead, methods are processed from top to bottom and return their result to the caller of the method. Listing 10.2 shows an updated function, setTimeoutFor3s, that delays its own execution by 3 seconds using setTimeout.

Listing 10.2 Nonblocking method with simulated delay

```
setTimeoutFor3s = function(value) {                    ◁— This needs some
  var result = value;                                       time to finish.
  setTimeout(function(){
    result += 3;
    console.log('Result after timeout', result);
  }, 3000);
  return result;
}
Meteor.methods({
  'nonBlockingMethod': function(){
    console.log('Method.nonBlockingMethod');

    var returnValue = 0;                               This always prints 0
    returnValue = setTimeoutFor3s(returnValue);        because Meteor won't wait
    console.log('resultComputation', returnValue);  ◁— for setTimeout to finish.

    return returnValue;
  }
});
```

At first the method call itself is added to the event loop and gets processed. The setTimeout function adds itself to the event loop as well, but it'll be delayed and can be processed only after the original method has already finished. This explains why the return value of the method is 0 and only after 3 seconds the correct result, 3, will be printed out (figure 10.4). Because the method has already finished execution it can't be returned, though. Therefore, the method can't do anything based on the return value.

Now you've seen what won't work. The next section introduces different ways to use asynchronous functions on the server side. Oftentimes you'll need to be able to

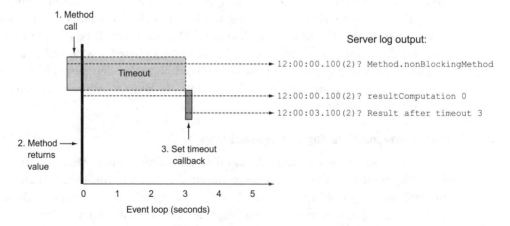

Figure 10.4 The callback function `setTimeout` is a new function on the event loop.

perform an asynchronous task inside a method call and be able to process the result and send it to the client. With Meteor there are different approaches to implementing asynchronous code that all share their dependency on *fibers*.

10.2 Asynchronous functions using fibers

Every method runs within a fiber (see section 10.2.1 for a definition) in Meteor, and the reason for that is to have a more synchronous coding style than you normally have if you're programming with Node.js. One problem with Node.js is that you often end up with the so-called pyramid of doom or callback hell. This happens because you have the event loop where every function call is registered as an asynchronous callback. If you, for example, create a connection to a database, perform a query, make a call to an external API, and then save the result and return a value, in the end you wind up having five callbacks. Let's look at the pseudocode in the following listing.

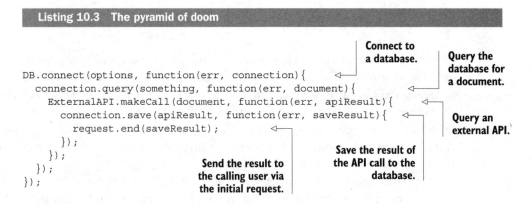

First you create a connection to a database; then you query the database for a document. This will possibly return the user's Twitter handle. Next comes an API lookup; let's say you retrieve the number of followers. This number will be stored in the database and the result will be returned to the user who initiated this flow of actions. Now imagine what listing 10.3 would look like with additional code that performs processing—it would be a nightmare to maintain. Luckily Meteor prevents you from using such complex structures.

10.2.1 Introducing multitasking to the event loop

By nature Node.js uses a single thread for everything it does. That's great because this avoids all the ugly aspects of multithreaded environments, but it creates a need for a solution to do things in parallel. A Zen-like approach of doing one thing after another is great as a personal life choice, but servers usually need to deal with multiple requests at the same time, especially when there are multiple CPU cores waiting for something to do.

Fibers are one possibility for introducing lightweight threading characteristics to Node.js with low overhead. There are several concepts that deal with long-running or parallel tasks like *futures, promises,* or the callbacks we looked at earlier. Because Meteor heavily relies on fibers, we'll limit our discussion to just them. In fact, fibers are one of the main reasons for Meteor's popularity. To explain how they work, we'll first look at the two main flavors of multitasking.

PREEMPTIVE AND COOPERATIVE MULTITASKING

To coordinate multitasking, you usually use a central scheduler to assign CPU cycles to threads. Schedulers have the power to suspend and resume threads whenever they see fit. With this preemptive approach to multitasking, resources may be evenly spread between processes. Unfortunately, the scheduler doesn't know when it's a good time to pause one task and resume another. If one thread requires a lot of CPU resources but the scheduler switches over to another that still needs to wait for an I/O operation to finish, it's not very efficient.

Inside the context of a process, it's much simpler to determine whether a task is currently waiting for the result from another operation (for example, calling a remote API or writing to the database) and handing over the CPU to another task that can use it. This is called *cooperative multitasking.* Each cooperative thread may yield (that is, give resources) to others while they need to wait. This is different from the commonly used preemptive multitasking (for example, when the operating system's scheduler decides that one thread must give resources to another thread).

FIBERS AND THE EVENT LOOP

Fibers introduce cooperative multitasking to the event loop. They're exclusive to the server and can't be used in the browser. Fibers are sometimes referred to as *green threads,* because unlike regular threads that are scheduled by the operating system, fibers are managed by the single-threaded Node.js server.

You'll hardly ever need to create a fiber yourself in a Meteor application because they're built into the platform so that fibers are used automatically. By default, Meteor creates a dedicated fiber for each DDP connection. Because each client uses a single DDP connection, you can say it creates one fiber per client.

Listing 10.3 showed how for every callback the pyramid gets bigger and bigger. To avoid that, you can wrap all functions inside a fiber (see following listing).

> **Listing 10.4 Using fibers to avoid the pyramid of doom**

```
Fiber(function(){
  var connection, document, apiResult, saveResult = null;

  DB.connect(options, function(err, con){
      connection = con;
  });

  connection.query(something, function(err, doc){
    document = doc;
  });
```

```
ExternalAPI.makeCall(document, function(err, res){
  apiResult = res;
});

connection.save(apiResult, function(err, res){
  saveResult = res;
});

request.end(saveResult);

}).run()
```

The code in listing 10.4 looks a lot easier to follow. Even though you're using asynchronous functions, within a fiber the execution is synchronized. The synchronous execution doesn't affect or even block other fibers (see figure 10.5)—no more pyramid is visible. Meteor uses exactly the same approach behind the scenes.

Even if you weren't aware of it, every time you use find() on a collection within a server method, you actually execute a nonblocking database query:

```
var user = Meteor.users.findOne({name: 'Michael'});
return user.name;
```

To access the database and return a result, Meteor automatically wraps the instructions in a fiber. The downside of this is that it becomes more complicated to use asynchronous external APIs. In section 10.1.2 we looked at a simple example where we used setTimeout to simulate an asynchronous function call. Unfortunately, the method finished and returned a value before the asynchronous call did. To change that, you can use fibers.

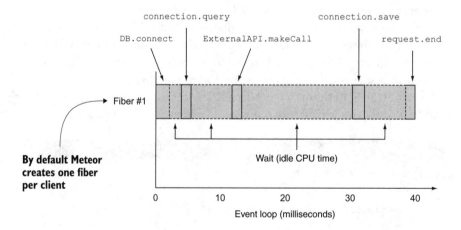

Figure 10.5   Meteor uses a fiber inside the event loop for each DDP connection.

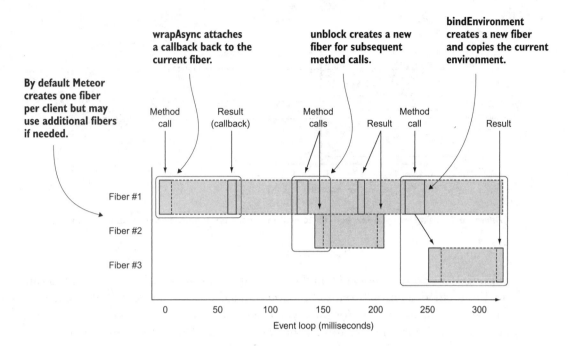

wrapAsync attaches a callback back to the current fiber.

unblock creates a new fiber for subsequent method calls.

bindEnvironment creates a new fiber and copies the current environment.

By default Meteor creates one fiber per client but may use additional fibers if needed.

Figure 10.6   Making asynchronous calls using fibers

You interact with Meteor's internally used fibers via three commands (see figure 10.6):

- wrapAsync—Attaches a callback back to the current fiber
- unblock—Enables multiple operations to execute in parallel within a single fiber
- bindEnvironment—Creates a new fiber to maintain the current environment (for example, global variable values)

10.2.2   *Binding callbacks to a fiber with wrapAsync*

Meteor creates a new fiber per client request, so you could assume that all code is already executed within a fiber. But callbacks break out of a given fiber and return their result without the previous context (such as which user made a request in the first place). Hence, a common error message in Meteor is "Meteor code must always run within a fiber." When dealing with callbacks, you can use the Meteor.wrapAsync function to ensure that the result from the callback stays within a certain fiber. You can wrap any other function in a fiber using wrapAsync. Without passing a callback as an argument, it calls a function synchronously; otherwise, it actually is asynchronous. Only when a callback is provided will Meteor be able to restore the environment captured when the original function was called, effectively putting the result into the same fiber.

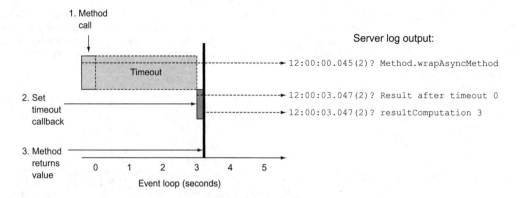

Figure 10.7   Using `wrapAsync` in order to wait for a callback to provide a method's return value

Listing 10.5 shows an updated method named `wrapAsyncMethod` we're going to call. In this method, an asynchronous function with a callback is invoked. With the help of a fiber, it's possible to wait for the asynchronous function to complete and only then the execute the method, returning the correct value. This helper function automatically runs the async function in the current fiber (see figure 10.7).

Listing 10.5   Calling a function using `wrapAsync`

```
setTimeoutFor3sCb = function (value, cb) {
  var result = value;
  Meteor.setTimeout(function () {
    console.log('Result after timeout', result);
    cb(null, result + 3)
  }, 3000);
}

Meteor.methods({
 'wrapAsyncMethod': function () {
   console.log('Method.wrapAsyncMethod');

   var returnValue = 0;

   returnValue = Meteor.wrapAsync(setTimeoutFor3sCb)(returnValue);    ⟵  Wait for
   console.log('resultComputation', returnValue);                         function
                                                                          to finish
   return returnValue;    ⟵┐ Returns 1
 }
});
```

NOTE   `wrapAsync` takes a standard callback function as the last parameter with an error and response parameter: `callbackFunction( err, result ){}`.

10.2.3 *Unblocking method calls for a single client*

If you call a method, it may perform several tasks. On the other hand, there are times when multiple tasks are performed by different methods and you want to call multiple methods in parallel for the same client. As you know, each client has an associated fiber and every method runs in it in a synchronous fashion, one at a time. If a client calls methodA and methodB afterward, the default behavior is to wait for methodA to finish before invoking methodB.

Let's assume you call a method two times, one after the other (from the same browser) and the method called is a long-running method that's blocking, as in the following listing.

Listing 10.6 Sequentially executing methods

```
block = function(value, cb) {
  Meteor.setTimeout(function(){
    cb(null, true);
  }, 3000);
}

Meteor.methods({
'sequential': function (value) {
    console.log('Method.sequential', value);
    Meteor.wrapAsync(block)(value);
    console.log('Method.sequential returns', value);
    return true;
  }
});
```

In a browser console you can now issue both method calls like this:

```
Meteor.call('sequential', 'first', function(err,res){
  console.log('done first');
});

Meteor.call('sequential', 'second', function(err,res){
  console.log('done second');
});
```

Did you notice anything? In this example the methods are called sequentially. The first callback function is executed after 3 seconds and the second callback 3 seconds after that. To execute the methods immediately and in parallel, you can use this.unblock() in the method, as shown in listing 10.7. If a method is still waiting for a result, using unblock allows Meteor to create a new fiber if the same client makes additional method calls.

Listing 10.7   Using `unblock` to let other functions continue

```
Meteor.methods({
  unblock: function(value){
    console.log('Method.unblock', value);

    this.unblock();

    Meteor.wrapAsync(block)(value);
    console.log('Method.unblock returns', value);
    return value;
  }
});
```

> Calling this.unblock allows the client to execute another fiber right away.

In this case, both methods run immediately and both callbacks will be executed after 3 seconds. Neither method has to wait for the other. Test it by calling the method from the browser using `Meteor.call`.

As you can see in figure 10.8, calling the `sequential` method will execute the first request and 3 seconds later the second, whereas the `unblock` method executes both requests at once.

10.2.4   Creating fibers with bindEnvironment

For certain operations, it's important to access the environment from which you made an asynchronous function call. Let's assume you have the `accounts` package added and you want to access the current `userId` in a simple method. As long as you do so asynchronously, you can do it easily like this:

```
Meteor.userId()
```

The second method call starts when the first is finished.

Both functions are called at the same time.

Figure 10.8   Running methods sequentially and using `unblock`

In the scope of a method, you can read the value for userId just fine because Meteor automatically attaches various variables to the fiber. Methods allow you to access the given environment at the time it was called via this. Through this invocation object, you can access different attributes and functions such as this.userId, which relates to the user that called the method. If you call a function that's executed outside the current fiber, you'll lose access to these environmental variables.

When calling an asynchronous function (setTimeoutFor3sCb) that takes 3 seconds to return its result, the original environment gets lost inside the callback. Suddenly this has lost access to userId because it relates to the global object instead of the invocation object.[1] That's the reason the first console.log can print out the current user ID to the terminal and the second attempt to log causes an error: "Meteor.userId can only be invoked in method calls." To illustrate the problem, take a look at the following listing.

Listing 10.8 Using `Meteor.userId()` in a callback for a method

```
Meteor.methods({
  'unboundEnvironment': function () {
    console.log('Method.unboundEnvironment: ', Meteor.userId());

    setTimeoutFor3sCb(2, function () {
      console.log('3s later: ', Meteor.userId());
    });
  }

});
```

Prints ID of the user calling the method

Generates an error message

When using asynchronous functions in a method that needs to be able to access the current environment, you can use Meteor's bindEnvironment function. bindEnvironment creates a fiber and attaches the correct environment automatically. In our example, it's sufficient to change the method as shown in listing 10.9. The entire callback function is wrapped in a Meteor.bindEnvironment() block.

Listing 10.9 Using `Meteor.userId()` in a bound callback for a method

```
Meteor.methods({
  'bindEnvironment': function () {
    console.log('Method.bindEnvironment: ', Meteor.userId());

    setTimeoutFor3sCb(2, Meteor.bindEnvironment(function () {
      console.log('Method.unboundEnvironment (3s delay): ', Meteor.userId());
    }));
  }
});
```

Binds the current environment of the method to the callback

Prints the ID of the user calling the method

---

[1] For a more in-depth explanation of the this keyword in JavaScript, take a look at http://stackoverflow.com/questions/133973/how-does-this-keyword-work-within-a-javascript-object-literal.

**Calling Meteor.userId from a
long-running method callback
results in an error.**

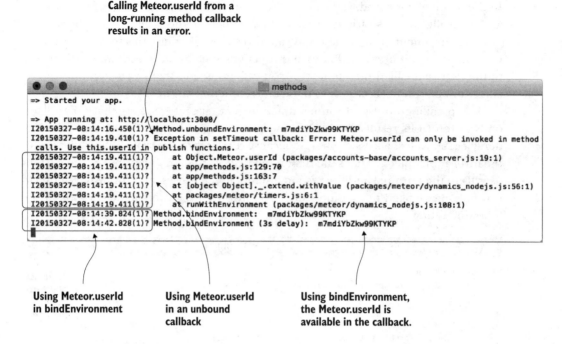

```
● ● ●                              ▓ methods
=> Started your app.

=> App running at: http://localhost:3000/
I20150327-08:14:16.450(1)? Method.unboundEnvironment:  m7mdiYbZkw99KTYKP
I20150327-08:14:19.410(1)? Exception in setTimeout callback: Error: Meteor.userId can only be invoked in method
 calls. Use this.userId in publish functions.
I20150327-08:14:19.411(1)?      at Object.Meteor.userId (packages/accounts-base/accounts_server.js:19:1)
I20150327-08:14:19.411(1)?      at app/methods.js:129:70
I20150327-08:14:19.411(1)?      at app/methods.js:163:7
I20150327-08:14:19.411(1)?      at [object Object]._.extend.withValue (packages/meteor/dynamics_nodejs.js:56:1)
I20150327-08:14:19.411(1)?      at packages/meteor/timers.js:6:1
I20150327-08:14:19.411(1)?      at runWithEnvironment (packages/meteor/dynamics_nodejs.js:108:1)
I20150327-08:14:39.824(1)? Method.bindEnvironment:  m7mdiYbZkw99KTYKP
I20150327-08:14:42.828(1)? Method.bindEnvironment (3s delay):  m7mdiYbZkw99KTYKP
```

**Using Meteor.userId
in bindEnvironment**

**Using Meteor.userId
in an unbound
callback**

**Using bindEnvironment,
the Meteor.userId is
available in the callback.**

Figure 10.9   Callbacks in an unbound environment return an error when accessing `Meteor.userId`.

Figure 10.9 shows a call to both an unbound and a bound environment. Because the value for `Meteor.userId` gets lost in the callback, the unbound example throws an error message whereas the second call to the bound method succeeds.

Most of the time, it's sufficient to use `wrapAsync` for calling asynchronous functions. Only when you need to access the given environment and can't pass all required variables to a function call should you use `bindEnvironment`. Most of the time, using `wrapAsync` is fine.

Look back at chapter 7, where we discussed the publication of aggregated data to the client. In this scenario, we also had to use `bindEnvironment` to make sure that the publication isn't blocked by waiting for the result from MongoDB.

10.3   *Integrating external APIs*

Many applications rely on external APIs to retrieve data. Getting information regarding your friends from Facebook, looking up the current weather in your area, or simply retrieving an avatar image from another website—there are endless uses for integrating additional data. They all share a common challenge: if APIs must be called from the server, calling the API usually takes longer than executing the method itself. You saw in the previous section how to deal with this theoretically—now we'll integrate an external API via HTTP.

Based on the IP address of your visitors, you can determine various information about their current location, such as coordinates, city, or time zone. There's a simple API that takes an IPv4 address and returns all these tidbits as a JSON object, and it's called Telize (www.telize.com).

10.3.1 Making RESTful calls with the http package

To communicate with RESTful external APIs such as Telize, you need to add the `http` package:

```
$ meteor add http
```

Although the `http` package allows you to make HTTP calls from both the client and the server, the API call in this example will be performed from the server only. Many APIs require you to provide an ID as well as a secret key to identify the application that makes an API request. Even though you won't need any credentials for this example, in many other cases you will, and then you should run your requests from the server. That way, you never have to share secret keys with clients. Figure 10.10 explains the basic concept. A user requests location information for an IP address (step 1). The client application calls a server method called `geoJsonforIp` (step 2) that makes an asynchronous call to the external API using the `HTTP.get()` method (step 3). The response (step 4) is a JSON object with information regarding the geographic location associated with an IP address, which gets sent back to the client via a callback (step 5).

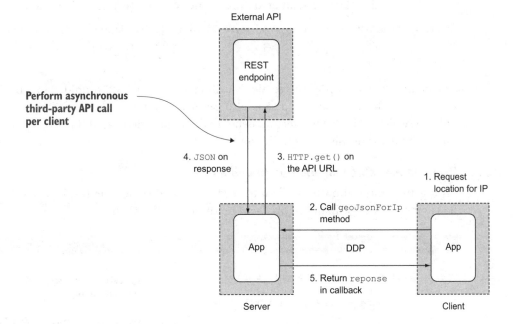

Figure 10.10 Data flow when making external API calls

10.3.2 *Using a synchronous method to query an API*

Let's add a method that queries telize.com for a given IP address, as shown in listing 10.10. This example includes only the bare essentials for querying an API.

> **Listing 10.10   Querying an external API using a synchronous method**

```
Meteor.methods({                                        The method expects
  'geoJsonForIp': function (ip) {                        a valid IPv4 address.
    console.log('Method.geoJsonForIp for', ip);
    var apiUrl = 'http://www.telize.com/geoip/' + ip;       Construct
    var response = HTTP.get(apiUrl).data;                    the API URL.
    return response;                          Query
  }                                           the API.
});
```

Once the method is available on the server, querying the location of an IP works by calling the method with a callback from the client:

```
Meteor.call('geoJsonForIp', '8.8.8.8', function(err,res){
  console.log(res);
});
```

Although this solution appears to be working fine, there are two major flaws to this approach:

- If the API is slow to respond, requests will start queuing up.
- Should the API return an error, there's no way to return it back to the UI.

To address the issue of queuing, you can add an `unblock()` statement to the method:

```
this.unblock();
```

As you know from the previous sections, calling an external API should always be done asynchronously. That way, you can also return possible error values back to the browser, which will solve the second issue. Let's create a dedicated function for calling the API asynchronously to keep the method itself clean.

10.3.3 *Using an asynchronous method to call an API*

Listing 10.11 shows how to issue an `HTTP.get` call and return the result via a callback. It also includes error handling that can be shown on the client.

> **Listing 10.11   Dedicated function for asynchronous API calls**

```
var apiCall = function (apiUrl, callback) {
  try {                                              try...catch allows you
    var response = HTTP.get(apiUrl).data;            to handle errors.
    callback(null, response);
  } catch (error) {                    A successful API call returns no error but
                                       returns the contents from the JSON response.
```

```
  if (error.response) {                                    ◁⎯⎤  If the API responded with
    var errorCode = error.response.data.code;                   an error message that
    var errorMessage = error.response.data.message;             contained a payload
  } else {                                               ◁⎯⎤
    var errorCode = 500;                                        Otherwise use a generic
    var errorMessage = 'Cannot access the API';                 error message.
  }
  var myError = new Meteor.Error(errorCode, errorMessage);  ⎤  Create an error
  callback(myError, null);                                     object and return
}                                                              it via callback.
}
```

Inside a try...catch block you can differentiate between a successful API call (the try block) and an error case (the catch block). A successful call may return null for the error object of the callback; an error will return only an error object and null for the actual response.

There are various types of errors and you want to differentiate between a problem with accessing the API and an API call that got an error inside the returned response. This is what the if statement checks for: in case the error object has a response property both code and message for the error should be taken from it; otherwise you can display a generic error 500 that the API couldn't be accessed.

Each case, success and failure, returns a callback that can be passed back to the UI. To make the API call asynchronous, you need to update the method as shown in listing 10.12. The improved code unblocks the method and wraps the API call in a wrapAsync function.

Listing 10.12 Updated method for making asynchronous API calls

```
Meteor.methods({                                        ⎤  Avoid blocking
  'geoJsonForIp': function (ip) {                           other method calls.
    this.unblock();                          ◁⎯⎯⎤
    var apiUrl = 'http://www.telize.com/geoip/' + ip;
    var response = Meteor.wrapAsync(apiCall)(apiUrl);  ◁⎯⎤  Asynchronous call to
    return response;                                        the dedicated API
  }                                                         calling function
});
```

Finally, to allow requests from the browser and to show error messages, you should add a template similar to the following listing.

Listing 10.13 Template for making API calls and displaying errors

```
<template name="telize">                                  ⎤  Set the
  <p>Query the location data for an IP</p>                    data
  <input id="ipv4" name="ipv4" type="text" />                context.   If location has an error
  <button>Look up location</button>                                     property, display type
                                                                        and message.
  {{#with location}}                            ◁⎯⎤
    {{#if error}}                                        ◁⎯⎤
      <p>There was an error: {{error.errorType}} {{error.message}}!</p>
```

```
  {{else}}
    <p>The IP address {{location.ip}} is in {{location.city}}
      ({{location.country}}).</p>
  {{/if}}
{{/with}}
</template>
```

The JavaScript required to connect the template with the method call is shown in listing 10.14. A `Session` variable called `location` is used to store the results from the API call. Clicking the button takes the content of the input box and sends it as a parameter to the `geoJsonForIp` method. The `Session` variable is set to the value of the callback.

Listing 10.14   Template helpers for making API calls

```
Template.telize.helpers({
  location: function () {
    return Session.get('location');     ◁─┐  The API response
  }                                        │  is stored inside a
});                                        │  Session variable.

Template.telize.events({
  'click button': function (evt, tpl) {
    var ip = tpl.find('input#ipv4').value;
    Meteor.call('geoJsonForIp', ip, function (err, res) {
      if (err) {
        Session.set('location', {error: err});   ◁──┐  The method call sets
      } else {                                       │  the Session variable to
        Session.set('location', res);      ◁─────────  the callback value.
        return res;
      }
    });
  }
});
```

10.4   *Uploading files to a collection*

Although uploading files is one of the most common functions used on the web, implementing this functionality isn't trivial. You can store uploaded content in various places (see figure 10.11), and each option has its pros and cons:

- The local filesystem
- Remote storage
- The application's database

Most developers find that the local filesystem is the natural solution for storing files (Option A). It's already there, it's reasonably fast, and it can hold as much content as space is available. Many hosting providers don't offer access to the local filesystem due to both security and performance reasons. Imagine a malicious script starting to write hundreds of megabytes to fill up disk space, effectively causing a denial of service for

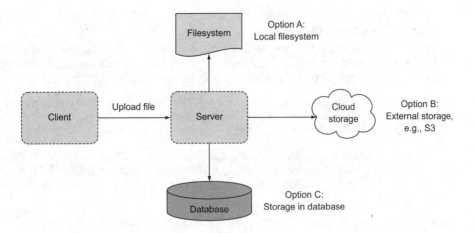

Figure 10.11   File storage and upload options for Meteor applications

all applications hosted on this instance. In practice this means that when deploying your application to a service such as meteor.com you won't be able to store data on the local disks; you need to upload files to a different location. A better solution for applications on the web is a separation of applications and data storage.

These days, cloud storage providers (Option B) are common because they offer a lot of advantages: they're fast and highly available, and redundant storage will keep your files safe. At the same time, setting up your application with them is a bit complicated and they can be costly. Cloud storage providers are a great option for scaling out production applications, but if you want quick results, you might consider another option.

A third possibility is to store files in the application's database (Option C). Unlike the filesystem you always have access to it, and having all data in a single place makes backups a breeze. Unfortunately, using the database for storing files is highly inefficient because it's slow and takes significantly more space than saving directly to the filesystem. MongoDB is designed to store files, but they're limited to the maximum document size of 16 MB. Storing files within collections requires some overhead, so the actual maximum file size is around 12 MB. MongoDB can be configured to use the GridFS filesystem, which allows you to use files of any size. Either way, it remains an inefficient yet convenient way to store files.

For small files such as avatar images or building prototypes, the database is a viable option, and it gives developers the most portable and simplest solution to implement. In the next section, you'll implement Option C (see the accompanying sidebar for other ways to implement uploads).

Useful package for file uploads

Although storing files in the database is convenient and easy to implement, it's hardly advisable for most production scenarios. For better performance and scalability, both the local filesystem and cloud storage providers are a much better fit.

`tomi:upload-server` allows users to upload files to the local filesystem, and when used in combination with `tomi:upload-jquery`, it also enables a full UI that also works well on mobile devices (this package implements Option A).

`CollectionFS` comes with various storage adapters that allow you to store files in the local filesystem (`cfs:filesystem`), in a MongoDB using the GridFS filesystem (`cfs:gridfs`), or in an S3 bucket (`cfs:s3`) (`CollectionFS` can be used to implement any of the three options).

When uploading files to a cloud provider, you might not want to first upload to your server and then forward to the actual storage. The client can also upload directly to Google Cloud, Rackspace, or others. The `edgee:slingshot` package implements the required functionality and works in combination with Option B.

10.4.1 *Uploading files to the database*

In this example you'll create a template to select a file, which will be uploaded directly to a MongoDB collection. Files can then be published and subscribed to just like any other database content. Image data will be stored in a Base64-encoded format so that it's simple to display images in the browser.

Each file document will have a `name` property and the file contents in a field called `base64`.

REQUIREMENTS AND LIMITATIONS

There are no additional requirements for uploading files to the database except from the usual Meteor components: an application and a database. You'll be using the HTML5 FileReader API in the browser to upload files, so not all browsers are supported, namely Internet Explorer 8 and 9.[2]

TEMPLATES

All that's needed for uploading files is an `input` element. You don't even need a button because the upload can start immediately when a file has been selected (listing 10.15).

For displaying images normally, you'd pass a URL to the `src` attribute of the `img` tag. Because this image isn't accessible from a URL, you can also pass the Base64-encoded content directly to the `src` attribute. For displaying multiple images from a collection, you can use an `{{#each}}` block—again, just as you do for any other database content.

---

[2] You can check which browsers support the FileReader API at http://caniuse.com/#feat=filereader.

Listing 10.15 Template code for uploading files

```
<template name="upload">
  <h2>Upload a file</h2>
  <input type="file" id="file-upload" />
</template>

<template name="file">
  {{#with file}}
    <h2>{{name}}</h2>
    <img src="{{base64}}" />
  {{/with}}
</template>
```

LIMITING PUBLICATIONS TO A SINGLE FILE

The first step is to create a new collection that will be used to store files:

```
FilesCollection = new Mongo.Collection('files');
```

This collection should be available on both client and server. Perform a `meteor remove autopublish` to avoid sending all files to all clients. This collection will become extremely big!

> **NOTE** When publishing files from collections, take care to limit the publication to a single file to avoid sending hundreds of megabytes to each connected client.

The required code to set up a publication for a single file only is shown in listing 10.16. The requested filename is passed to the publication via a `Session` variable. This means that only a single image can be displayed at a time. If you need to display multiple images from the `FilesCollection`, you must adjust the function to take an array of names.

Listing 10.16 Code for publishing and subscribing to a single file

```
if (Meteor.isServer) {
  Meteor.publish('files', function (file) {
    console.log("publish", file);            Publication is based
    return FilesCollection.find({            on the filename.
      name: file
    });
  });
}
                                             Passing the Session
if (Meteor.isClient) {                       variable will result
  Tracker.autorun(function (computation) {   in a single file being
    Meteor.subscribe('files', Session.get('file'));   returned.
  });
}
```

Now that files from the database can be sent to the client, it's time to implement the upload process.

USING THE FILEREADER API TO UPLOAD IMAGES TO A COLLECTION

By taking advantage of HTML5's native capabilities, you won't need any Meteor-specific code for uploading files in the client. Selecting a file will trigger the upload and hand the file's contents to a server-side method to store it in the database. As you can see in the following listing, the code looks a bit complicated, so we'll go through it line by line.

Listing 10.17　Using FileReader to upload a file

```
if (Meteor.isClient) {
  Template.upload.events({
    'change #file-upload': function (event, template) {
      var file = event.target.files[0];
      var name = event.target.files[0].name;

      var reader = new FileReader();
      reader.onload = function (file) {
        var result = reader.result;
        Meteor.call('saveFile', name, result);
      }
      reader.readAsDataURL(file);
    }
  });
}
```

The code listens for changes to an input field with the ID `file-upload` in the uploads template. Although the FileReader API allows multiple files to be uploaded at one time, this code supports only a single file at a time. The actual file is accessible via the current event: `event.target.files[0]`. You can access the filename via the `name` property of the object; this gets assigned to a variable. An instance of FileReader is created (`reader`). The `onload` event is triggered when the file was successfully read, which is when you can send the file contents to the server method `saveFile`. The method takes two arguments: the filename and a Base64 string that holds the file contents (`result`).

To tell FileReader to load the file, you use the `readAsDataURL()` function. This function reads binary data and automatically encodes it into Base64. When this action finishes successfully, the `onload()` event is triggered.

If you want, you can perform additional validations before calling the server method, such as validating that the file in question is indeed an image:

```
if (!file.type.match('image.*')) {
  alert('Only image files are allowed');
  return;
}
```

The corresponding server method, `saveFile` (listing 10.18), should look quite familiar to you; the only difference from the examples you saw earlier is that `buffer` holds a lot more data and is Base64 encoded. All data is sent via DDP to methods, and this is no exception. The upload is done completely via WebSockets and doesn't use traditional HTTP.

Listing 10.18 `saveFile` **method for storing files in a collection**

```
if (Meteor.isServer) {
  Meteor.methods({
    'saveFile': function (name, buffer) {
      FilesCollection.insert({
        name: name,
        base64: buffer
      })
    }
  });
}
```

All that's left to do is display image content.

DISPLAYING IMAGES STORED IN A COLLECTION

At this point the remaining code is simple enough. The image will be returned like any other collection document:

```
if (Meteor.isClient) {
  Template.file.helpers({
    'file': function () {
      return FilesCollection.findOne();
    }
  });
}
```

You added the template earlier, so you can test your new upload functionality now.

Remember that this easy solution isn't suitable for large files and high-traffic environments, but it's quite useful for implementing quick and portable upload functionalities.

10.5 Summary

In this chapter, you've learned that

- Even though Node.js is nonblocking by design, it's possible to write blocking code in Meteor applications.
- Meteor uses fibers to make it easier to write asynchronous code.
- When writing asynchronous code on the server, you'll probably use `unblock()` and `wrapAsync`. There are only rare cases where you should use `bindEnvironment`.
- Calls to external APIs using the `http` package should be made asynchronously to avoid blocking.
- Asynchronous server functions may return errors back to the client via callbacks.
- There are various options for handling file uploads. Without using community packages, the easiest way is to use the application's database.

Part 3

Leaving the crater

The final two chapters of this book discuss building, debugging, and deploying applications. Chapter 11 explains how the build process works and teaches you how to turn a web application into an app for phones and tablets. In chapter 12 you'll learn about the prerequisites for successful deployments, simple load testing, and scaling options for Meteor applications.

Building and debugging

This chapter covers

- Customizing the Meteor build process
- Debugging using the server shell and
  `node-inspector`
- Creating browser applications
- Creating mobile applications

With the rise of the smartphone, web applications no longer require a web browser because they also come as mobile applications. Meteor wouldn't be an appropriate tool for building modern applications if it didn't offer support for mobile platforms as well. Platforms that are capable of running Meteor applications can be the server, browser, and even mobile devices like iOS and Android.

Although there is no need to create an EXE file or application binaries, even interpreted languages like JavaScript require some source code processing before they can be run. One of the most familiar steps in building a JavaScript project is *minification*, which reduces source files to a minimum so that network traffic is minimized at the cost of readability.

Turning source code into runnable applications is the job of a build tool, and in Meteor it's called *Isobuild*. This tool works mostly behind the scenes and allows you to focus on coding rather than setting up build chains.

In this chapter, we take a close look of two main aspects of Isobuild:

- How the Meteor build process works
- How to build apps for various platforms

Additionally, this chapter introduces debugging techniques that will allow you to get a better understanding of what happens inside the application when it's running.

When you complete this chapter, you'll be able to customize your workflow and put your application on iOS and Android devices.

11.1 *The Meteor build process*

Whenever a Meteor project is run, Isobuild gets busy behind the scenes. It needs to combine all files that contain HTML and JavaScript source code, put together styling information, and merge the results intelligently with the content from all packages present within the project. The output is an application that can be run on development or production systems.

Let's revisit the graphic introduced in chapter 1 that showed the various parts that make up the source of a Meteor application (see figure 11.1). Building an application

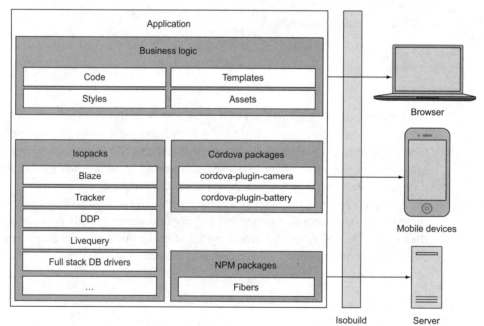

Figure 11.1 **Isobuild takes all parts that compose a Meteor application and turns them into applications for various platforms.**

means taking the contents from the box on the left side and processing them so they may run on any or all of the platforms shown on the right. Isobuild takes care of this transformation. It's a complete tool chain for turning source code into programs that may run on various platforms.

For a platform to be isomorphic, all functionality that's added via packages must behave the same on multiple—or ideally all—components of the stack. Certainly there are exceptions—for example, accessing the phonebook of a mobile phone on a server platform is hardly possible. But most other functions, like fetching contents from a web service, must be called in exactly the same way, regardless of where they take place. Instead of you having to use `jQuery.get()` in a browser and `http.request()` on the server, Meteor provides an abstract API that allows you to use `HTTP.get()` anywhere and achieve the same results. It's not just the same language that's used across the entire stack—it's the same API so that the same code can run anywhere.

Why does Meteor have its own build system?

The JavaScript world knows a large number of build tools—npm, `jake`, `bower`, `grunt`, and `gulp`. Why doesn't Meteor use one of these instead of Isobuild?

Building Meteor applications requires a build tool that works equally well for server and client code. Most tools focus on only one of these environments, so they're a poor fit for a full-stack platform, especially when they must cater to the isomorphic nature of the code.

Packages for Meteor aren't limited to using JavaScript, Spacebars, and CSS but also use CoffeeScript, Jade, or LESS. These require an additional build step to translate the contents into the former languages. Furthermore, *Isopacks* may contain not only code but also assets such as font files or images. That means injecting resources into the client bundle becomes necessary.

Another shortcoming of package managers is the *paradox of choice*. With many packages offering similar functionality, it becomes hard to tell which is the best (and still maintained) option to choose. The Meteor Development Group addresses this issue by using a two-level namespace for packages. Every package that prefixes a curator in the `curator:packagename` style is considered a community package. Once these become widely tested and commonly accepted, they drop the curator prefix and are considered safe bets, thereby making it much easier for developers to pick the most reliable package from a list of alternatives.

Because none of the existing solutions were capable of satisfying all the requirements for a full-stack build and package manager, Meteor 0.9 introduced the Isobuild system.

All the code we've written in the previous chapters and all assets that were added (remember the images we used for the fridge in chapter 2?) are considered business logic. For some Meteor functionality we use packages (*Isopacks*) and—if needed—also npm packages. The default target platforms for all Meteor applications are server and browser, and neither supports Cordova packages. These are needed to access mobile hardware such as the camera or contacts from the phone's address book when you build an application for mobile platforms. Therefore, we'll look at Apache Cordova/ PhoneGap in more detail later in this chapter.

> **NOTE** Apache Cordova is an open source project that turns HTML5-based applications into mobile apps and provides a JavaScript API to access device functionality available to native apps but not from inside a web browser. Adobe PhoneGap is a fork of this project and offers additional, for-pay features. In the context of this book and for using Google search, both names are used interchangeably.

11.1.1 Build stages

Whenever you run a Meteor application using the `meteor run` command, the build process is triggered. While the Meteor server is running, any changes to the application code will trigger a rebuilding of the application code. Up until this point we haven't paid close attention to what actually happens with our code during the build process, so now we'll look under the hood.

Meteor goes through the following build stages:

1 Read project metadata.
2 Initialize the catalog.
3 Resolve constraints.
4 Download missing packages.
5 Build local packages.
6 Save changed metadata.

Let's have a look at each of these stages.

STAGE 1: READING PROJECT METADATA

Before the build process performs any actions, it reads the current project configuration. Every Meteor project has certain metadata that's stored in the .meteor directory. There are four files that hold all relevant information for the build process. You can edit them manually, but the standard way to modify them is by using Meteor's CLI tool (see table below).

Table 11.1 Files used to store project metadata and their corresponding CLI commands

Filename	Modified by command	Contains information on…

.meteor/packages	`meteor list`
	`meteor add`
	`meteor remove`
		Meteor packages used by this project, one per line

.meteor/platforms	`meteor list-platforms`
	`meteor add-platform`
	`meteor remove-platform`
		Target platforms to build the project for

Table 11.1 Files used to store project metadata and their corresponding CLI commands *(continued)*

Filename	Modified by command	Contains information on...
.meteor/release	`meteor create` `meteor update`	Meteor release version to be used for this project
.meteor/versions	`meteor update`	Package requirements and versions determined by the Version Solver component of Isobuild

Every project has a base version of the Meteor framework,[1] which is stored inside the release file. It gets updated when you first create a new project and every time you perform an `update` command in the project root folder. This is the starting point for the Version Solver component that determines which package versions are known to work well together (refer back to chapter 9 for more details on Version Solver).

Whenever you add or remove a package with the `meteor` command, it'll trigger an edit of the packages file. By default new projects start with the three packages `meteor-platform`, `autopublish`, and `insecure`. Packages can depend on other packages. For example, the `meteor-platform` package consists of multiple others, but they aren't listed inside the packages file. They are managed implicitly by Isobuild.

Adding a new package will add a new line at the end of the file, so the contents of this file are ordered chronologically, not alphabetically.

In the versions file, Meteor keeps track of all packages that are needed to build the current project, regardless whether they were added explicitly or came in as a dependency. Therefore, a package such as `tracker` isn't listed inside the packages file but only inside versions. If you wish to update all packages used in your project to the latest version, you use `meteor update`. You shouldn't edit this file manually—it'll be managed by Isobuild.[2] Packages in the versions file are ordered alphabetically; they're the result of processing the packages file that takes place in stage 3.

> **NOTE** In case you only need to update packages to their latest version but not the Meteor release, add the `--packages-only` option to the `update` command.

When you issue a `meteor run` command, the first thing that happens is that those four files are read.

STAGE 2: INITIALIZING THE CATALOG

In the build context, the *catalog* is basically the versions file. Here all the Isopacks required to build the project are listed. When a new package is added to or removed from the packages file and `meteor run` is called, the appropriate package needs to also be

---

[1] Instead of the word *platform* we'll use *framework* here to avoid confusing target platforms with the Meteor platform.

[2] When you add a package with a specific version constraint using `meteor add`, the contents of the versions file will be updated. Because it doesn't affect the build process, we won't go into the specifics of this case.

added or removed from the versions file. In case a package brings in additional dependencies, then those need to be brought in as well, which happens in the next stage.

STAGE 3: RESOLVING CONSTRAINTS

The purpose of the *resolving constraints* stage is to determine dependencies in regard to both packages and versions. All locally available packages are stored inside the Meteor installation folder and not the current project folder. To resolve constraints, each package configuration is read. If a package configuration references another package or a version that's not available locally, additional packages are marked as required and will be retrieved in the next stage.

STAGE 4: DOWNLOADING MISSING PACKAGES

In case packages aren't present on disk yet, Meteor will attempt to download them automatically from the internet. All packages will be stored in the Meteor installation folder rather than the current project folder. That way, all Meteor projects on the same machine can share packages.

Eventually the full set of required Isopacks is available so that the build process can begin.

STAGE 5: BUILDING LOCAL PACKAGES

When all packages are available on the build system, they're built for the current project. Code and assets (fonts, images, and so forth) will be added to the project in the .meteor/local folder. Also, source maps are created for each JavaScript file. Source maps allow you to view the original sources in the browser, even if the files used are minified.

STAGE 6: SAVING CHANGED METADATA

Once all build steps have been executed, the current state is persisted inside the versions and packages files.

RINSE AND REPEAT: WATCHING FOR CHANGES

Although technically not a build stage, the run command will continue to monitor any changes to application files and reexecute the build process if needed. Meteor handles client and server changes differently. Client changes are processed and get sent directly to the browser using *hot code push*. All changes that affect the server cause an actual relaunch of the application. Note that this also executes all Meteor.startup() functions in the server context.

Meteor uses an advanced method to detect file modifications that's similar to the way it uses the MongoDB oplog to monitor changes to the database. On Mac OS X, a kernel extension named kqueue is used; on Linux inotify informs Meteor of all file operations that took place. On Windows there is no such mechanism available.

When Meteor can use either kqueue or inotify, it falls back to a 5000 ms interval to check for possible changes it may have missed, which is much easier on CPU and disk operations than the default setting of 500 ms. On remote filesystems that are mounted via NFS or shared with a virtual (such as a Vagrant[3]) machine, the kernel

---

[3] See appendix A for more details on how to use Vagrant.

extensions may miss changes. If it takes up to 5 seconds for the Meteor process to pick up on any changes, it's likely that the watcher doesn't work properly. In these rare cases you can use two environment variables to define polling behavior (that is, regularly checking for changes). In the same terminal session where you'll start the `meteor` process, issue the following commands to force polling regardless of whether `kqueue` or `inotify` is found, and set the interval to 10 seconds:

```
$ export METEOR_WATCH_FORCE_POLLING=t
$ export METEOR_WATCH_POLLING_INTERVAL_MS=10000
```

> **NOTE** The environment variable `METEOR_WATCH_FORCE_POLLING` expects a single `t`, which sets it to `true`; otherwise it defaults to `false`. The polling interval is defined in milliseconds, and when not set, it defaults to 5000 ms (500 ms if polling is forced).

11.1.2 Running with the –production flag

If you're using a more complex file structure for your project, you can see that using `meteor run` will hardly change the number or structure of your files at all. They'll simply be copied over to the .meteor/local/build directory structure.

This behavior is convenient for development purposes on a local system because a simple copy operation doesn't add a lot of overhead for each file change. In production environments, though, the fewer files you need to serve, the better the initial page loads are. Therefore, in a web environment all files of the same type are usually merged so that only three files must be sent to the browser:

- One JavaScript file
- One CSS file
- One HTML file

Also, the contents of these files are minified, which again decreases transfer times. Unfortunately, merging and minifying source files can lead to some unexpected behaviors such as messed-up styles or crashing applications. To avoid surprises when supposedly finished code is deployed, run a local project with the `--production` flag:

```
$ meteor run --production
```

Using this flag triggers additional build steps. All code that's sent to the client will be merged into a single file for each type (JS, CSS, HTML) and given a random, 41-character name. Server code isn't merged because these files aren't sent over the network and combining them wouldn't yield noticeable performance benefits.

The additional build steps make restarting the server and performing hot-code pushes slower, so use `--production` for testing purposes rather than during development.

> **Debug-only packages**
>
> Some packages add functionality that's useful only in a development context. In case they expose easy access to internal data or execute tests, they can even be danger-ous to deploy to production. For this purpose packages can set a `debugOnly` flag that advises Meteor to exclude those packages from the build process when running with the `--production` option.

11.1.3 *Load order*

With the freedom of creating files and folders using any directory hierarchy, it's important to understand precedence in Meteor's loading process. Especially when cli-ent files are merged using the `--production` flag, having the wrong load order can lead to crashes and bugs.

Meteor's load order is based on both naming conventions and folder hierarchy. This load order is applicable only the business logic of an application. The load order in packages is defined manually inside the package definition (refer to chapter 9 for more details).

As a rule of thumb, Meteor loads files in subdirectories before files in parent direc-tories. The deeper a file is inside a project hierarchy, the sooner it gets loaded. Conse-quently, files in the root directory are loaded last. Within the same hierarchy level or directory, files are loaded in alphabetical order by filename.

There are some exceptions to this general rule:

- All files in folders named lib/ are loaded before all other folder contents. If multiple lib folders exist, they're ordered by level (deepest first) as well as alphabetically. As such, client/lib/file1.js gets loaded before client/scripts/ views/file2.js, even though the general rule suggests that file2 should be loaded first due to the position in the hierarchy.
- The client/compatibility/ directory is reserved for libraries that rely on vari-ables declared with var at the top level being exported as globals. Files in this directory are executed without being wrapped in a new variable scope. These files are executed before other client-side JavaScript files but after the contents from lib/.
- All files that start with main.* are loaded after everything else: client/lib/valida-tions.js comes before client/lib/main.helper.js.
- Any content inside the private/, test/, and public/ directories isn't automati-cally loaded and won't be processed by the build process.

Depending on whether Meteor is running in the server or client context, some files may not be loaded at all. Meteor ignores certain folder contents to prevent sending all code to the browser, even if it's never executed there. Table 11.2 lists all folders that are either ignored on the server or not even sent to the client.

Table 11.2 Directories ignored in server and client contexts

Excluded in server context	Excluded in client context
client/	server/
public/	public/
private/	private/
tests/	tests/

Figures 11.2 and 11.3 show the load order in action. Each file is logging its name to the console once it's loaded. As you can see, only two files are loaded on the server (common.js and server.js), whereas the client loads a total of eight JavaScript files. All directories with the same hierarchical level are sorted alphabetically and loaded in order. The special directories private, public, and test are excluded from loading any JavaScript code.

The client uses a more sophisticated file structure. Regardless of their position inside the hierarchy, all contents from directories named lib come first, which is why its files come before everything else. Then all files from the deepest hierarchy level to the highest are loaded; on same level directories and files are sorted alphabetically. That means client/views/edit/edit.js comes before client/views/client.js. All files with a main.* prefix are moved to the very end of the loading cycle. So even if

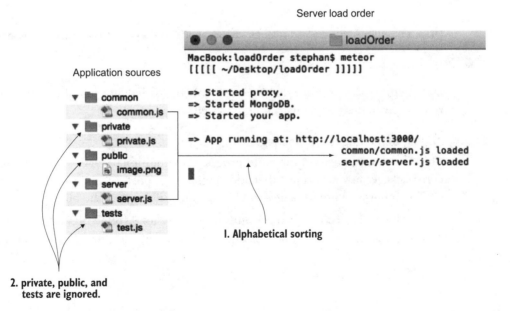

Figure 11.2 Visualizing the load order for JavaScript files on the server using console messages

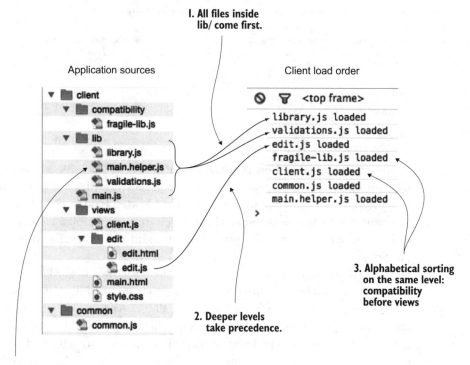

Figure 11.3 Visualizing the load order for JavaScript files on the client using console messages

main.helper.js is stored inside lib/ it will only be loaded after all other files. All these rules apply to the server environment as well.

11.1.4 *Adding build stages via packages*

The easiest way to extend the build process with additional stages is to add one of the core packages to your project that add language support.

The following core packages can be used to add stages to the build process:

- The package `coffeescript` adds transpiling[4] of *.coffee files to JS.
- The package `less` or `stylus` adds processing of *.less or *.sty files to CSS.

---

[4] The term *transpiling* is used to describe source-to-source compilation. Generally, when compiling a file the level of abstraction is reduced—for example, when turning C code into Assembly. When transpiling the level of abstraction stays the same—that is, when going from CoffeeScript to JavaScript.

For additional language support, a variety of community packages are also available. Check the official package repository to see whether your preferred language is available already.

As a third option, you can choose to write your own package that enhances the build process.

COFFEESCRIPT

Many JavaScript developers prefer using CoffeeScript instead of plain JavaScript. Coffee uses a different syntax with fewer brackets and semicolons and requires transpiling into plain JavaScript so it can be executed in the browser and inside Node.js.

Using CoffeeScript with a Meteor project is as simple as adding the `coffeescript` package:

```
$ meteor add coffeescript
```

Once the package is available in a Meteor project, all files with a .coffee extension are automatically transpiled (translated) into JavaScript whenever they're modified. That way, regular JavaScript files can be used along with code written in CoffeeScript—for example, when adding external libraries to a lib/ folder.

Except for the fact that Meteor supports another file extension and adds a translation stage, the rest of the build process stays exactly the same, including the load order of files.

LESS OR STYLUS

Static style files using CSS are supported by Meteor out of the box. If you add the corresponding packages, the dynamic styling languages LESS and Stylus can also be used. These languages are called *preprocessors*, and they're used to enhance style sheets with variables and mixins. Mixins allow you to use style snippets that can be easily reused, thus shortening the overall code that you have to write. In combination with using variables, this makes customizing designs much easier, which is why many developers prefer dynamic preprocessors over plain CSS.

LESS and Stylus need to be translated into plain CSS for a browser to be able to interpret them. Let's start by adding either of the packages using the CLI:

```
$ meteor add less
$ meteor add stylus
```

As a result of adding either of the packages, files with a .less or .sty extension are properly identified and processed by Meteor. Both preprocessors behave exactly the same in regard to the build process.

Meteor concatenates all style files into one, following the aforementioned load order. To gain more control over the load order, you can import individual files from a style file. If a file has the extension *.import.less or *.import.sty, then Meteor won't process it during the build unless these files are directly referenced from a style file.

In practice you'll end up with a single styles.less file that may look similar to listing 11.1. Obviously the referenced files must exist in order to import them.

Listing 11.1   Sample style file using the LESS preprocessor

```less
@bg-color: #ff9900;                               ◁──      Declaring
                                                            a variable
.rounded_top_mixin {                              ◁──
    -webkit-border-top-left-radius: 5px;
    -webkit-border-top-right-radius: 5px;                  Declaring
    -moz-border-radius-topleft: 5px;                       a mixin
    -moz-border-radius-topright: 5px;
    border-top-left-radius: 5px;
    border-top-right-radius: 5px;
}
.tab {                                                     Using a variable
    background: @bg-color;                        ◁──
    .rounded_top_mixin;                           ◁──      Using a mixin
}

@import "variables.import.less";                  ◁──      Importing additional
                                                           .less files
```

11.1.5 *Adding a custom build stage*

In version 1.1, the possible ways to extend Meteor's build stages are limited to watching for changes to files with a specific extension. Changes to a file may trigger an action associated with the watcher configured for the specific file extension, such as transpiling one language to another.

Essentially adding a custom build stage requires using a package. Build steps are added during stage 5, the building of local packages. In the package.js file `Package` `.registerBuildPlugin()` is used to identify that a package extends the build process. Listing 11.2 shows the code used by the `coffeescript` package as an example.

- `name` is the identifier for this build stage. A package may contain multiple build plug-ins as long as they have unique names.
- `use` references Meteor Isopacks that this build stage may depend on as a string or array of strings.
- `sources` contains an array of strings that defines which files are part of the plug-in.
- `npmDependencies` is an object that holds `npm` package names and versions that the plug-in may depend on.

In case you need to write your own build plug-in—say, for transpiling TypeScript (another shorthand notation for JavaScript) to plain JavaScript—you need to replace the `coffee-script` npm dependency with the `ts-compiler` module. Additionally, you need to adjust the name and source file accordingly.

Listing 11.2   Registering a build plug-in with CoffeeScript support in package.json

```
Package.registerBuildPlugin({
  name: "compileCoffeescript",
  use: [],
```

```
sources: [
  'plugin/compile-coffeescript.js'
],
npmDependencies: {"coffee-script": "1.7.1", "source-map": "0.1.32"}
});
```

A single source file is used for this plug-in.

Two npm modules are required to execute the plug-in.

In the source files of a build plug-in, you can use `Plugin.registerSourceHandler()` to define what actions to execute if files with a particular extension are changed. If the plug-in is supposed to monitor files with a .ts extension, then it must be specified as a source handler. Listing 11.3 outlines the essentials parts of a build plug-in. Using `compileStep`, it's possible to either read or write to the currently processed files.[5]

> **Listing 11.3 Skeleton for transpiling TypeScript to JavaScript during the build**

```
//file: plugin/compile-typescript.js
var typescript = Npm.require('ts-compile');


Plugin.registerSourceHandler('ts', handler);


var handler = function (compileStep) {
    var fileContents = compileStep.read().toString('utf8');
    // transpiling logic, result stored inside jsCode
    compileStep.addJavaScript({
        path: outputPath,
        sourcePath: compileStep.inputPath,
        data: jsCode
    });
};
```

Required npm modules must be included via NPM.require.

The file extension is used without the first dot.

compileStep gives the handler access to the current file.

addJavaScript writes the result of the build step into a JavaScript file.

NOTE As of version 1.1 there's a limitation on the source handler that only one build plug-in per file extension can be used. There can't be multiple plug-ins that add a build step for JavaScript files, for example.

If you add a package to a project that turns TypeScript or CoffeeScript into JavaScript, the `build` and `run` process will look like this:

1 Isobuild determines which file has changed.
2 It looks at the filename extension and checks if a `compileStep` is associated with it. There may only be one step per file extension.
3 If an associated `compileStep` is found, Isobuild executes it and saves the output as defined by the build plug-in.

---

[5] The official documentation for using `compileStep` can be found at https://github.com/meteor/meteor/wiki/CompileStep-API-for-Build-Plugin-Source-Handlers.

4 If you use the `build` command or run Meteor with the `--production` flag, merging and minification run independently and after completing all steps of the build plug-in.

11.2 Accessing running applications

In previous chapters you've used the browser console to send commands to a running application, such as to check the values of a `Session` variable. In this section, we'll explore possible options to access the server side of a running application as well to allow better debugging capabilities.

11.2.1 Using the interactive server shell

Whenever you issue `meteor run` in a terminal session, you can view all server output in the same terminal window. All console logging that takes place on the server side is shown, but it doesn't allow you to send any commands. Instead, whenever you need to check the current state of variables you can add a `console.log()` to the JavaScript files, which triggers a server restart.

For locally running applications, the Meteor CLI tool can open an interactive shell session, where you can send commands to the server just like inside the browser console.

INVOKING THE INTERACTIVE SHELL

Open a terminal session and navigate to the Meteor project folder. Run the server using the following:

```
$ meteor run
```

You can now see all server messages scroll by as the project starts up. Open a second terminal session and navigate to the same project folder. Now issue this command:

```
$ meteor shell
```

This command opens up an interactive shell, as shown in figure 11.4.

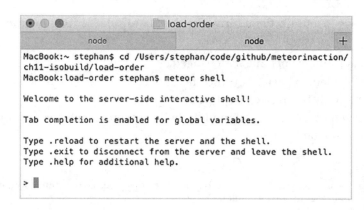

Figure 11.4 Invoking the interactive server shell using the `meteor` command

USING THE INTERACTIVE SHELL

All shell commands start with a leading dot. They can be used to execute any code that you would otherwise put inside a file. For example, during development you can query external APIs, call helper functions, or easily remove content from the database using `Collection.remove()`. That way, you can also use the Meteor syntax instead of the slightly different MongoDB syntax and you don't need an additional MongoDB connection using RoboMongo or `meteor mongo`.

The shell supports autocompletion of all Meteor globals when you use the Tab key. You can also access a complete history of all commands by using the up and down arrow keys. The shell history is stored in the project folder in the .meteor/local/shell-history file. Using the `.save` and `.load` commands, you can store a sequence of commands for reuse. All commands from the current session will be saved. This can be useful for saving scenarios like filling in fixtures or resetting the application state to a certain point. Saving and loading requires a unique name. To store a sequence of commands under the `bootstrap` identifier, you could use the following:

```
> PostsCollection.insert({title: 'first test article'})
'i4xZb8WM8Lr63KwA4'
> PostsCollection.insert({title: 'second test article'})
'PvRkekuDuBn6Wx5kY'
> .save bootstrap
```

Whenever you want to re-execute these commands, you can do so by issuing `.load bootstrap` inside the shell. The saved REPL[6] files can be found in the project/ .meteor/local/build/programs/server/ folder. Multiple shells may be opened for the same project.

> **NOTE** Both the shell-history file and the REPL files are ignored by Git by default. If you want to add them to your source code repository, you must adjust the .gitignore file accordingly.

11.2.2 Debugging using node-inspector

If you need to perform more sophisticated server-side debugging of an application, `node-inspector` is a handy utility. It's a browser-based debugger interface for Node.js that you can use to set breakpoints, inspect source files, step through program execution, and inspect values and variables.

Passing the `debug` command to the `meteor` CLI tool provides a simple way to use `node-inspector`. Make sure you are in a project's root directory and that it's currently not running. Then issue this command:

```
$ meteor debug
```

---

[6] REPL stands for Read-Eval-Print-Loop and refers to the fact that it isn't a fully interactive shell where, for example, your commands could query additional user input during execution. They're simply read and executed, and the result is printed to the screen.

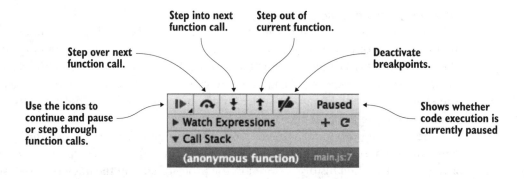

Figure 11.5 The icons on the top of the right sidebar enable stepping through functions and pausing execution.

Any WebKit-based browser is capable of running `node-inspector`, which means both Chrome and Safari can be used to access the debugging URL. You can't use Firefox or Internet Explorer.

> **NOTE** Accessing the application using http://localhost:3000 is still possible in debug mode. Additionally, you can open the debugger interface using http://localhost:8080/debug?port=5858.

Once the server starts up, you can access both the app and the debugging interface. If you don't see your application starting up, go to the debugging URL and check the current execution status. If code execution is paused, you'll see a message icon at the top of the right sidebar, just like in figure 11.5. Click the pause arrow at the left of the icon bar to continue program execution.

The application will run as usual, but you'll now be able to use the debugging console to inspect what happens during code execution on the server. Two of the most important tools are setting breakpoints and inspecting and modifying variable content.

Breakpoints are markers that define where code execution should be paused so that each step can be executed individually to identify the actual behavior of a function or code section. You can set them either in the browser window by clicking an individual line number of a file or by using the `debugger;` statement. Listing 11.4 shows a simple example where the variable `status` is assigned the value `initialized`, and immediately after code execution is paused. Using `node-inspector`, you can then inspect the content of the `status` variable.

Listing 11.4   Setting breakpoints using `debugger;`

```
if (Meteor.isServer) {
  Meteor.startup(function () {
    var status = 'initialized';
    debugger;
    if (status === 'initialized'){
      status = 'done'
    }
    console.log('status is now ' + status);
  });
});
```

When running with meteor debug, this will cause the app to pause.

Hover the mouse cursor over the variable name, and its contents will be displayed in a yellow pop-up as well as on the right side under Scope Variables (where you can change the value to something else). For setting breakpoints or inspecting variable content from other files, open the file navigator using the top-left icon (see figure 11.6).

TIP If `node-inspector` doesn't seem to behave like it should, try refreshing the browser. If that doesn't work, restart Meteor with the `debug` command again.

`node-inspector` is a powerful tool that enables you to gain valuable insight into your application's behavior. To understand all its features, take a look at the documentation at the project's GitHub page: https://github.com/node-inspector/node-inspector.

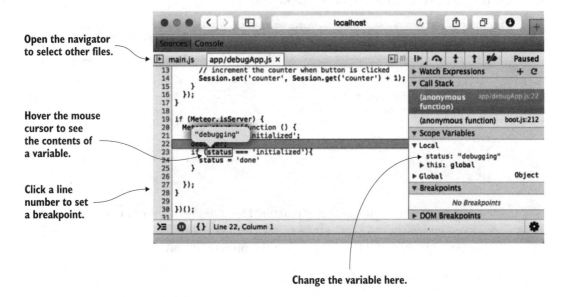

Open the navigator to select other files.

Hover the mouse cursor to see the contents of a variable.

Click a line number to set a breakpoint.

Change the variable here.

Figure 11.6   Inspecting and changing the contents of a variable with `node-inspector`

11.3 *Creating browser applications*

Applications may support one or more platforms. By default, all new projects have the server and browser platforms enabled. As mentioned earlier, you can view a list of all supported platforms for a project by issuing this command:

```
$ meteor list-platforms
```

Unless you've added additional platforms already, the output will show `browser` and `server`. To deploy an application to a server, you have to bundle it first. The output is similar to that of `meteor run --production`, but there's no need to run continuously and watch for file changes.

> **NOTE**   In version 1.0 Meteor projects must always contain the server platform. It's not possible to build for the browser platform only.

11.3.1 *Application configuration using Meteor.settings*

Earlier we talked about storing configuration data like API keys and secrets only on the server side. But there are scenarios where multiple server environments exist—dedicated development, testing, and production environments. Each may require different settings, which is why it's not efficient to store configuration data in the code files but rather in a configuration file. Meteor can take a JSON file and expose its contents via the `Meteor.settings` object. That means you can use code like `Meteor.settings.oauth.twitter.apikey` instead of a string. The following listing shows the structure of a configuration file for Meteor settings.

> **Listing 11.5 Setting configuration options for applications via settings.json**

```
{
  "oauth": {
    "twitter": {
      "apikey": "123abc",
      "secret": "abc123"
    }
  },
  "public": {
    "version": "v1"
  }
}
```

Meteor doesn't use a settings file by default. The settings file must be specified on the command line using the `--settings` parameter.

To use a file named settings.json, start the project with this:

```
$ meteor run --settings settings.json
```

Alternatively, you can store the JSON configuration object in an environment variable called `Meteor.settings`. Either way, you can access properties of the settings object, as shown in listing 11.6.

NOTE When you're using `Meteor.settings` always provide the settings object upon start of the Meteor server or you'll run into errors.

Listing 11.6 Using `Meteor.settings` with values from a JSON configuration file

```
if (Meteor.isServer) {
  console.log("Using the following API Key for Twitter");
  console.log(Meteor.settings.oauth.twitter.apikey);
}
```

The configuration file isn't available on the client, but you can access all configuration settings stored inside a public field by using `Meteor.settings.public`. Any content that is stored outside the `public` field won't be accessible on the client and can be safely be used for sensitive configuration settings.

Using different settings files, you can easily run applications in staging and production environments with different databases and API connections.

11.3.2 Building Meteor projects

Meteor can create bundles of an application using the `meteor build` command. The output is a fully contained Node.js application in the form of a tarball. If needed, the `build` command can be changed to create a directory with the same contents as the tarball.

Creating the bundle is as simple as navigating to the application root directory and calling the command with an argument specifying you want to create the output file.

TIP When you're creating a tarball, it's usually fine to place the output in the current project folder, but for various reasons it might be better to put it elsewhere. First, you could accidentally add it to the source code repository unless you explicitly add a rule to ignore this file. Second, if you decide to create a directory instead of a file or build for another platform, the resulting files will be interpreted as additional source files when you use `meteor run` and produce error messages.

To place the archived bundle file for your Meteor application at the parent folder of the current project in a directory called builds, use the following commands:

```
$ cd myMeteorProject
$ meteor build ../builds
```

The tar.gz file contains the compiled Meteor application, which you can put on a server, extract, and run (see chapter 12 for more details).

You'll notice that the entire directory structure has changed significantly from the original project organization (see figure 11.7). Instead of client, server, and public folders, you'll now see two main folders: programs and server. All relevant code is located in the programs folder, organized by platforms. In the server folder, all modules, packages, and assets are stored. The contents from the assets and private folders

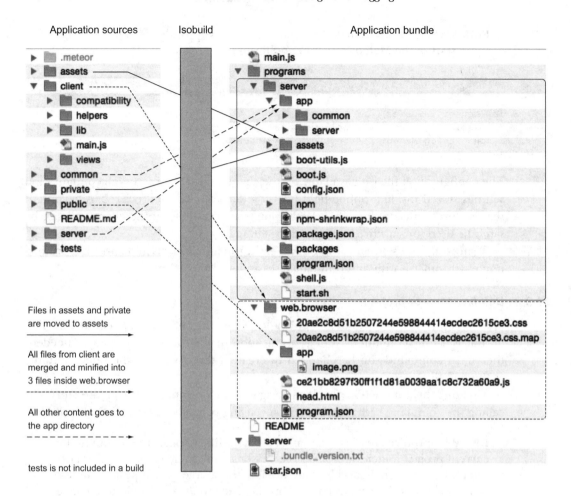

Figure 11.7   The output of `meteor build`

are treated differently because they're moved into an assets directory inside the bundle. All other contents are moved to the app directory; the tests folder is an exception because it isn't put into production bundles.

All resources that are sent to the browser are stored in the web.browser folder. Running `meteor build` implies using the `--production` option, so there are three important files: one each for HTML, CSS, and JavaScript. Also, the static resources from the public directory are copied for the client platform and can be found in the app directory.

You'll notice several other files are available that weren't present before, such as main.js. These files are generated automatically and include the main components needed to run the project as a regular Node.js application.

Although `meteor build` is simple to use, it does have some limitations in regard to portability. As long as you don't rely on platform-specific, binary `npm` modules, you shouldn't experience any problems moving an app from a Mac OS X development system to an Ubuntu Linux server. In some advanced cases that require truly portable Node.js applications, `demeteorizer` is the more flexible tool. Take a look at chapter 12 for further information on how to use it.

11.4 Creating mobile applications

Apps running on smartphones and tablets are often similar to web applications. Instead of using a browser, they embed the application in an app container. That way, they combine aspects of server/client-oriented websites based on HTML5 and native apps, which is why they're called *hybrid* apps. Meteor leverages the power of Cordova to add mobile platform support.

11.4.1 Hybrid apps with Cordova

Cordova[7] is a framework that converts HTML, JavaScript, and CSS into a native application that can run on mobile platforms such as iOS or Android. It provides a native wrapper around a web view (think of it as an embedded browser) and offers access to hardware features like the camera or GPS. To a user, apps built on Cordova look and behave exactly like native apps. They're distributed via app stores, so in order to sell mobile Meteor apps you must be part of Apple's or Google's developer program.

Because it's an Apache project, Cordova is open source and free to use. There's also PhoneGap, which is often used to describe the same tool. Technically PhoneGap is a distribution of Cordova that's maintained by Adobe and offers some paid features. For the purpose of putting Meteor applications on mobile devices, we'll refer only to Cordova from here on, but on Google and Stack Overflow most of the time you can use both terms interchangeably.

CORDOVA FEATURES

The most important advantage Cordova can add to a Meteor app is the web browser shell that'll make it look and behave like an app. This shell allows apps to be bought in the app stores and started without you having to know which server URL to navigate to.

By using plug-ins, Cordova can access a device's hardware or exchange data with other apps on a device. These plug-ins provide APIs to use the camera, access contacts, or even enable in-app purchases.

---

[7] If you want to learn more about Cordova, refer to Raymond K. Camden's *Apache Cordova in Action* (Manning, 2015).

A full list of all available plug-ins for Cordova can be found at http://plugins
.cordova.io/. Some of the plug-ins are available as Meteor packages as well. The Meteor
Development Group provides the following:

- `mdg:camera`—Allows an app to access the device's camera
- `mdg:geolocation`—Provides a reactive interface to the device's GPS location
- `mdg:reload-on-resume`—Delays hot-code pushes until the app is closed and
  reopened

CORDOVA LIMITATIONS

Although Cordova makes it easy to turn HTML5 applications into mobile apps, it's still
the same as browsing a website. Don't expect the same performance from the DOM
rendering as from a graphic-intensive action game written in Java. That said, many
apps will certainly do fine with modern devices.

Because Cordova only shells web applications, it doesn't provide a UI framework or
enforce design guidelines.

11.4.2 *Adding mobile platforms*

Meteor supports two mobile platforms: Android and iOS. When either of them is
added to a project, the `build` command will take care of creating not only a tarball but
also a valid Android Studio or Xcode project. During development, there's no need to
open either of those tools because Meteor is capable of running an application inside
simulators as well.

PREREQUISITES

Before you can add mobile platforms to a project, you must install the SDKs for each
platform on your development machine. The iOS SDK is available only on Mac OS X
and requires you to also install Apple's Xcode. It's not possible to build iOS applications on Linux or Windows. You install the SDKs by using these `meteor` commands:

```
$ meteor install-sdk ios
$ meteor install-sdk android
```

You have to accept the license agreement for the iOS SDK. If you get an error message, try opening Xcode and click on the agreement. The Android SDK has a dedicated configuration interface, which can be invoked by the `meteor` CLI tool as well.
You can use this interface to download updates or manage devices that can be used
with the simulator. It's not necessary to perform any configuration before you can
start bringing an application to Android, so we won't look into the details of this
tool. Should you ever need the Android SDK Manager, you can start it with this
command:

```
$ meteor configure-android
```

ADDING PLATFORMS

Making a Meteor application run on mobile devices requires adding the corresponding platform to the project. To do so, use one or both of these commands:

```
$ meteor add-platform ios
$ meteor add-platform android
```

The Meteor build process will automatically be configured to include the required steps to produce mobile apps for either platform. But meteor run won't automatically run your application for a mobile platform; you need to add the platform name as an argument to the run command like this:

```
$ meteor run ios
$ meteor run android
```

This command will compile the application and open it in a simulated iPhone or Android device. Although the application itself won't make use of any UI guidelines for the platform, all input fields like drop-down lists and text boxes will rely on the devices' default interfaces (see figure 11.8).

If you prefer to run the Meteor app on an actual device, you'll need to use Xcode (https://developer.apple.com/library/mac/documentation/IDEs/Conceptual/App DistributionGuide/LaunchingYourApponDevices/LaunchingYourApponDevices.html)

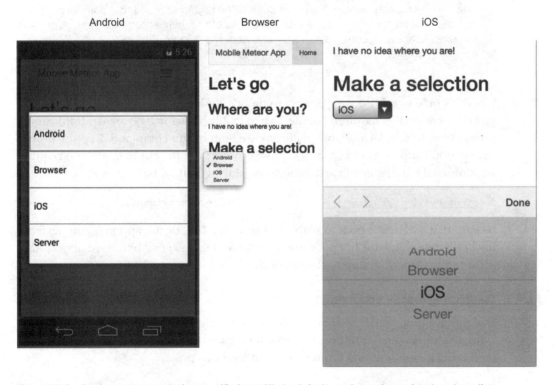

Figure 11.8 Cordova apps use device-specific input UIs by default, such as when using drop-down lists.

or follow the instructions for setting up an Android device for testing (http://developer
.android.com/tools/device.html#setting-up). The `run` command must include a device
as a parameter to tell Meteor to use actual hardware instead of a simulator:

```
$ meteor run ios-device
$ meteor run android-device
```

> **Submitting to the app stores**
>
> Meteor won't create a finished mobile application that can be submitted to the app
> stores. For both Android and iOS, you'll still need to complete the necessary steps
> for publishing the applications just as you would for any other mobile app. But you
> won't have to write any code in Xcode or Android Studio. You can only make the fin-
> ishing touches to distribute your app using these tools.
>
> The first prerequisite to get your mobile Meteor application on a smartphone or tablet
> is to join the developer program. For both platforms, doing so involves registration
> and paying a fee; you'll then be able to submit applications to the Google Play Store
> or the Apple iTunes Store.
>
> The specifics may change, so you should consult the official process of creating an
> application, but these are the basic steps you need to follow. Once you have a devel-
> oper account, you'll obtain a certificate that you can use to sign your application
> code. This certificate verifies that your application is your app and that someone else
> isn't distributing it under your name. The certificate usually accompanies a distribu-
> tion profile that lists company information and, most important, a unique identifier
> for your application.

When it's time to release your project to mobile devices, issue the `meteor build` command to create the required Xcode (when publishing for iOS) or Android Studio
project files. In fact, all available platforms are built by this command. Because mobile
devices don't allow users to enter URLs like browsers do, the `build` command requires
an additional parameter to specify the server during build time:

```
$ meteor build ../builds --server=http://mobile.meteorinaction.com
```

Be sure that a Meteor app is available at the server URL or the app may run perfectly
fine inside the simulator but not once it's deployed to an actual hardware device. Also,
before submitting your app to the stores check that the server URL is correct.

11.4.3 *Configuring mobile applications*

You can customize mobile applications by changing the default configuration. App
icons, launch screens, application meta information, and plug-in settings may be managed using a mobile-config.js file at the root level of a project.

APPLICATION META INFORMATION USING APP.INFO()

App.info() holds an object that contains further information regarding an app. It uses the following properties:

- id—Unique reverse-domain identifier
- version—Full version number using x.y.z notation
- name—Displayed on the device's home screen and used in app stores
- description—Used in app stores
- author—Used in app stores
- email—Used to further specify the author information in app stores
- website—Used to further specify the author information in app stores

All keys take a string value, as shown in the following listing.

Listing 11.7   Sample `App.info()` for a mobile app

```
App.info({
    id:          'com.meteorinaction.mobile.app',
    version:     '1.0.0',
    name:        'Meteor in Action Mobile App',
    description: 'This is a mobile app for Meteor in Action',
    author:      'Stephan Hochhaus',
    email:       'stephan@meteorinaction.com',
    website:     'http://meteorinaction.com'
});
```

ICONS AND LAUNCH SCREENS

To customize both the logo that's shown on the home screen of a device and the screen shown during the startup of an application, use the API commands App.icons() and App.launchScreens(). When those blocks are not filled, the default Meteor icons and launch screens are used. Different devices use different resolutions, which is why both commands take a variety of properties. For distribution in app stores, all screen sizes must have a dedicated icon and launch screen configured. Check the mobileApp project from this chapter's code samples for a full list of all currently supported device types. The following listing shows how they're used in the mobile-config.js file.

Listing 11.8   Setting up icons and launch screens in mobile.config.js

```
App.icons({
  'iphone':                'icons/iphone.png',
  'android_ldpi':          'icons/android-launcher.png',
});

App.launchScreens({
  'iphone':                'icons/splash-iphone.png',
  'android_ldpi_portrait': 'icons/splash-ldpi_portrait.png',
});
```

WHITELISTING URLs

In web browsers your application may request additional information from various URLs without you noticing it. For security reasons Cordova applications are not allowed to access arbitrary URLs. Only URLs that are whitelisted in the mobile-config.js file can be accessed. Each allowed URL is defined using `App.accessRule` using the syntax

```
App.accessRule(domainRule, {launchExternal: false})
```

The `domainRule` can be any URL, using placeholders for subdomains. Setting options is not required. The only possible option is `launchExternal`, which allows the Cordova apps to launch a URL in an external application on the mobile device. Listing 11.9 gives an example of typical access rules.

> **NOTE** Whenever your mobile application relies on content from external APIs, you must declare access rules in order to allow your app to access the remote URL.

Listing 11.9   Declaring URL access rules in mobile.config.js

```
App.accessRule('https://*.googleapis.com/*');        Allow access to Google
App.accessRule('https://*.google.com/*');            APIs such as Maps.
App.accessRule('https://*.gstatic.com/*');


App.accessRule('https://pbs.twimg.com/*');       ◄──  Allow access to Twitter
                                                      profile images.

App.accessRule('http://graph.facebook.com/*');       Allow access to Facebook's
App.accessRule('https://graph.facebook.com/*');      profile images.
```

CONFIGURING CORDOVA PLUG-INS

Besides Isopacks and `npm` modules, Meteor supports Cordova plug-ins. The mobile-config.js file can also be used to configure these plug-ins. You can set the configuration of the WebKit container via `App.setPreference()`. Technically it allows you to set values for the `preference` tag inside Cordova's config.xml file.

Cordova plug-ins can be configured using `App.configurePlugin()`. They also use a rather simple key-value style for configuration, so the command takes two arguments: the name of a plug-in and a config object providing key-value pairs.

The following listing shows how to configure both global preferences as well as a plug-in called `facebookconnect`.

Listing 11.10   Configuring app behavior and Cordova plug-ins

```
App.setPreference('BackgroundColor', '0xff0000ff');
App.setPreference('HideKeyboardFormAccessoryBar', true);

App.configurePlugin('com.phonegap.plugins.facebookconnect', {
  APP_ID: '1234567890',
  API_KEY: 'apikey'
});
```

11.4.4 *Adding mobile functionality*

Although turning an existing browser application into a mobile app isn't difficult, so far we haven't shown you how to add any mobile-specific functionality. Similar to the isServer() and isClient() methods, you can use a Meteor.isCordova() function to run code exclusively on mobile platforms:

```
if (Meteor.isCordova) {
  console.log('Printed only in mobile cordova apps');
}
```

Using this conditional is the simplest way to add mobile-only functionality, but it doesn't enable access to a device's features. To do so, you have to enhance the existing application.

Cordova is similar to Meteor because it uses a small core set of functionality that's extended by plug-ins. If a feature can be added by using an Isopack such as mdg:geolocation, its usage is like most other packages.

Any functionality that relies on a Cordova/PhoneGap plug-in should wrap code in a Meteor.startup() block. In case of mdg:geolocation, you'd need code like this:

```
Meteor.startup(function () {
  Geolocation.currentLocation();
});
```

Without going into the details of using specific packages, we'll look at another way to extend the application's functionality by integrating Cordova plug-ins into an app. There are two types of plug-ins: those that are bundled with the core (which can be identified by their name prefix, org.apache.cordova) and third-party plug-ins, which can be found in the official plug-in registry at http://plugins.cordova.io/ and on GitHub.

> **NOTE** Don't wrap mobile code inside an isServer() block or put it in the server folder because eventually it must run on the mobile client device.

Let's look at an example of how to use plain Cordova plug-ins with Meteor. We'll use the dialogs plug-in, which provides native UI dialog elements to an application. First, add it via meteor add. Because it's a Cordova plug-in, it uses the cordova: prefix by definition. Meteor doesn't perform the same consistency and compatibility checks as it does with Isopacks, so you must specify a specific version instead of relying on Version Solver to determine the correct one:

```
$ meteor add cordova:org.apache.cordova.dialogs@0.3.0
```

The dialogs plug-in will now be listed along with all other packages when issuing meteor list. Listing 11.11 shows how to create a native dialog based on Meteor's default project. In the event map you add an additional dialog to the change event on a select box and wrap it in an isCordova() block to prevent it from being executed in the browser. Meteor can use the plug-in as is; there's no need to wrap it in API calls. The same navigator.notification.alert that can be used in regular Cordova apps can be used here. It takes four arguments: the *dialog message* in the form of a string, a *callback function* when the alert is dismissed (here, null), a *dialog title* (which defaults to Alert), and the *button name* (which defaults to OK).

Listing 11.11   Adding the Cordova `dialogs` plug-in to a change event

```
Template.select.events({
  'change #platform': function (evt) {
    var selectedPlatform = evt.currentTarget.value;
    if (Meteor.isCordova) {
      navigator.notification.alert(
        'You picked ' + selectedPlatform,
        null,
        'Your choice',
        'I know'
      );
      navigator.notification.alert(
        'You selected',
        selectedPlatform
      );
    } else {
      console.log('selected ' + selectedPlatform)
    }
  }
});
```

Only execute this code block on mobile devices.

Create a dialog box.

Callback function when alert is acknowledged

Dialog box title

Button text

Message text

11.5   Summary

In this chapter, you've learned that

- Although JavaScript isn't a compiled language, Meteor apps need to be built before running them.
- When you use the --production flag with the run command, all files will be minified.
- The file load order is based on hierarchical position and filenames.
- The build process can be extended by using packages such as coffeescript or less.
- By default, all projects are built for a server-browser scenario.
- Adding mobile platforms extends the build process to create hybrid apps for iOS or Android using Cordova.
- Cordova plug-ins can be used directly with Meteor; they don't have to be wrapped inside Isopacks.

Going into production

12

This chapter covers

- Organizing your code to ease deployments
- Integrating testing frameworks using Velocity
- Estimating and testing load
- Understanding deployment options, from simple to highly available
- Using Meteor UP to deploy an application
- Using environment variables to configure the server
- Architecting highly available architectures

When all features are implemented and all bugs ironed out, it's time to go into production. This chapter covers all the essentials of deploying a Meteor application. We won't go into the specifics of server administration, but we'll explore typical architectures and possible options in regard to small as well as scalable deployments, so you know what to do when your app becomes a success.

In an ideal world, you'll already have thought about the "go-live" of your application even before you started writing a single line of code. If you haven't, now is the time to revisit expectations and requirements. You'll notice that your deployment options are greatly influenced by the requirements you have. But because most of the largest applications started small as well, we'll begin by looking at the simplest deployment scenarios and introduce larger scale and the complexity it introduces as a second step.

12.1 *Preparing for production*

At the most basic level, putting your project into production means copying it to a remote server and giving users access. From this moment on, you'll notice bugs, plan additional features, deploy patches, receive user feedback—you'll be working in two worlds: the production environment and the development environment. Before you copy code to any servers, let's walk through some essential techniques that are useful for running an application in production.

12.1.1 *Using version control*

From the moment you issue the first `meteor create` command, you're preparing for production. Unless you're at a hackathon and will never again look at the code you created, place your project under version control, especially if it consists of more than just a few lines of code or is developed by more than a single person. Systems such as Git, Subversion, or IBM ClearCase give you a safety net that also helps with development as well as deployment.

The benefits of source control for deployment may not be as apparent when you first copy your files to a server. But how do you know what revision is available to users and whether a bug raised from a paying customer still exists or has already been fixed before you go on a two-week vacation?

> **TIP** Add your Meteor project not at the root of your repository but in an app folder. That way, you can also add non-application resources such as configuration files to the same repository.

Once you're ready to go into production you should have a dedicated master branch that represents production-quality code and tag it every time you deploy it into production. That approach makes it easy to see what code base is used for your running app.

Using Git we'll walk you through the steps required. Many people do all work on the *master* branch, which makes merging changes much more complicated than it could be. Instead, use a branch for all development or error fixing and let only working code make it into the master branch.

> **TIP** When using Git be sure the master branch always contains only the most recent and stable code. No development work should be done on the master but on dedicated development or feature branches.

In a Git repository, a simple project may look similar to figure 12.1.

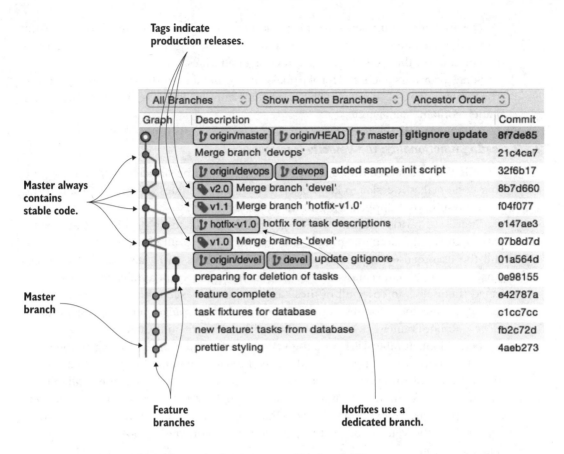

Figure 12.1 Using multiple branches for development and hotfixes in Git

All development takes place in a dedicated branch called *devel*. Once development is finished and all tests are passed, the code is merged over to master and is tagged with a version number (such as v1.0).

The advantage of using multiple branches is that you can add features to your application that you don't yet want to deploy but still be able to fix critical issues in your production code without risking mixing untested development code with a live environment.

In our scenario, you've successfully deployed stable code into production and tagged it v1.0. While working on the next version, 2.0, a critical issue is reported and requires a hotfix. To work on the hotfix, you create a new branch called *hotfix-v1.0*. Once you correct and test the code in the hotfix branch, you merge it back into master. All this is unaffected by anything that might happen in the devel context.[1]

---

[1] You can find a more in-depth explanation of this branching model at http://nvie.com/posts/a-successful-git-branching-model/.

The greater the number of people working on a project or the more complex your application becomes, the more branches might be used. Just be sure that you can easily keep track of the code used in production at all times.

Some providers such as Heroku make it the default to deploy your application from source control. Just as in the previous example, they assume that the master branch contains stable code.

12.1.2 Testing functionality: the Velocity framework

All code that you merge into the master branch should be sufficiently tested. Tagging your code makes it easier to keep track of testing candidates as well, especially if the person testing your application isn't the app's developer.

There are various flavors of testing, including unit testing, which isolates small parts of the application; integration testing, which ensures all parts work together well; and the user-focused approach of behavior-driven tests (BDT, also known as acceptance tests). In recent years, several testing tools for JavaScript applications have established themselves to cover all of these areas. With the exception of Tinytest, Meteor uses the same tools for testing that you may know from other projects: Jasmine, Mocha, Robot Framework in combination with Selenium, and Cucumber.

Take a look at table 12.1, which gives you an overview of the testing frameworks and what areas they're used for. It also lists the package name for using them within Meteor. Each of these frameworks has quite extensive documentation available, so we won't discuss their use, but we'll show you how to integrate them into your Meteor projects. To get a better understanding of how these individual tools work, you can visit the Velocity page at http://velocity.meteor.com or look at each project's documentation.

Table 12.1   Overview of functional test tools for Meteor

Framework	Package name	Unit testing	Integration testing	Acceptance testing
Tinytest	`tinytest`	Server, client (Isopacks only)	—	—
Jasmine	`sanjo:jasmine`	Server	Client	—
Mocha	`mike:mocha`	—	Server, client	—
Robot Framework	`rsbatech:robotframework`	—	—	Client
Cucumber	`xolvio:cucumber`	—	—	Client

Meteor's official testing framework is called Velocity. Technically it's a test runner that includes specific testing frameworks. Written by a team of developers in the Meteor

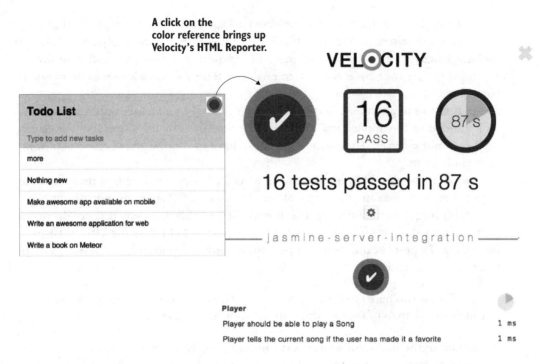

Figure 12.2 Velocity has an HTML reporter that overlays the actual application with a full test report.

community, Velocity lets you define automated tests[2] using any mix of established testing libraries.

The Velocity framework is added via packages, and it even integrates directly in the application's UI. Whenever you add a testing framework from table 12.1 to your applications, you also bring in Velocity. To use Jasmine, you'd issue the following:

```
$ meteor add sanjo:jasmine
```

All framework packages include an HTML reporter that displays the results of your tests in an overlay. This reporter is added by default in all frameworks except Jasmine. To add it explicitly for Jasmine, use this:

```
$ meteor add velocity:html-reporter
```

Running `meteor` will now display a green dot in the upper-right corner of the page. This is the HTML reporter, which can be accessed by clicking the dot, as shown in figure 12.2. The reporter shows the test results of all installed Velocity test frameworks. If

___

2 If you plan on doing regular updates to your production environment, it pays off to set up a continuous integration (CI) or continuous delivery (CD) environment to perform all tests at the push of a button and optionally deploy to your target systems. Take a look at Travis or Jenkins if you want to start using the benefits of a CI environment.

no tests have been defined yet, the Jasmine package allows you to create a set of sample tests. Once a test is available, this view shows each test result (pass or fail). It updates reactively if test results change. Integration and unit tests will typically be rerun every time your code is saved, to enable real-time feedback on whether code is passing or failing tests.

All tests live in a folder called tests at the root level of a Meteor application. They aren't added to the application when build is executed or the --production flag is used to run the server. That means you don't have to remove tests before deploying your application.

Although you should have unit tests in place, they don't ensure that users are able to perform all actions in your application without errors. When testing your application don't forget to include negative tests—test for what happens if users do unexpected things such as entering letters into a digit-only field. Use the 70/20/10 rule[3] for testing: 70 percent unit tests, 20 percent integration tests, and 10 percent acceptance, or end-to-end, tests.

> **TIP** Unless you have specific reasons to use Mocha or Robot Framework, you can cover all areas of testing with both Jasmine and Cucumber.

At the end of the day, testing your code and tracking issues is all about transparency. You need to know whether the application is ready for launch. If there are still open issues, you need to decide whether they'll prevent your application from going into production or if they're acceptable. Only code that's sufficiently tested and free of any bugs that prevent it from going into production should be tagged for deployment.

12.1.3 *Estimating and testing load*

If you haven't thought about the expected number of users for your application, now is the time. Certainly you have a good understanding of the users of your application in terms of functionality, but now you'll have to focus on scale by asking three questions:

- How many (concurrent) users do you have?
- How much data (and load) does a single user generate?
- Where are your users?

WORST, BEST, AND REALISTIC SCENARIOS

Even though it may be hard to guess the exact number of users, chances are you can at least give somewhat reasonable numbers for the first months. A common approach to estimating the visitors of a site is to assume three scenarios: best case, worst case, and realistic case. In a best case, you come up with the maximum number of users you

---

[3] See also this entry at the Google Testing Blog: http://googletesting.blogspot.de/2015/04/just-say-no-to-more-end-to-end-tests.html.

can expect if your marketing campaign is extremely successful. You shouldn't consider slashdotting[4] unless you explicitly aim for it. The worst case marks the low end of the spectrum, where the least number of people accesses your site, whereas the realistic scenario is somewhere in the middle. If you already have a similar web presence, you can use your existing server logs as a starting point.

To illustrate how to estimate the number of users, let's consider an online game where users play a game of Scrabble against one another. Our worst-case scenario expects 100 users per day (3,000/month), realistically 1,000 a day (30,000/month) will be playing, and in the best scenario there might be 10,000 per day (300,000/month).

What do these numbers tell you? At first you'll use them to calculate possible storage requirements. If every user can upload an avatar image and you expect them to have detailed statistics about each game played as well as the words they used, you'll use 1 MB per user as your baseline. That tells you that you need between 3 and 300 GB of storage for your application (see table below).

Table 12.2 User estimates for a deployment

	Worst case	Realistic case	Best case
Users/month	3,000	30,000	300,000
Users/day	100	1,000	10,000
Storage/user	1 MB	1 MB	1 MB
Overall storage requirements	3 GB	30 GB	300 GB

Unless you figure out the number of concurrent users, you can't come up with any sensible server requirements when it comes to load or memory. Making assumptions and using simple math, you can determine a number of concurrent users, which is an essential figure when designing your server setup.

ESTIMATING CONCURRENT USERS

To determine the required resources, you need to know a bit more about your users' behavior. The numbers alone don't tell you whether all players are evenly distributed or whether they're only active each Saturday night. This information is important because you must also design your deployment to handle any spike loads, if you can know about them in advance.

Your Scrabble application will be a casual game, so you expect users to mostly play during their nonworking hours. That means more traffic between 12 a.m. and 1 p.m. (for a quick game during lunch break) and in the evening, from 6 p.m. to 11 p.m. That leaves you with a six-hour window in which most games will be played. Because

---

[4] The Slashdot effect, also known as slashdotting, occurs when a popular website links to a smaller site, causing a massive increase in traffic. See http://en.wikipedia.org/wiki/Slashdot_effect.

you're still estimating, you can safely ignore all times outside this window and pretend all users stay inside it.

For the number of concurrent users, you'll have to make one more assumption: the average time a user spends playing.

In a worst-case scenario, you have now 100 users who are distributed across six hours. From the beta tests, you know that players typically spend 10 minutes playing the game, and that on average four players take part per game. Six hours translate into 360 minutes. You'll use this number to calculate the maximum concurrency by taking the number of users within your window and dividing it by the duration of the number of games that fit into the time window:

Concurrent Users = Expected number of users / (Time Window / Average Game Length)

Now you know that your servers should be capable of handling 3, 28, or 278 concurrent users, depending on the scenario (see table below).

Table 12.3   Calculating concurrent users

	Worst case	Realistic case	Best case
Users	100	1,000	10,000
Time window (mins)	360	360	360
Average players per game	4	4	4
Average game length (mins)	10	10	10
Concurrent games (rounded)	1	7	70
Concurrent users (rounded)	3	28	278

The next step is to conduct load testing to figure out the amount of server resources needed to serve that many concurrent users.

LOAD TESTING

Load testing is a complex task, especially if some of the processing is outsourced to a client, as is the case with Meteor. Traditional tools that generate HTTP load such as Apache Bench (ab) or Siege can't be used to test JavaScript applications reliably.

The solution is to use load simulation by generating DDP messages that would be sent from the clients or to simulate the clients directly, such as using PhantomJS. `meteor-load-test` (https://github.com/alanning/meteor-load-test), the first load-testing tool for Meteor, sends DDP messages to stress an application. It uses Grinder, a Java load-testing framework that can also be used to flexibly test APIs. `meteor-down` (https://github.com/meteorhacks/meteor-down) is an alternative tool that allows you to write Node.js applications that can directly subscribe to Meteor publications and execute methods.

An example for using PhantomJS in combination with CasperJS is `meteor-parties-stresstest` (https://github.com/yauh/meteor-parties-stresstest). The most important part of load testing is to monitor the results and know how to interpret them.

As a result of a load test, you can get to know important information about your application. It'll become clear where possible bottlenecks sit and whether your servers should have a bigger CPU or more RAM. Because this topic can become overwhelming very quickly, a simple way to perform a load test is to find out how the application scales.

Try to find out whether your application scales in a linear fashion. Let five users run concurrently against your app and see how much CPU and memory the server consumes. Now increase by five users and check again. Perform this test at least two more times; the more values you have, the more accurate your predictions will be. Increase the number of users until you max out either RAM or CPU on the machine under load.

Eventually you should have values for 10, 20, 50, and perhaps more concurrent users. Then you can draw a simple diagram that shows how the server behaves under load. This will tell you what to look for in a server and give you an idea of the cost to expect.

LOCATION

Last but not least, you should take into consideration where your users are located. If you deploy an application where the user base comes from a small geographic region, then you should take care that your hosting isn't thousands of miles away. Reducing network times is still an important factor to improve user experience, so make sure your servers stay close to your users.

If your users come from all over the world, you should take a look at hosting that supports multiple servers in different geographical locations. Alternatively, a content delivery network can help to reduce network traffic.

> **TIP** Network latency is a huge factor that impacts user experience. Be sure to not only use sufficiently dimensioned servers but also place them as close to your target users as possible.

12.1.4 *Server administration*

Most software developers aren't interested in running and managing servers, and they shouldn't. Thankfully you don't have to be a server expert—there are many Platform-as-a-Service (PaaS) offerings where you rent a Meteor or Mongo instance rather than managing your own server. You do need to know enough about the overall architecture, though, so you'll be able to estimate the effort and cost involved in running your application.

If you don't choose a full-service PaaS provider, you must decide who will manage the application servers, monitor the load and possible outages, apply security updates, and renew SSL certificates. Cloud providers often take care of these things, but you'll have to pay for the comfort.

BACKUP

What happens when your servers crash and all data is lost? Your application source code is safe in your version control system, but all user-contributed data is gone unless you have some sort of backup strategy in place. Typically there are two types of data that need to be backed up with a Meteor project:

- MongoDB/your database
- File uploads

Backing up MongoDB is fairly straightforward. You could create a replica set and run another MongoDB instance off-site to achieve pretty much instant backups. Alternatively, you perform a traditional backup. For a typical backup of MongoDB, you can use `mongodump` and `mongorestore` to back up and restore the database.

Backing up files isn't different from any other web project. Just make sure you include all relevant configuration files as well, if they aren't under version control (where they should be!). If your hosting doesn't come with a backup solution, it's best to create your own rolling backup—for example, using rsnapshot (http://www.rsnapshot.org/). Be aware that even though cloud providers claim to be secure, they too may lose data and it's always safer to have your own backup, especially if you can't afford to lose important customer data. Running off a RAID-1 drive is not a substitute for regular (daily or at least weekly) backups.

12.1.5 Checklist

You can use this simple checklist to make sure you're ready to go into production. You should be able to answer all questions with yes.

1 Are you using a version control system for your code?
2 Are there no issues with your software that prevent a go-live?
3 Do you know how many (concurrent) users to expect?
4 Did you conduct load testing to determine how much CPU/memory a single user requires?
5 Did you calculate the amount of required disk space?
6 Do you know where your users are located?
7 Do users only exchange data via the database? If not, do you have a plan to secure traffic between server instances?
8 Do you have dedicated and trained staff to manage the servers?
9 Do you have a backup strategy planned?
10 Did you test your backup strategy by performing a successful restore?

12.2 Setup and deployment

Now it's time to put your application on a live server. Depending on the criticality of your application and the number of users you expect, you can choose between three main deployment options. To help you decide on an approach, table 12.4 shows the pros and cons of each.

Table 12.4 Pros and cons of Meteor server options

Deployment to	Advantages	Disadvantages
Meteor.com	Easiest deployment No hosting cost	No guaranteed availability No custom URL
Cloud provider (such as Modulus, Heroku, or Nodejitsu)	Low administration overhead Quick and easy scalability Pay per actual usage	Limited control over configuration options
Manual setup (such as Amazon EC2, Rackspace, or your own hardware)	Full flexibility Ability to reuse existing resources across different applications	Requires administration knowledge Scaling requires more time

For quick prototypes, the Meteor.com infrastructure is the easiest way to go, although it's not a good choice for production use because you get no guaranteed availability and scaling is rather complicated. Your application may be offline or unresponsive at any time. On the other hand, it's a free option and so you'll probably use it at some point.

If you don't want to spend significant overhead on system administration, one of the existing cloud providers might be a good fit. Besides not having to work on system configurations, they often offer push-button scalability that allows you to add more instances almost instantly. Keep in mind that you won't be able to control all settings of the underlying infrastructure because it's often shared among multiple applications. Some unconventional requirements may come at a hefty price, if they're possible at all.

When you're familiar with running servers and have dedicated people who can fix things on short notice, a manual setup is the most flexible. If you're hosting multiple projects, it can become the best option, even if no exotic configuration settings are required. You'll have to put some more thought into what resources you require, though—you pay for the entire setup, not just your usage. Adding more instances also takes significantly more time than clicking a single button.

12.2.1 *The simplest deployment: meteor.com*

To deploy to meteor.com, all you need is the Meteor CLI tool. When your application is ready, the following command will send it to the Meteor.com infrastructure:

```
$ meteor deploy <subdomain>
```

Replace <subdomain> with the name of the subdomain that's going to be used to access your application. Meteor.com uses developer accounts to make sure that once you've deployed to a free subdomain nobody else will be able to overwrite your application. The subdomain will be connected to your Meteor.com developer account. If

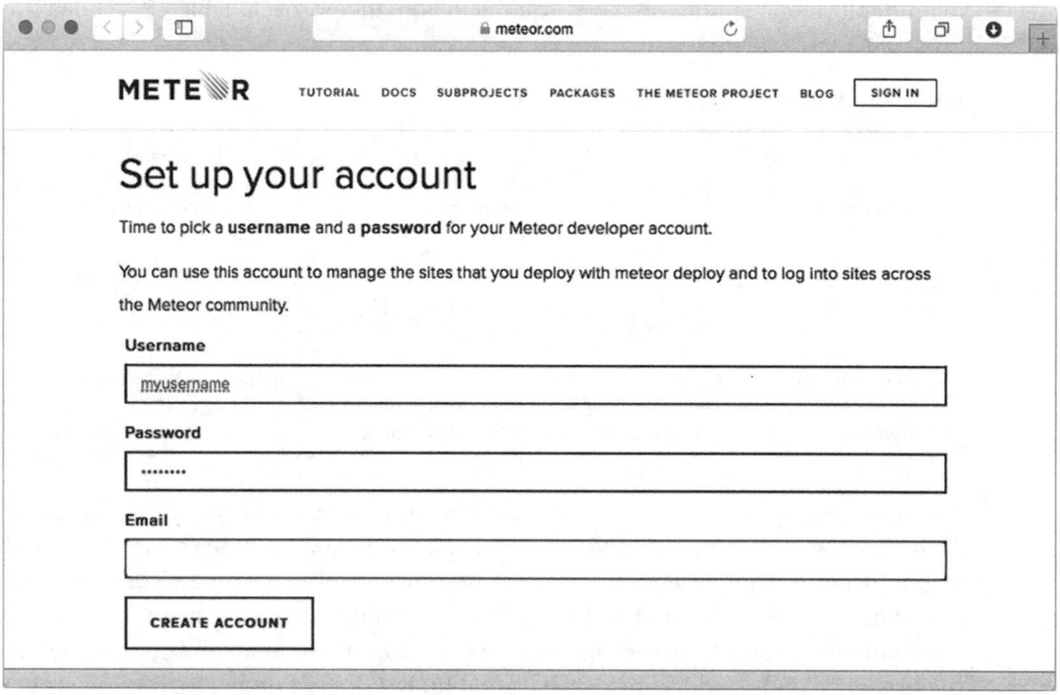

Figure 12.3   Setting up your Meteor developer account

you don't have one yet—which is generally the case for a first deployment—you'll be asked to automatically set one up during the deployment process. All you need to do is provide your email address, and you'll then be able to set a username and password on the meteor.com website (see figure 12.3).

  If you have multiple developers who are able to deploy to a meteor.com subdomain, you can add them to an *organization*. Every member of the organization will have the same permissions on your project.

> **NOTE**   In case you need to debug a deployed application, you can also use `meteor deploy <subdomain> --debug`, which will allow you to use the browser-based debugger and keep your breakpoints.

When you try to deploy to an existing subdomain, `meteor deploy` will prompt you to enter a username and password to authenticate. Once you're successfully authenticated, Meteor will remember your account on the local system. That way, you don't need to log in for subsequent deployments, even if they're to other sites that are associated with your current login account. You can see a list of all subdomains you're authorized for by entering this:

```
$ meteor list-sites
```

```
●  ●  ●                    📁 myApp — bash — 110×25
MacBookPro:myApp stephan$ meteor deploy mysampleappon
To instantly deploy your app on a free testing server, just enter your
email address!

Email: mail@meteorinaction.com
Deploying to http://mysampleappon.meteor.com.
Now serving at http://mysampleappon.meteor.com
                                        -
You can set a password on your account or change your email address at:
https://www.meteor.com/setPassword?5CwrvpAfMg

MacBookPro:myApp stephan$ meteor logs mysampleappon
[Tue Nov 04 2014 13:36:11 GMT+0000 (UTC)] INFO STATUS null -> starting
[Tue Nov 04 2014 13:36:11 GMT+0000 (UTC)] NOTICE Starting application on port 13188
[Tue Nov 04 2014 13:36:11 GMT+0000 (UTC)] INFO STATUS starting -> running
[Tue Nov 04 2014 13:40:31 GMT+0000 (UTC)] INFO HIT / 91.52.215.18
[Tue Nov 04 2014 13:40:32 GMT+0000 (UTC)] INFO HIT /20ae2c8d51b2507244e598844414ecdec2615ce3.css 91.52.215.18
[Tue Nov 04 2014 13:40:32 GMT+0000 (UTC)] INFO HIT /819f96ffbb57aa2351efdbf57c2ea8b6cb0e89bd.js 91.52.215.18
[Tue Nov 04 2014 13:40:33 GMT+0000 (UTC)] INFO HIT /favicon.ico 91.52.215.18
[Tue Nov 04 2014 13:40:47 GMT+0000 (UTC)] INFO HIT / 91.52.215.18
[Tue Nov 04 2014 13:40:47 GMT+0000 (UTC)] INFO HIT /20ae2c8d51b2507244e598844414ecdec2615ce3.css 91.52.215.18
[Tue Nov 04 2014 13:40:47 GMT+0000 (UTC)] INFO HIT /819f96ffbb57aa2351efdbf57c2ea8b6cb0e89bd.js 91.52.215.18
[Tue Nov 04 2014 13:40:48 GMT+0000 (UTC)] INFO HIT /favicon.ico 91.52.215.18
[Tue Nov 04 2014 13:41:06 GMT+0000 (UTC)] INFO HIT /_GALAXY_ 91.52.215.18
MacBookPro:myApp stephan$ ▮
```

Figure 12.4 Deploying and accessing the logs from the command line

To manage an application on the meteor.com infrastructure, you can use the CLI tool to access the server log files (see figure 12.4) and even the database shell. This is done with the following commands:

```
$ meteor logs <subdomain>
```

and

```
$ meteor mongo <subdomain>
```

> **NOTE** Although it's convenient to use the meteor.com infrastructure, it's not yet ready for production-grade deployments.

Getting a MongoDB connection string for meteor.com

Let's say you deployed an application to meteor.com to test it with other users and it becomes a great success. Now you want to migrate your data away to a dedicated database, but you don't know how to access the remote database.

When you pass the `--url` parameter to `meteor mongo`, the return value is a MongoDB connection string—for example:

```
$ meteor mongo --url mysubdomainname.meteor.com
mongodb://client-b4898462:4f69301a-8be4-7196-a2db-23816e785e9e@
   production-db-a2.meteor.io:27017/mysampleappon_meteor_com
```

This URL can be used in any MongoDB client such as Robomongo or passed to the `mongodump` command to access and extract data. The URL expires after one minute, though, so you need to use it quickly or the username and password will be denied. As such, it's not useful to share this connection string via email with others.

12.2.2   *All-inclusive hosting: cloud providers*

Although dedicated Meteor hosting isn't widely available yet, there are already many platforms to run Node.js applications. Because Meteor applications can be quickly converted to run on a plain Node.js server, you can use any provider that's capable of hosting Node.js.

If you're using the infrastructure of a cloud provider (see table 12.5 for a short list), there's no need to set up any components and processes on your own. Oftentimes providers will also offer MongoDB in their portfolio, which allows you to host all components with a single company.

Table 12.5   Node.js-as-a-Service providers

Provider	URL
Modulus	https://modulus.io/
Heroku	www.heroku.com/
Nodejitsu	www.nodejitsu.com/

To get Meteor up and running with a Node.js provider, you need to prepare your application for the deployment process. The preparation depends on your provider of choice; some can directly host a Meteor app, but most of them require you to convert your project to a regular Node.js application first.

HIGHLY PORTABLE NODE.JS BUNDLES WITH DEMETEORIZER

The `demeteorizer` project was started by the engineers behind the cloud provider Modulus. Demeteorizer wraps and extends the `build` command by creating a standard Node.js application.

To create highly portable Node.js bundles with `demeteorizer`, you first need to install it on your development system. Because it comes in form of a node module, it can be installed via npm:

```
$ npm install -g demeteorizer
```

Once `demeteorizer` is available on your system, it works similarly to the `build` command introduced in chapter 11. Navigate to your project root folder and call it from the command line:

```
$ cd myMeteorProject
$ demeteorizer -t myApp.tar.gz
```

In contrast to the `build` command, `demeteorizer` creates a directory by default, which is why the –t switch is needed to create a tarball. By default it'll create a new

The difference between meteor build and demeteorizer

Both commands create a Node.js application, but there's a subtle but important difference. `meteor build` creates an application that includes `npm` modules. `demeteorizer` doesn't bundle any `npm` modules but includes a meta file (packages.json) that specifies which `npm` modules are needed to run the application.

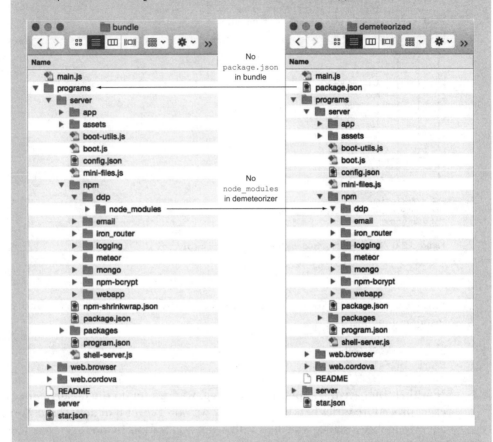

Most providers that offer Node.js hosting require a package.json file and install `npm` modules using `npm install` rather than including them with the application sources. Therefore, `demeteorizer` is required when deploying to a regular Node.js provider.

directory called .demeteorized, where it creates a structure like the one shown in figure 12.5.

The resulting archive can be uploaded and extracted to the server. Some providers such as Modulus.io will allow you to directly upload the archive via a web interface. Thanks to the presence of the package.json file in the root of the project, either all node modules will be installed automatically—if your provider supports it—or you'll

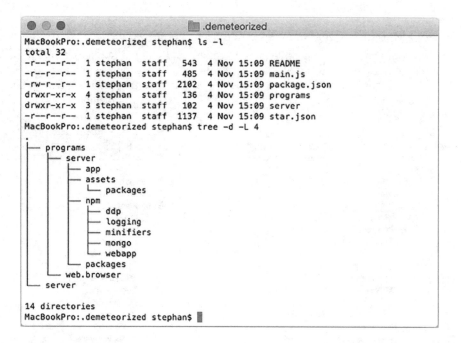

```
MacBookPro:.demeteorized stephan$ ls -l
total 32
-r--r--r--  1 stephan  staff   543  4 Nov 15:09 README
-r--r--r--  1 stephan  staff   485  4 Nov 15:09 main.js
-rw-r--r--  1 stephan  staff  2102  4 Nov 15:09 package.json
drwxr-xr-x  4 stephan  staff   136  4 Nov 15:09 programs
drwxr-xr-x  3 stephan  staff   102  4 Nov 15:09 server
-r--r--r--  1 stephan  staff  1137  4 Nov 15:09 star.json
MacBookPro:.demeteorized stephan$ tree -d -L 4
.
├── programs
│   ├── server
│   │   ├── app
│   │   ├── assets
│   │   │   └── packages
│   │   ├── npm
│   │   │   ├── ddp
│   │   │   ├── logging
│   │   │   ├── minifiers
│   │   │   ├── mongo
│   │   │   └── webapp
│   │   └── packages
│   └── web.browser
└── server

14 directories
MacBookPro:.demeteorized stephan$ ▌
```

Figure 12.5 The resulting folder structure of `demeteorizer`

navigate to the root folder of the project on the deployment server and issue the install command:

```
$ cd /var/www/myDemeteorizedApp
$ npm install
```

Now that you have the application running, you can set up the database. Because the exact procedure varies between providers, we won't cover it in detail here. You can use any MongoDB instance you like with your application; it doesn't even have to be hosted with the same provider.

MONGODB-AS-A-SERVICE

Sometimes it's necessary to split the hosting of Meteor and MongoDB. A Node.js provider might not offer a feature for MongoDB that you'd like to use (such as oplog tailing), or perhaps they're too expensive compared to the competition. In that case, there are many MongoDB-as-a-Service providers (see table 12.6) that might just be for you. Some start with a completely free plan, which makes them an ideal starting point for small projects; you can easily scale at a later stage with usually a single click.

Table 12.6 MongoDB-as-a-Service providers

Provider	URL
MongoLab	https://mongolab.com/
Compose.io	www.compose.io/
MongoSoup	www.mongosoup.de/en/
ObjectRocket	www.objectrocket.com/
Elastx	http://elastx.com/

ADVANTAGES

You don't need to know a lot about MongoDB and its internals, so using a provider will get you started very quickly. Minimal overhead for administration is involved. You get all the features of high availability and load balancing out of the box, so you can focus on your application alone. Also, switching to the next bigger database size is easy.

Oftentimes less commonly used features are cheaper with a specialized database provider, and for low-traffic sites there are even free tiers with some of them.

DOWNSIDES

Network latency between your application servers and the MongoDB instances will be much higher compared to hosting your own database on the next machine. But because many providers use Amazon or Rackspace infrastructure, there may be no noticeable effect at all if you're using the same infrastructure for your own servers as well.

The comfort of not having to administer the infrastructure will cost you, especially if you go beyond the sizes available on the price list. For optimum performance, you'll want to include oplog tailing for your Meteor application, but some providers charge a hefty extra for it because it requires a dedicated replica set and they can't use a shared shard for your data.

12.2.3 Full flexibility: manual setup

Setting up Meteor manually on a server is straightforward. If you're running Ubuntu, Debian, or OpenSolaris on your server, it gets even easier with `meteor-up`, also known as `mup`. If you can't use `mup` or need more flexibility, all it takes to start running your project on your own servers is a regular Node.js server in combination with the bundling functionality discussed in the previous section.

METEOR-UP

`meteor-up` is a community project. The tool lets you both set up servers and deploy Meteor. First you initialize a new project, configure the environment, initiate the server installation, and finally deploy your project. Additional information can be found at GitHub: https://github.com/arunoda/meteor-up.

You install `meteor-up` via npm:

```
$ npm install -g mup
```

Use a terminal to navigate to your Meteor application folder and initialize a new project with this command:

```
$ mup init
```

Now you have two JSON files in the current directory:

- *mup.json*—This file is used to define the servers that'll be used as deployment targets and to specify what components to install.
- *settings.json*—This file is used to define deployment-specific configuration options available in Meteor.settings. It can be used for API keys or server credentials, for example.

Although it you don't have to use settings.json, you must adjust the contents of mup.json to reflect your own server setup. You'll use two hosts in this example (listing 12.1), but you don't want to set up MongoDB on either of them.

Listing 12.1 mup.json configuration

```
{
  // Server authentication info
  "servers": [                          ⟵  You can define one or
    {                                        multiple servers that will
      "host": "host1.meteorinaction.com",    be used for deployment.
      "username": "stephan",
      //"password": "password"          ⟵  SSH keys or passwords
      // prefer pem file (ssh based authentication)    may be used for
      "pem": "~/.ssh/id_rsa"            ⟵  authentication.
    },
    {
      "host": "host2.meteorinaction.com",
      "username": "stephan",
      "pem": "~/.ssh/id_rsa"
    }
  ],

  // Install MongoDB in the server, does not destroy local MongoDB on future
     setup
  "setupMongo": true,                   ⟵  mup can also set up a
                                            MongoDB without replication.

  // WARNING: Node.js is required!
  // Only skip if you already have Node.js installed on server.
  "setupNode": true,

  // WARNING: If nodeVersion omitted will setup 0.10.36 by default.
  // Do not use v, only version number.
  "nodeVersion": "0.10.36",            ⟵  PhantomJS isn't required
                                            but is used in conjunction
  // Install PhantomJS in the server        with some packages.
  "setupPhantom": true,                ⟵
```

```
                   // Application name (No spaces)
                   "appName": "meteorinaction",
```
If you deploy multiple Meteor instances to the same machine, you can differentiate between them using different names.

```
                   // Location of app (local directory)
                   "app": "/Users/stephan/Code/meteorinaction",
```
Path to your application source code on the local machine, not the server

When using an external MongoDB, define the connection string as an environment variable; if used, the oplog must also be declared.

```
                   // Configure environment
                   "env": {
                     "ROOT_URL": "http://www.meteorinaction.com"
                     "PORT": "3000"
                     "MONGO_URL": "mongodb://user:password@192.168.2.210/meteor"
                     "MONGO_OPLOG_URL": "mongodb://ploguser:password@192.168.2.210/
                                   ➥ local?authSource=admin"
                   },

                   // Meteor Up checks if the app comes online just after the deployment
                   // before mup checks that, it will wait for no. of seconds configured below
                   "deployCheckWaitTime": 15
                 }
```
Environment variables to be used for this application

Optionally specify the port Meteor should use.

Number of seconds to wait to see whether a deployment was successful

With the settings you see in listing 12.1, mup will deploy to the servers host1.meteori-
naction.com and host2.meteorinaction.com using an SSH key for the user "stephan".
For security reasons. you should avoid using passwords and rely on the more secure
SSH keys.[5]

NOTE Although it's tempting to use passwords for test deployments, you
should consider switching to SSH keys instead of passwords for production
deployment.

In this example, you'll set up both MongoDB 2.6 and Node.js in version 0.10.36. You'll
also install PhantomJS, which is used by some packages like spiderable to improve
visibility for search engines. The application name is used to identify the node process
on the server. You can use mup to deploy multiple node processes to the same machine
from different mup.json configurations, and the application name is how you can differentiate between them. The location of your app relates to the project you want to
deploy from your local workstation or laptop. Using the environment variables, you
can fine-tune the Meteor runtime environment.

In case you have a multicore server, you may want to deploy multiple Meteor
instances on the same machine so that all cores are used. In that case you need to use
a different port and application name for each instance, which in turn requires multiple

---

[5] SSH keys can be used on Linux, Mac OS X, and Windows. You can read more about working with keys at
https://help.ubuntu.com/community/SSH/OpenSSH/Keys.

mup.json files. To avoid any conflicts, use a dedicated directory for each core. For a dual-core system, the structure might look like this:

```
.
├── client
├── core1
│   └── mup.json
├── core2
│   └── mup.json
├── public
├── server
└── settings.json
```

The content of both mup.json files would be exactly the same—only the application name and the setting for the PORT environment variable would be different.

Without a local MongoDB instance, you need to specify the URL for the database as an environment variable. If you're using the oplog, you can define it there as well.

Once the configuration is finished, you can set up the environment using the following:

```
$ mup setup
```

This will take care of all server configurations and installation for you. Meteor Up also ensures that all server processes are started upon boot. Additionally, it uses forever to restart a node in case it crashes. It doesn't yet copy your application over to the server.

Bundling and deploying the application is the final step (see figure 12.6):

```
$ mup deploy
```

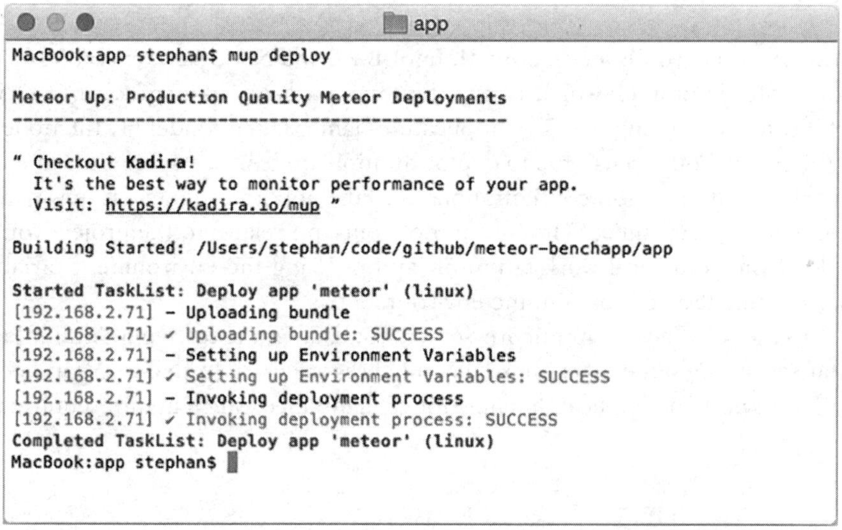

```
● ● ●                          📁 app
MacBook:app stephan$ mup deploy

Meteor Up: Production Quality Meteor Deployments
------------------------------------------------

" Checkout Kadira!
  It's the best way to monitor performance of your app.
  Visit: https://kadira.io/mup "

Building Started: /Users/stephan/code/github/meteor-benchapp/app

Started TaskList: Deploy app 'meteor' (linux)
[192.168.2.71] - Uploading bundle
[192.168.2.71] ✓ Uploading bundle: SUCCESS
[192.168.2.71] - Setting up Environment Variables
[192.168.2.71] ✓ Setting up Environment Variables: SUCCESS
[192.168.2.71] - Invoking deployment process
[192.168.2.71] ✓ Invoking deployment process: SUCCESS
Completed TaskList: Deploy app 'meteor' (linux)
MacBook:app stephan$ █
```

Figure 12.6   Setting up a server with Meteor Up

Besides `init` and `deploy` there are commands for starting and stopping the application (`start`/`stop`/`restart`) and a way to access the Node.js logs (`logs`). When passing the `-f` option to `logs`, you can monitor the log file continuously, similar to using the `tail -f` command.

12.3 Connecting the pieces

When running an application server, you can configure a number of things. You may need to change the port a server listens on, define the root URL, or include connection details to the database server or mail transports. All settings that need to take effect upon server start are passed to Meteor in form of environment variables.

12.3.1 Environment variables

Depending on which packages you use with your application, you can set environment variables that'll influence the way your Meteor application behaves. The most common environment variables are listed in the table below.

Table 12.7 Common environment variables

Variable name	Description
PORT	Network port to bind to (default: 3000)
BIND_IP	IP address to bind to (default: all)
ROOT_URL	Base URL for the application
MONGO_URL	Connection string for MongoDB
MONGO_OPLOG_URL	Connection string for MongoDB oplog
MAIL_URL	SMPT connection string for the mail server (default: STDOUT)
NODE_ENV	Some cloud providers use this, typically set to `production`

Most cloud providers have a web interface for you to define names and values of environment variables (see figure 12.7).

12.3.2 Connecting Meteor to MongoDB

Once you have a running Node.js server and a MongoDB instance, you can configure Meteor so it knows how to access the database. You can specify both the regular database and oplog access individually by using the variables `MONGO_URL` and `MONGO_OPLOG_URL`, respectively. Both use the same syntax of a standard MongoDB connection string:

```
mongodb://<username>:<password>@<host>/<database>?<options>
```

- `mongodb://` is the required prefix and indicates that this is a string in the standard connection format.
- `username:password@` are optional. If present, they'll be used to log into a specific database.

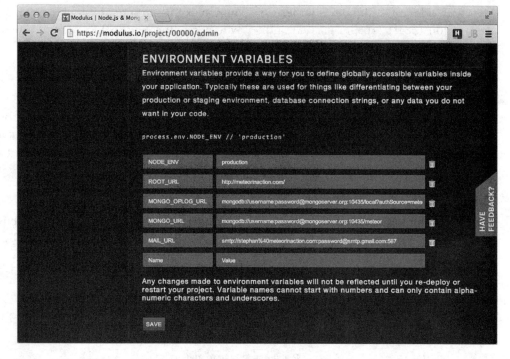

Figure 12.7   Defining environment variables with Modulus

- host is the only required part. If no port is specified, the default will be used (27017). You can define multiple hosts, separated by a comma.
- /database is required in combination with username:password and specifies the database you want to log into after successfully connecting to the server. If not specified, the admin database is used by default.
- options are connection options in the form of name=value pairs separated by &.

Let's assume the environment described in the table below.

Table 12.8   Example MongoDB connection information

Key	Value
MongoDB server address	`mongo.local.lan`
Database name	`meteordb`
Database user	`meteoruser`
Database password	`drowssap`
Oplog user	`ploguser`
Oplog password	`drowssap`

Based on those values, the connection strings look like this:

```
$ export MONGO_URL=mongodb://meteoruser:drowssap@mongo.local.lan/meteordb
$ export MONGO_OPLOG_URL=mongodb://oploguser:drowssap@mongo.local.lan/
local?authSource=admin
```

Notice that in the MONGO_URL definition you specify the database Meteor is going to use, which is meteordb. In contrast, the name of the application database is irrelevant for the MONGO_OPLOG_URL—it always uses local. This is because the oplog is kept in the local database. Because users can't authenticate against the local database, you need to pass another option, authSource, to the connection string in order to use the admin database as the authentication source instead.

12.4 Scaling strategies

System architecture is as complex as writing software. Without going into too much detail, this section introduces you to the main concepts of scalability. There are two different aspects:

- *Reliability*—No single component failure will break the system.
- *Availability*—Every request can be processed.

At first glance it may look as though both are the same, but they serve quite different purposes. Both can be translated to high availability (HA), but reliability focuses on redundant components and availability is often achieved by means of load balancing.

12.4.1 Active-passive high availability with redundancy

When an application is running in production, it's expected to be available 24/7. Depending on the nature of your application, you'll start losing users or even money when your application isn't available. That's why most production deployments will be architected to be highly available. It boils down to your setup not having any single points of failure. Each single component may go down at any point in time without any significant impact for the user. Operations will be able to continue even without an admin having to fix things immediately. Not only is this approach helpful in a case of failure, but also regular updates can be applied without taking the entire system offline. Figure 12.8 illustrates the steps required to achieve highly available applications.

You often find active-passive combinations in HA environments: one server does the actual work and another stands idly by, ready to take over should the first server ever go down. If you find yourself maxing out server resources—meaning a single server isn't able to handle all requests anymore—you'll need to scale vertically (also known as scaling up), which means you add more server resources such as CPU or memory. If you were running on Amazon EC2, you'd upgrade your server from a medium to a large instance. But you can't scale up forever; if you're very successful you'll reach a point where no single server will be able to handle the load by itself.

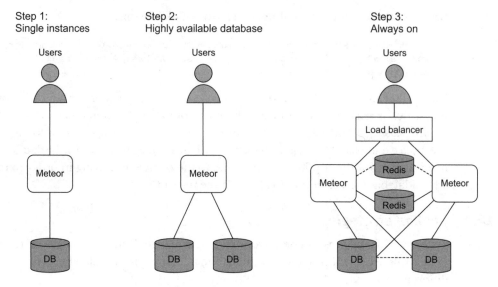

Figure 12.8   From single instances to high availability

ACTIVE-ACTIVE HIGH AVAILABILITY WITH LOAD BALANCING

If only a single instance can ever be active at the same time, it doesn't leave you with any real options to handle more load. Exchanging a small server for a bigger one usually takes time, which is why you should consider scaling horizontally (scaling out) as well.

In load-balanced environments, you find servers running as active-active pairs, meaning both servers actively get and process requests. Unfortunately, managing dependencies gets more complicated if both active servers influence the data or processing that's currently going on with the other server. In the Scrabble application introduced earlier in this chapter, you need to consider how two players on two different servers could be able to play the same game.

12.4.2 Single-component deployments

When you run Meteor locally, there's a single Meteor application and a single MongoDB instance. This offers the advantage of having a fairly simple setup that doesn't share any session data or users between multiple machines. It also makes an ideal setup for development environments, because you know exactly where to look in log files and locate potential bugs. There's no need to first analyze on which of your servers errors might have happened or whether any balancing components may have caused their own bugs.

The downside of having single instances is that this architecture isn't failsafe and it doesn't scale. If your MongoDB goes down, the entire application will stop working properly. The same goes for the Meteor server. Also, as the number of (concurrent) users increases, you only have one real scaling solution: buy a bigger server.

12.4.3 *Redundancy and load balancing*

The first step to better scalability and high availability is to make sure the database is always available. If you use a PaaS provider for your database, they'll ensure that you can always access your data. If you need to set up a highly available database yourself, or if you want to know more about what goes on inside a MongoDB cluster, check out appendix B.

The second step in achieving high availability is making sure the application itself is always accessible. This requires scaling out Meteor servers. Because the Meteor application server is a Node.js server, all of the principles for hosting Node.js applications apply to Meteor as well. Depending on the expected number of users, you should set up two or more server instances. Because you can't ask users to either access server 1 or server 2, you can add an automatic dispatcher or load balancer that distributes all requests to a single URL across all application servers.

BALANCING LOAD

It's a common best practice to run web applications behind load balancers. A large range of established tools is available, reaching from open source software such as HAProxy or nginx to dedicated hardware boxes from F5 or Cisco. The principle is the same as with query routers in MongoDB[6]: any number of actual worker processes (or applications) run as a logical group and all requests from clients are sent to either of these workers.

Meteor is different from the traditional way of serving web pages. In the traditional approach, connections are stateless; it makes no difference which application server responds to any request in a series. With Meteor, though, each connection maintains state and therefore switching between servers for different requests of the same client will break things, because any information regarding the context is lost. No matter which load-balancing approach you choose to implement, you must ensure that a client doesn't move across servers unless you have a way to exchange state information between all nodes.

The simplest form of keeping a user on the same server is to remember a user in the load balancer—for example, by associating an IP address with an application server. All requests from IP 192.168.2.201 will go to server A only, no matter how much load it currently has. Alternatively, the load balancer can set a cookie to remember which server a client should stick to.

COMMON LOAD-BALANCING ALGORITHMS

Knowing the most important algorithms for distributing requests will help you choose the best for your application. Many people are familiar with *round robin*, which means that all requests are evenly distributed between servers by count: Request 1 goes to server A, the second request to server B, the third to server A again, 4 to B, and so on. That works well if all your servers have the same specs, but if one of them is more

---

[6] See appendix B for more information on query routers in MongoDB.

powerful, a *weighted round robin* might be the better choice. You might configure server A to retrieve twice as many requests because it has double the memory and CPU.

Unfortunately, these algorithms don't take into account any load a server might currently have—for example, because users have ended their session already. Typically a load balancer won't know about the status of the nodes it redirects requests to. Some can determine how long a server takes to respond and avoid sending any more users to an already unresponsive server. A load balancer may also be configured to distribute users based on the actual number of connections. That brings the *least connection* algorithm into play; the load balancer actively checks how many users are currently connected to a server and distributes users evenly.

All algorithms have their specific uses. If in doubt, the best way is to start out with round robin and enable session stickiness. Consult appendix C for configuration examples.

SINGLE THREADS

To help you avoid dealing with the complexity of multithreaded architectures, Node.js was designed to run in a single thread. That means it will only run on a single core and a single thread of the CPU, regardless of how many cores exist. That's a major roadblock for scaling up—you can't simply use a bigger machine with more CPUs if your application is becoming slow; you have to scale horizontally. Although there's a Node.js cluster package, it isn't yet production ready.[7] If you happen to have a multi-core server, you can take advantage of all cores by running multiple Meteor processes on the same server. Using different ports, the load balancer will be able to distribute requests between multiple instances on the same machine just like it would between different physical servers. Usually the operating system will take care of running the different processes on different cores, but if you want direct control over which Meteor instance runs on which core, you can use the `taskset` package on Linux.

> **TIP** Running multiple instances of Meteor on the same server will allow you to use more than a single CPU core, but it won't provide true high availability unless you use two or more separate servers.

SECURE CONNECTIONS: SSL

Although Node.js supports SSL connections, Meteor itself does not. To provide secure connections, SSL can still be used on the load balancer facing the clients. All traffic between the load balancer and the application server will then be unencrypted, which is referred to as *SSL offloading*. All messages between a user and the datacenter will still be fully secure, but inside the datacenter you need to trust the provider of the infrastructure.

Be careful when load balancing across datacenters. If the load balancer is located in the United States but it redirects to a Meteor server in Japan, it must not terminate SSL in the U.S. but instead redirect the SSL request to Japan and use a local load

---

[7] As of this writing the Node.js cluster package was marked as Stability: 1 – Experimental.

balancer to offload the SSL. Otherwise, the users may see an HTTPS connection, but in truth it will go halfway across the world just like any other unsecured request.

In many environments nginx is used for SSL offloading, so it shields the Meteor application from handling any infrastructure concerns and concentrates on a single purpose: running the application.

SESSION STATE

Coming back to our Scrabble game, we assume four players are logging in on two load-balanced servers. Two of the players are now on server A and two on server B, but they should all join the same game. The simplest way to share information between all instances is to use the database as the central place of information exchange. Though from the application perspective it may seem like an ideal approach, it adds a lot of load to the database servers, requiring many disk operations for reading and writing, which can eventually lead to a noticeable lag for the user. After all, it doesn't make sense to persist data that's only short-lived, such as the position of your opponent's mouse cursor or whether they're currently typing.

A better solution to exchanging volatile data between application servers is to use Redis, an in-memory database. In a nutshell, Redis is a simple key-value storage. It's similar to MongoDB because it supports sharding and provides a means to fail over to another server if the primary process is unavailable. The key difference is that all data is kept in memory, which removes all disk I/O and makes Redis a fast and efficient way to store all session-relevant data.

PROXY SERVERS

Although technically not part of high availability, a good way to increase performance and eventually enable your application to run with less resource usage is to introduce proxy servers.

Node.js is great for serving dynamic content, but it doesn't work equally efficiently for static files. All resources that are the same for all users should be served by a proxy server instead. That includes image files, fonts, and ideally also CSS and JavaScript files. If the requirements aren't too demanding, both load balancing and serving static content can be accomplished by a single process such as `nginx`.

12.4.4 Bulletproof availability

In comparison, it's relatively easy to design a system to be 99 percent available. That gives you 3.65 days a year or over 7 hours a month that your application may be offline. Going from two 9s to five 9s (which means from 99 to 99.999 percent) reduces possible unavailability of your application to less than 5.5 minutes in an entire year. Achieving the last 1 percent is exponentially more expensive and rarely worth the effort, unless your application is of vital importance to health or business.

Probability is a driving factor for any decision in system architecture. The more components are highly available, the less likely it is that the entire system will shut down. Of course, network routers can fail as well. Brownouts may happen; even entire datacenters have been flooded in the past. If you absolutely can't live with any outages, then you should go the extra mile and make sure your servers are in separate datacenters and all cables are connected redundantly. For most use cases, though, it's sufficient to worry about server processes and leave the infrastructure to your provider.

12.5 Summary

In this chapter, you learned to

- Use version control and a dedicated branch for managing production-ready code.
- Reuse established JavaScript testing frameworks with the Velocity framework.
- Make assumptions to estimate the expected load and determine the required architecture.
- Decide whether to use a PaaS provider or set up your own infrastructure.
- Use environment variables to determine what components the application server connects to.
- Understand that an availability of 99 percent is relatively easy, but going beyond requires a lot of effort.

appendix A
Installing Meteor

This appendix covers

- Prerequisites for installing Meteor
- How to install Meteor on a development machine

In this appendix we'll highlight the prerequisites of Meteor and walk you through installing it. Unless you're on Windows, you can issue a single command to get started with Meteor, but we'll cover all major platforms.

A.1 Prerequisites

In contrast to many other web development tools, Meteor is a self-contained installation and doesn't require any particular software to be present. The installer will put Node.js as well as MongoDB in your home directory so they won't conflict with any other instances installed by package managers such as brew or apt-get. To ensure a fully working environment, Meteor will always use the binaries it installed.

Currently supported platforms include the following:

- Mac OS X 10.7 and later
- Microsoft Windows 7, Windows 8.1, Windows Server 2008, and Windows Server 2012
- Linux (x86 and x86_64 systems)

BSD and other operating systems aren't supported. Using virtualization—for example, by running a Vagrant box (we'll discuss Vagrant in a moment)—it's possible to install Meteor and start developing on unsupported systems as well.

If you can't install Meteor or prefer to run it on the cloud, you can use Nitrous (http://nitrous.io/). It offers an IDE in the cloud without the need to install anything locally.

A.2   Installing Meteor on Linux and Mac OS X

Meteor supports Mac OS X 10.7 and later as well as Linux x86 and x86_64 systems. The installation for the supported systems involves entering just one line in the terminal:

```
$ curl https://install.meteor.com/ | sh
```

This code downloads and installs the entire Meteor platform onto the system and makes the CLI tool globally available (see figure A.1).

For the installation you shouldn't need to have administrator privileges, but you may have to provide your password for Meteor to be able to create a symbolic link to /usr/local/bin/meteor so all users on your computer can use the meteor command.

> **TIP**   If you ever need to uninstall Meteor, you can do so by deleting the file /usr/local/bin/meteor as well as the .meteor/ directory inside your home directory.

Figure A.1   Installation of Meteor on Mac OS X

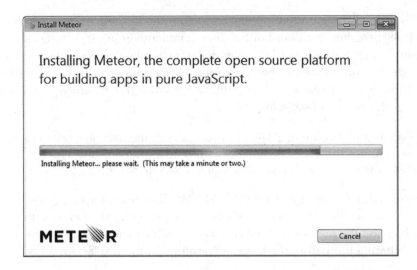

Figure A.2   Installing Meteor on Windows

A.3   *Installing Meteor on Windows*

Download the official Meteor installer from https://install.meteor.com/windows. A simple double-click on the InstallMeteor.exe file starts the installation process (figure A.2). During the process you'll be asked to provide your Meteor developer credentials or create a new account. You can skip this step if you want to.

Once the installation has finished you can use the Meteor CLI tool just as you would on a Linux or Mac OS X system.

A.4   *Running Meteor using Vagrant*

If you want to run Meteor on an unsupported platform or use the same operating system for testing as you'll use on your production servers, then you can use a virtual machine to enhance your development environment. One possible way is to use Vagrant, which allows you to use portable development environments in the form of virtual machines that are tightly integrated into your host system. That way, you can easily exchange files and run commands such as meteor.

You can download the Vagrant installer from https://www.vagrantup.com. You'll also need to install Oracle's VirtualBox, which you can find at https://www.virtualbox.org. Furthermore, you should have an SSH client installed. This can either be PuTTY or the ssh command provided by Cygwin.

Once you've finished your installations, you can add a Ubuntu Linux box to your system with this command:

```
C:\Users\stephan\> vagrant init hashicorp/trusty32
```

This will create a configuration file named Vagrantfile in the current directory. This file is a Ruby program (with most of the lines commented out) and contains the configuration settings for your machine. Besides some general configuration settings, it includes the blueprint that should be used for setting up the virtual machine—in this case, a 32-bit image of Ubuntu 14.04 (codename: Trusty Tahr), which is provided by HashiCorp, the creator of Vagrant.

> **TIP** Even if you're running a 64-bit OS, you can still use a 32-bit guest OS with Vagrant, but not vice versa. In some cases it'll be more efficient to use 32 bit, especially if you assign only a small amount of RAM to the guest.

The default value for the guest's RAM is 512 MB, and it uses a single core of your CPU, which is usually sufficient for small development environments. But if you need to increase the memory size or core count, you can adjust the Vagrantfile and add the following just before the last end (resulting in the two last lines both having end in them):

```
config.vm.provider "virtualbox" do |v|        RAM size in MB
  v.memory = 1024                     ◄─┘
  v.cpus = 2              ◄─┐  CPU cores to assign
end                           to the guest
```

To open your Meteor application in your Windows browser, you need to set up port forwarding. To do so, uncomment (remove the # symbol) the line starting with `config.vm.network` and adjust the settings as follows:

```
config.vm.network "forwarded_port", guest: 3000, host: 3000
```

You can also assign an IP address to the virtual machine by adding the following line to the configuration file:

```
config.vm.network :private_network, ip: "192.168.33.31"
```

That way, you can access the Vagrant machine just like any other remote server via SSH.

When the Vagrant box is running, this will forward all requests to your local machine (host) on port 3000 to the virtual box (guest) on port 3000. Just navigate your browser to http://localhost:3000 once you've started Meteor inside the virtual box.

To start your virtual box, issue this command (see table A.1 for an overview of the most common commands):

```
C:\Users\stephan\> vagrant up
```

Vagrant will now fetch the box blueprint defined in the Vagrantfile from the internet and store it as a reusable image (which will speed up all future executions of the vagrant up command). You'll only need to be connected to the internet for the initial download of the box image. Vagrant will set up your virtual machine and allow you to access it via SSH (the default password for most boxes is `vagrant`):

```
C:\Users\stephan\> vagrant ssh
```

Table A.1   Common Vagrant commands

Command	Description
init	Initializes the current directory to be a Vagrant environment by creating an initial Vagrantfile if one doesn't already exist. Passes the box name as an argument.
up	Creates and configures guest machines according to your Vagrantfile.
ssh	Uses SSH to access a running Vagrant machine and gives you access to a shell.
suspend	Saves the exact point-in-time state of the machine so that when you resume it later, it begins running immediately from that point, rather than doing a full boot.
resume	Continues running a suspended Vagrant box.
halt	Shuts down the running machine Vagrant is managing.
destroy	Stops the running machine and destroys all resources that were created during the machine creation process. After running this command, your computer should be left at a clean state, as if you'd never created the guest machine in the first place.

From here on, you're basically inside a real, virtualized Linux system. The beauty of using Vagrant is that files are instantly shared, so you can use your editor of choice on Windows and also use your local browser. By default, your user's home directory is shared with the virtual box so that all files you store in C:\Users\<your username>\ are accessible inside the guest system within /vagrant.

You can now install Meteor in the same way as described in the previous section.

Vagrant can be used to clearly separate the Meteor environment from the rest of your system.

appendix B
The anatomy of MongoDB

This appendix covers

- Scalable MongoDB architectures
- How to set up MongoDB with oplog tailing

Out of the box, Meteor works hand in hand with MongoDB. If you consider hosting your own database server, you should first know the basic components of a MongoDB installation, how it scales, and how it integrates with Meteor.

This appendix introduces you to more advanced topics. They assume you have a basic understanding of system architecture and administration. By the end of this appendix, you'll be familiar with the most important aspects of setting up and running your own MongoDB instance.

Figure B.1 The simplest way to use MongoDB with Meteor

B.1 The MongoDB components

A MongoDB database is fairly simple. You access it via an endpoint, authenticate with a user and password, and query for what looks like JSON objects. The simplest way to deploy MongoDB is to use a single instance (see figure B.1).

In a production environment, where you want to make sure the database is always available, you need to look behind the scenes to identify the requirements for high availability. Although the database itself is often referred to in singular, there are in fact multiple processes running. With MongoDB we differentiate between the following components:

- mongod
- mongos
- mongoc

B.1.1 mongod: databases and shards

The mongod process is the database process and takes care of data replication. In the simplest setup, it's the only process required for running MongoDB. Once a database becomes too big for a single instance, it needs to be scaled out. MongoDB does that by splitting the data between multiple servers, the so-called shards. Shards typically contain only a part of the overall database, a subset of all available documents.

Imagine you're going to store a worldwide phonebook in your database. Because there are a lot of entries, you'll partition the data to be stored across three servers. The entries for names starting with A–J will be placed on shard 1, K–S on shard 2, and T–Z on shard 3. Each of the shards contains roughly the same amount of data to evenly balance the load.

B.1.2 mongos: query routing

Because there are now multiple database processes, a routing component will be needed to direct requests to the appropriate mongod instance. The Meteor application should have only a single connection and be unaware of any internal database. In a sharded cluster, the way an application can access the database is through a process called MongoDB Shard, or simply mongos. From an application point of view, it behaves just like the mongod process and takes care of distributing data to the correct shard. The application won't know whether it was redirected to any other mongod instance.

If you decide to add a new entry in the phonebook, your application will need to access the database through mongos and write a new entry. But how does mongos know where to redirect the request and store the data?

B.1.3 mongoc: configuration servers

A sharded cluster also needs an instance that knows which data resides in which shard. This is where mongoc comes in. This process is referred to as the config server and technically it's a special kind of mongod instance. It's crucial that the config servers be available at all times, although they don't handle a lot of load because the routing instances cache all relevant data for performance purposes. When the routing servers are started, they contact the config servers to retrieve cluster metadata. Sometimes a

MongoDB database will use balancing techniques to split or migrate some data to another shard, which is when data gets written to the configuration servers. The creators of MongoDB recommend using three mongoc instances in a production environment. If you decide you don't want to use sharding, you don't have to use any configuration servers.

In the phonebook example, the mongoc process ensures that all documents starting with R are stored on shard 2, so the mongos instance knows to redirect the application's write request to the corresponding machine.

B.1.4   *Replica sets*

When designing for high availability, you can't risk losing a single shard. To prevent the unavailability of data when any single process dies, you can use *replica sets*. Replica sets can have members of three types:

- *Primary*—All write operations are performed on the primary member only. The primary member also maintains the oplog, which is the foundation of all replication action and is used by Meteor as a better alternative to the poll-and-diff approach.
- *Secondary*—Secondary members maintain an identical dataset from the primary. In case the primary member becomes unavailable, they can take over as a new primary. Failover requires the remaining members to vote on the new primary.
- *Arbiter*—Although technically not a real member of a replica set, the arbiter has a vote when electing a new primary member. It doesn't maintain a copy and can't become a new primary member. An arbiter is a special mongod process.

Each replica set requires a dedicated mongod process. Multiple processes can run on the same physical or virtual machine, but they must use different ports.

In the phonebook example, you have three mongod instances running on each of the shards. The primary replica set is the one that's writable, and depending on the exact configuration of the cluster all others will be used as backups for automatic failovers or even as read-only instances for optimum load balancing.

When a primary replica set becomes unavailable, it can automatically be replaced by a secondary member. The remaining nodes will vote on which secondary member will be the new primary. Because a member can't vote for itself, an uneven number of members is required in a replica set. When you have three replica sets and one goes down, the remaining two will elect the new primary. If for whatever reasons you need to use an even number of replica sets—for example, when two are sufficient and you don't want the additional network and disk I/O overhead of another instance—then using an arbiter will help reach an uneven number. Otherwise, if there's an uneven number of sets already, you most likely don't need an arbiter. Consequently, there should never be more than one arbiter associated with one replica set. Arbiters vote, but they don't put additional load for replication processes on either of the machines. There's no need for an arbiter in figure B.2 because an uneven number of replica set members (three) exists.

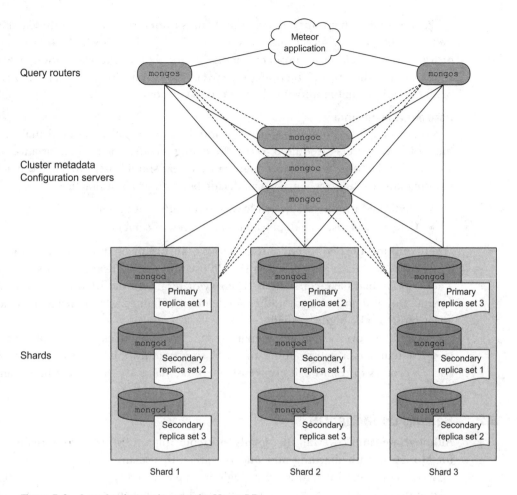

Figure B.2 A production-ready setup for MongoDB

OPLOG

Replica sets aren't limited to sharded deployments. Even in single shard deployments—such as when you're running the `meteor` CLI tool—replica sets are useful because they enable the oplog (operations log), which is an important way to enhance the performance of a Meteor application running on multiple servers.

In the phonebook example, an administrator might want to import a whole batch of names and other data directly into the database without going through the web application. Also, two instances of the application could be running in parallel, so both can change data at the same time. In both cases, the application will only know about any changes if and when it makes a dedicated request (such as "find all entries"). The standard behavior for Meteor is to poll the database every 10 seconds.

Performing such an operation regularly puts unnecessary load on the database as well as on the Meteor server and adds noticeable lag, which is why Meteor is capable of using a much cleverer approach: hooking directly into the replication stream by subscribing to the oplog. The oplog is a special collection that keeps a rolling record of all operations that modify the data stored in your databases.

COMPONENT DISTRIBUTION

A production-grade MongoDB consists of multiple servers, physical or virtual. A minimum of three servers is required to run the config servers. The `mongod` instances could also run on the same servers, although typically you should use a dedicated machine. For the query routing `mongos`, you can decide between two best practices:

- Dedicated routing servers, at least two on different servers
- One `mongos` instance deployed on each Meteor server

When running on dedicated routing servers, all instances must listen to the same address, because each Meteor server should use only one dedicated connection string. Therefore, a load balancer such as HAProxy or nginx should be used in front of the `mongos`. Doing so introduces another single point of failure, which means the load balancer must also be highly available.

To avoid an overly complex scenario, you can simply decide to install `mongos` on every Meteor server you're going to use. Using system tools, you can configure the `mongos` process to restart if it ever crashes, which makes this approach much simpler to manage.

B.2   Setting up MongoDB

Although we can't cover all the details for deploying a fully production-ready cluster for MongoDB with sharding and query routers, this section covers the specifics for Meteor. We'll focus on setting up a single instance with a replica set so that you can take advantage of tailing the oplog. You'll find further instructions on how to set up MongoDB in the official documentation or by checking out *MongoDB in Action* (Manning, 2011), by Kyle Banker.

SETTING UP OPLOG TAILING

The oplog is stored in a system database called `local`. If you haven't defined any replica sets, you won't have a collection called `oplog.rs` (see figure B.3). To initialize the collection you must define a replica set, but you don't need to add multiple members—you can use a single primary member only.

Each `mongod` instance has its own configuration.[1] First open the `mongodb` configuration file /etc/mongodb.conf. At the very end of the file add two lines:

```
replSet=rs0
oplogSize=100
```

---

[1] If you're running multiple `mongod` processes on the same machine, make sure you're editing the correct config file.

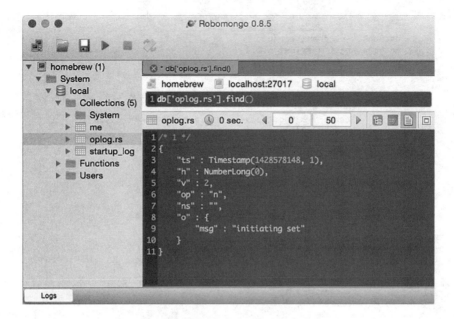

Figure B.3   Accessing the oplog with Robomongo

The first parameter defines the name of the replica set (replSet) to be used by this mongod instance. oplogSize defines the amount of disk space to be used for the collection, 100 MB in this example. If you don't specify oplogSize it defaults to 5 percent of your free disk space.

Next, restart the mongod process and open a mongo shell. You can use either a tool such as Robomongo or the command line. Once you're connected, switch to using the local database:

```
> use local
```

The next step is to initialize the replica set and thereby enable the oplog:

```
> rs.initiate({
  _id: "rs0",
  members: [{
    _id: 0,
    host: "localhost:27017"
  }]
})
```

You can always check the status of the current replica set by using rs.status() and view the full configuration and member list using rs.config(). After a successful initialization, these commands should show a replica set with a single member, similar to figure B.4.

rs.status() shows no active replica set.

rs.initiate() configures the replica set with localhost.

rs.status() shows a healthy replica set.

The command prompt includes the current name and status of this server's replica set.

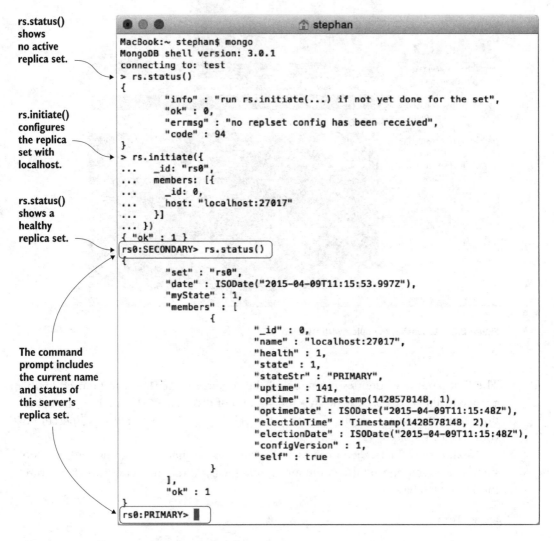

```
● ● ●                          🏠 stephan
MacBook:~ stephan$ mongo
MongoDB shell version: 3.0.1
connecting to: test
> rs.status()
{
        "info" : "run rs.initiate(...) if not yet done for the set",
        "ok" : 0,
        "errmsg" : "no replset config has been received",
        "code" : 94
}
> rs.initiate({
...    _id: "rs0",
...    members: [{
...      _id: 0,
...      host: "localhost:27017"
...    }]
... })
{ "ok" : 1 }
rs0:SECONDARY> rs.status()
{
        "set" : "rs0",
        "date" : ISODate("2015-04-09T11:15:53.997Z"),
        "myState" : 1,
        "members" : [
                {
                        "_id" : 0,
                        "name" : "localhost:27017",
                        "health" : 1,
                        "state" : 1,
                        "stateStr" : "PRIMARY",
                        "uptime" : 141,
                        "optime" : Timestamp(1428578148, 1),
                        "optimeDate" : ISODate("2015-04-09T11:15:48Z"),
                        "electionTime" : Timestamp(1428578148, 2),
                        "electionDate" : ISODate("2015-04-09T11:15:48Z"),
                        "configVersion" : 1,
                        "self" : true
                }
        ],
        "ok" : 1
}
rs0:PRIMARY> █
```

Figure B.4   Initializing a replica set from the `mongo` **shell**

As you can see in figure B.4, two additional collections will be created: `oplog.rs` and `system.replset`. Also, the shell prompt will change to reflect the replica set name and its member status (`rs0:PRIMARY`).

MongoDB now automatically tracks all write operations in the `oplog.rs` collection. Once the specified size is reached, it'll purge old entries.

SETTING UP AN OPLOG USER

By default, MongoDB doesn't require a user to authenticate. In such an environment you can also access the oplog without credentials, so you could skip this step. But in production environments you should add users to provide a means of access control.

For the purpose of tailing the oplog, you need a dedicated user that's allowed to access the `local` database, which is where the `oplog.rs` collection is.

> **NOTE** Even though the oplog user has access to the `local` database, it's technically created inside the `admin` database. This is because the `local` database doesn't allow any users to be created inside it.

Create an oplog user with the following command:

```
db.createUser({                          Set the desired
    user:'oplog',              ◁──┘       username.
    pwd:'password',                   ◁────────┘   Set a password.
    roles:[
        { role: "read", db: "local" }   ◁──┐  Read privileges on
    ]                                       └  the local database.
})
```

appendix C
Setting up nginx

> **This appendix covers**
> - Setting up nginx as a load balancer
> - Serving static content from nginx
> - Enabling SSL for Meteor applications

Although Node.js—Meteor's underlying server technology—is great for handling events, it's not optimized to handle static content such as images well. Even though it's possible to use SSL with a Node.js application, it's not yet possible with Meteor. The fact that Node.js is a single-threaded application that won't take advantage of the full power of multicore processors might be enough to convince you that scaling Meteor will be complicated.

Thankfully it doesn't require much to build a production environment for running a Meteor application that takes care of all these shortcomings. In this appendix, you'll learn how to use the lightweight web server nginx to accomplish all you need to run a rock-solid Meteor project.

C.1   Load balancing with nginx

Some of the most popular choices for running software load balancers are nginx and HAProxy. Both are available as free open source packages, but because HAProxy

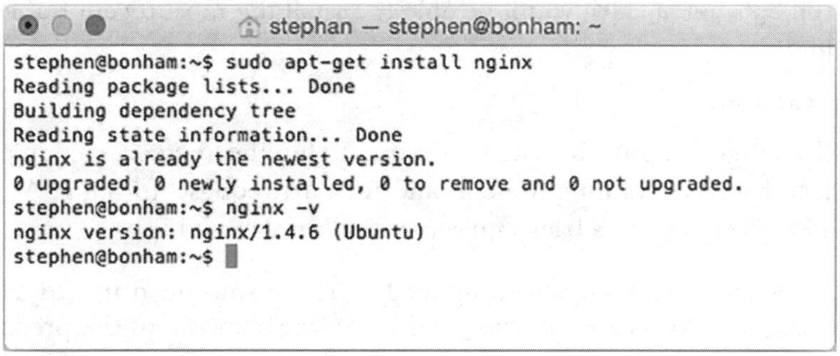

```
● ● ●              🏠 stephan — stephen@bonham: ~
stephen@bonham:~$ sudo apt-get install nginx
Reading package lists... Done
Building dependency tree
Reading state information... Done
nginx is already the newest version.
0 upgraded, 0 newly installed, 0 to remove and 0 not upgraded.
stephen@bonham:~$ nginx -v
nginx version: nginx/1.4.6 (Ubuntu)
stephen@bonham:~$ █
```

Figure C.1 Installing nginx

is built as a load balancer and nginx is a web server that's also capable of load balancing, HAProxy provides more advanced features should you need them.[1]

Our example uses nginx because it's more versatile and it can do everything you need to ensure your Meteor application is always available. You can reduce the complexity of your setup by just adding a single application to address all your production challenges.

C.1.1 Installing nginx on Ubuntu

On all major Linux distributions, nginx can be installed using a package manager. On Ubuntu and Debian the command is as follows:

```
$ sudo apt-get install nginx
```

Meteor uses WebSockets, and nginx only supports WebSockets starting with version 1.3, so ensure that you're using a recent version (see figure C.1).

C.1.2 Installing on Debian 7 (Wheezy)

On Debian 7 (Wheezy), the default nginx version is too old to support WebSockets, so you should install it from the Dotdeb repository instead. Simply add these two lines to the end of the /etc/apt/sources.list file:

```
deb http://packages.dotdeb.org wheezy all deb-src http://packages.dotdeb.org
wheezy all
```

Then issue these two commands to fetch and install the Dotdeb GPG key:

```
$ wget http://www.dotdeb.org/dotdeb.gpg
$ sudo apt-key add dotdeb.gpg
```

---

[1] Note that the commercial variant nginx plus offers more advanced functionality, but it's not available as open source. More details on the differences between the free and the paid versions of nginx can be found at http://nginx.com/products/feature-matrix/.

Once you run `apt-get update` you'll be able to install the most recent stable version of nginx with this:

```
apt-get install nginx
```

Next, you'll configure nginx to listen to requests for the meteorinaction.com site, define back-end servers running Meteor, and forward requests to them. Also, nginx mustn't send any requests to a back-end server that's not available.

> **NOTE** Debian 8 (Jessie) ships with nginx 1.6. There's no need to add additional repositories; you can use `apt-get install nginx` without the preparatory steps.

C.2   *Configuring as a load balancer*

Similar to Apache, nginx uses a general server configuration file and ideally every virtual host should be configured inside an individual file. You don't have to touch the general main config file—you'll create an additional configuration file for your Meteor application.

C.2.1   *Creating a site configuration file*

First, you create a new file in the /etc/nginx/sites-available directory named meteorinaction.com. To listen to any requests, you define the server name and port at which nginx should listen.

Also, you want to redirect all incoming requests to have a *www* prefix.[2] The corresponding file is shown in the following listing.

Listing C.1   nginx site configuration

```
server {
    listen       80;                                          Listen on
    server_name  meteorinaction.com;                          port 80.
    return       301 http://www.meteorinaction.com$request_uri;
}

server {
  listen 80;
  server_name www.meteorinaction.com;
}
```

Listen on port 80.

Apply this configuration only when meteorinaction.com is requested.

Redirect the request to the www-subdomain, maintain the URI string, and use a 301 HTTP status.

Apply this configuration to www.meteorinaction.com and all other requests.

---

[2] Although it's convenient for users to drop the *www* from an address, any site running on a "naked" top-level domain can create scalability issues. If you don't use a subdomain, the DNS system will lock you into assigning a single IP address to your domain, which is why we rewrite all traffic to use a subdomain. Users can still access your site without it; they'll be automatically redirected. Find out more at www.yes-www.org/why-use-www/.

C.2.2   *Defining Meteor servers*

To let nginx know which servers to forward requests to, you use a module called `upstream`. Because any server configuration can use any `upstream` group, it must not be inside a `server {}` block. At the very beginning of the configuration file, place the following block:

```
upstream meteor_servers {          ◁───  Choose a unique name for
    server 192.168.2.221:3000;     ◁───  your upstream group.
    server 192.168.2.222:3000;           Each line corresponds to
    ip_hash;                       ◁───  one Meteor server instance.
}                                        Specify how to
                                         distribute requests.
```

You can think of `upstream` as an array of servers. Each line starting with `server` defines a new instance. The first parameter is the actual address of the server. The machine running nginx must be able to access it, but it's not required that the upstream server can be accessed from the internet. Therefore, you can also use a local Meteor instance at 127.0.0.1 as an upstream. In this example, both instances are accessible only from a private network in the 192.168.2.0/24 range.

 All incoming requests will now be distributed equally between both back-end servers. You can further specify parameters such as weight to fine-tune the settings for your environment. Across all requests you need to keep in mind that they're stateful and that moving between servers may break a user session. The easiest way to make sure users aren't moving back and forth between servers from one request to another is to use the `ip_hash` directive. By adding it to your configuration block, you tell nginx to always send requests from the same IP to the same upstream server.

> **NOTE** If you expect many requests from the same IP, using the `ip_hash` directive may result in uneven distribution of users across your servers. In that case you should include the sticky module in your nginx configuration in combination with the `least_conn` directive instead. You can find out more at https://bitbucket.org/nginx-goodies/nginx-sticky-module-ng/overview. Alternatively, HAProxy might be the better solution for you.

C.2.3   *Forwarding requests to the back-end servers*

Once nginx listens to requests and knows about the upstream servers, you can define how you want to forward requests. In the configuration block for www.meteorinaction .com, you add a new location for root (/) (see the following listing).

Listing C.2   Location for request forwarding in nginx

```
server {
...
location / {
    proxy_pass http://meteor_server;
    proxy_redirect off;
```

```
    proxy_http_version 1.1;
    proxy_set_header X-Forwarded-For $proxy_add_x_forwarded_for;
    proxy_set_header Host $http_host;
    proxy_set_header Upgrade $http_upgrade;
    proxy_set_header Connection "upgrade";
  }
}
```

Let's go through this configuration line by line:

- `proxy_pass` is used to tell nginx that it should forward requests to this location. It uses the name of the upstream group (`meteor_server`) and not a real URL.
- `proxy_redirect` can be used to rewrite the URL request in more complex scenarios. It's not needed in your setup so you switch it off.
- `proxy_http_version` sets the HTTP version to 1.1 (the default is 1.0), which is required for WebSockets functionality.
- `proxy_set_header` allows you to add or modify some headers that'll be sent to the Meteor server. `X-Forwarded-For` contains the IP address of the user making the request. Especially when nginx is on the same host as your Meteor server, you need to set this. `Host` passes the hostname for the actual request to the Meteor server. Both `Upgrade` and `Connection` are used to allow forwarding of WebSocket connections.

C.2.4   Activating the nginx site

The final step in configuring the load balancer is to activate the site. First you'll create a symbolic link of the configuration that'll be placed in the /etc/nginx/sites-enabled/ directory:

```
$ sudo ln -s /etc/nginx/sites-available/meteorinaction.com
 /etc/nginx/sites-enabled/meteorinaction.com
```

Next you test if the configuration is good to go by calling nginx with the -t parameter:

```
$ sudo nginx -t
```

If there are no errors, you can reload the configuration without having to restart nginx:

```
$ sudo nginx -s reload
```

C.3   Serving static content with nginx

Even if you only expect a small number of users, serving content from a content delivery network or using a reverse proxy to serve static files can greatly decrease wait times for the users of your application. If your application is already using an nginx load balancer, it requires just some lines of configuration to enable it as a reverse proxy.

Meteor shouldn't have to serve any static files, so you'll configure nginx to process all requests for media files and images as well as CSS and JavaScript files. Additionally you'll enable gzip compression.

C.3.1 Serving CSS and JavaScript

The `meteor build` command automatically minifies and compiles all CSS and Java-Script files and places them in the folder bundle/programs/web.browser. If nginx is to serve these files, they must be accessible from the nginx server. If Meteor is deployed to a different server, you can either copy the files to the nginx machine or configure a folder share using Network File System (NFS). If you copy the files, remember that you need to repeat this every time you deploy the application. Because each `build` command will create new random filenames, there's no need to delete the old files; this allows for a smoother transition between deployments.

To configure serving static application files and styles, you must define a new location block in your nginx configuration file:

```
server {
    ...
    location ~* "^/[a-z0-9]{40}\.(css|js)$" {    ◁──── This catches all requests for files with names that are 40 characters long and end with js or css.
        root /home/meteor/app/bundle/programs/web.browser/app;    ◁──── No logging of these files to reduce disk I/O
        access_log off;
        expires 30d;    ◁──── Clients may cache these files for 30 days.
        add_header Pragma public;    ◁──── Adds a header that sets Pragma to public
        add_header Cache-Control "public";    ◁──── Adds a header for Cache-Control to be set to public
    }
}
```

The files can be found in this directory. points to the `root` line.

During the bundling process, all CSS and JavaScript files get a new and unique name consisting of 40 characters (letters and digits), and only they will be served from the proxy. Adjust the value for `root` to the directory where nginx can find these files. Logging will be deactivated for these static files and clients may cache these files for 30 days (`expires` in combination with the added headers for Pragma and Cache-Control are responsible for this). The next bundling process will result in new filenames, so you won't run into clients having stale cached files even if you deploy a new version of your app before the 30 days of caching are over.

> **NOTE** Nginx must have direct access to the files created by Meteor in order to be able to serve them as a proxy. If nginx can't access these files locally, you need to leave out this configuration block.

C.3.2 Serving media files and images

The contents of the public folder should also be served from nginx. Because the public folder is accessible at the root of your application, you'll use file extensions to determine whether a request will be served statically or from Meteor. The configuration is similar to the block you saw earlier:

```
location ~ \.(jpg|jpeg|png|gif|mp3|ico|pdf) {
    root /home/meteor/app/bundle/programs/web.browser/app;
    access_log off;
    expires 30d;
    add_header Pragma public;
    add_header Cache-Control "public";
}
```

You may add all file extensions to the regular expression in the location line. During the bundling process, all contents from the public folder go into bundle/programs/web.browser/app so you must use this as the root path for the location.

Again, if nginx has no access to these files locally, you should copy them over manually, use a shared storage such as an NFS export, or leave out this configuration part.

C.3.3 *Enabling gzip compression*

The last optimization for serving static files from an nginx reverse proxy is enabling gzip compression. Even when minified, text files can be compressed efficiently; in particular, users with less bandwidth (such as mobile users) benefit greatly from using compression. Configuration is done outside any location blocks but inside a server block:

```
server{
    ...
    gzip on;
    gzip_disable "msie6";
    gzip_vary on;
    gzip_proxied any;
    gzip_comp_level 6;
    gzip_types text/plain text/css application/json application/x-javascript
        text/xml application/xml application/xml+rss text/javascript;
}
```

The first line activates gzip compression and the second disables it for Internet Explorer 6. Enabling vary and proxied ensures that even requests going through proxy servers that may be used along the way to the client will be handled correctly. In this example, you set the compression level to 6 (on a scale from 1 to 9). Finally, you define the MIME types that should be compressed.

C.4 *Setting up SSL with nginx*

Because Meteor doesn't support SSL, you'll configure nginx for SSL offloading, which means the SSL connection will terminate at the load-balancing proxy server. It doesn't matter whether you use a self-signed certificate or one that was issued by Thawte, StartSSL, or any other certificate authority (CA). You must copy both the certificate file (with the .crt extension) and the key file (with the .key extension) to your nginx server.

Your Meteor application and server will run exactly the same as before—no changes required. The only configuration you'll need to make is in the nginx site file.

In the server configuration block you'll switch the port to 443, turn SSL on, and configure the certificate files to be used (see the following listing).

Listing C.3 SSL setup for nginx

```
server {                                Listen on default
    listen 443;              ◁          SSL port 443.
    server_name www.meteorinaction.com;              Enable SSL.
    ssl on;                                    ◁
    ssl_certificate /path/to/my.crt;              ◁      Path to the
    ssl_certificate_key /path/to/my.key;     ◁              certificate file
    ssl_verify_depth 3;     ◁
                                    When using concatenated      Path to the
    ...                             certificates, the depth      key file
}                                   must be adjusted.
```

Just like in the non-SSL configuration, you have to define both the port and server name. When `ssl` is set to `on`, you must also provide a certificate and a key file. Sometimes the instructions issued by a CA ask you to combine multiple files into one. In order for nginx to accept and verify this combined file, you should adjust the `ssl_verify_depth` parameter. This parameter defines the maximum number of intermediate certificate issuers—that is, the depth of how many CA certificates may be looked up while verifying the client certificate. When combining your own with a primary and a secondary intermediate certificate, the depth should be 3; self-signed certificates have a depth of 0.

Additionally, you should add a server that listens on port 80 and forwards all non-SSL traffic to the SSL port:

```
                                                    Add both variants with
                                                    and without www.
server {
    listen        80;
    server_name   meteorinaction.com www.meteorinaction.com;          ◁
    return        301 https://www.meteorinaction.com$request_uri;        ◁
}
                                                    All requests are forwarded
                                                    to the URL containing www.
```

Now your configuration file should have two server blocks: one that listens on port 443 and the other that listens on port 80 and forwards all requests to the SSL server. Test and reload the configuration and you're good to go.

> **NOTE** This SSL configuration is very limited—there are ways to make connections even more secure. Take a look at the code accompanying this book for a full example that'll provide maximum security while being compatible with most browsers.

index

JavaScript Application Design
A Build First approach
by Nicolas G. Bevacqua

    ISBN: 9781617291951
    344 pages, $39.99
    January 2015

Node.js in Action
by Mike Cantelon, Marc Harter,
   T.J. Holowaychuk, Nathan Rajlich

    ISBN: 9781617290572
    416 pages, $44.99
    October 2013

Node.js in Practice
by Alex Young and Marc Harter

    ISBN: 978-1-933988-05-4
    424 pages, $49.99
    December 2014

Ionic in Action
Hybrid Mobile Apps with Ionic and AngularJS
by Jeremy Wilken

    ISBN: 9781633430082
    325 pages, $44.99
    September 2015

YOU MAY ALSO BE INTERESTED IN

Rails 4 in Action
Revised Edition of Rails 3 in Action
by Ryan Bigg, Yehuda Katz,
   Steve Klabnik, Rebecca Skinner

ISBN: 9781617291098
576 pages, $49.99
August 2015

jQuery in Action, Third Edition
by Bear Bibeault, Yehuda Katz,
   Aurelio De Rosa

ISBN: 9781617292071
504 pages, $44.99
August 2015

HTML5 in Action
by Rob Crowther, Joe Lennon,
   Ash Blue, Greg Wanish

ISBN: 9781617290497
466 pages, $39.99
February 2014

AngularJS in Action
by Lukas Ruebbelke

ISBN: 9781617291333
192 pages, $44.99
July 2015

For ordering information go to www.manning.com